ENGLAND: AN ANTHOLOGY

THE ENGLISH ASSOCIATION

(FOUNDED 1906)

President 1943 : THE HON. HAROLD NICOLSON, C.M.G., M.P.

Chairman of Committee : NOWELL C. SMITH, M.A.

AIMS AND ACTIVITIES

1. To unite and introduce to one another those who are interested in English Language and Literature, whether as writers, teachers, artists, actors, or administrators ; and to act as a link between groups engaged in specialized English work.

2. To uphold the standards of English writing and speech ; to contribute to English letters, scholarship, and research ; to discuss methods of English teaching ; and to encourage especially the work of younger members.

3. To spread as widely as possible the knowledge and enjoyment of English Literature.

4. To put these aims into practice by providing lectures, readings, discussions, social functions, a magazine and other publications ; and to organize occasional visits to dramatic performances and places of literary interest.

(*a*) The financial year runs from January 1 to December 31, and a subscription paid at any time during the year entitles a member to the Association's magazine *English* (three numbers) and the Presidential Address.

(*b*) The annual subscription to the Central Body is 10*s.* 6*d.*, or with *Essays and Studies* and *The Year's Work in English Studies* (post free), £1 : 1*s.*

Life Membership (which does not cover *Essays and Studies* and *The Year's Work in English Studies*) is £5. Life Membership subscription can be compounded on the basis of a deduction of 1*s.* 6*d.* for every annual subscription paid.

(*c*) The annual subscription of a full member of a Branch is fixed within certain limits by the Branch, and is usually 7*s.* 6*d.*, or with *Essays and Studies* and *The Year's Work in English Studies* (post free), 18*s.*

(*d*) Subscriptions to the Central Body should be made out in favour of the English Association and sent to Barclays Bank, 95 Victoria Street, Westminster, S.W.1. Further information will be given to intending members, or they will be placed in communication with the Hon. Secretary of any Branch by the Secretary, 3 Cromwell Place (Second Floor), London, S.W.7.

ENGLAND
AN ANTHOLOGY

WITH AN INTRODUCTION

BY

HAROLD NICOLSON

PUBLISHED FOR THE

ENGLISH ASSOCIATION

BY

MACMILLAN & CO. LTD

1944

PRINTED IN GREAT BRITAIN
BY R. & R. CLARK, LIMITED, EDINBURGH

INTRODUCTION

Anthologies are not always acceptable, since the individual reader is apt to resent either the omission of some favourite passage or the inclusion of poems which to him seem unrepresentative or dull. The present collection, which has been compiled by a Committee of the English Association, has been chosen with a definite purpose in mind ; it is an attempt (and in my judgment a successful attempt) to indicate how diverse and yet how similar have been the impressions which English poets of many centuries have derived from English life and character. It is an example, on the one hand, of the continuity of English literature, and on the other of its variety. For, although the instruments which form the vast orchestra of English poetry are diverse both in strength and form, the main themes are strangely recurrent and one can detect throughout the centuries a resonant continuity of tone.

The anthology is divided into eight main categories, each one of which reflects some definite aspect of our national expression. We have the town and the country ; we have sport and war ; we have reflection and humour ; we have art and character. It might be objected that English poetry is, in its essence, reflective rather than intellectual, rural rather than urban ; and it might be urged that such themes as war and comedy can be expressed only in the minor categories of patriotic or humorous verse. It is thus useful to be reminded by this anthology that our poets throughout the ages have sought to interpret, rather than to escape from, contemporary life ; that Crabbe could write more realistically, and no less beautifully, than Goldsmith about the English village ; that Masefield and Scawen Blunt could compose sincere poems about hunting or coursing ; that Mrs. Meynell could electrify a London fog and Bridges write lovely lines about the snow on London pavements ; or that Tennyson or Kipling could raise patriotic verse to the level of true national poetry. It is useful also to be reminded that our conception of an ideal national character is a continuous conception, and that Wordsworth's "Happy Warrior" is the prototype of Kipling's "If". And thus it is interesting, in an anthology as catholic and as varied as the present collection, to trace the similarity of tone and feeling which, from Chaucer to Bridges, informs and inspires the vast organic growth of English poetry.

The poems here collected constitute a cross-section of our literature during the last five hundred years. Is it possible, by studying such a cross-section, or sample, to make any deductions regarding the specific quality of English poetry or to decide in what respects it differs from the poetry of other ages and of other nations? I think it is possible. I believe that a foreigner reading this sample of English poetry, and comparing it with a similar anthology of French, German, or Italian poems, would find that there occur certain recurrent attitudes, certain constant moods of sensitiveness or attention, which are more characteristic of the English than of any other poets.

There is, in the first place, the constant preoccupation with Nature—the unceasing reaction against urban life. There were moments, of course, when our poets could sing, as John Dyer sang, the glories of the coming Industrial Revolution, or prefer to "hunt books in the Charing Cross Road". But in general they have sought to become

"... lost to human things
To blend at last with Nature and to hear
What song she sings
Low to herself when there is no one there."

It is a commonplace with poets of every age and nation to feel distracted by the smoke and noise of towns and to seek in the fields and forests for that solitude which alone can soothe their tautened nerves. But the love of Nature which for so many centuries has inspired and fortified our English poets has a quality more intimate and more natural than that which marks the nervous reactions of foreign writers. That quality may be due, in the first place, to the deep instinct for privacy which is one of the more distinctive elements in the English character. And in the second place it may be ascribed to a particular, and it may be a catholic, sense of communion with the soil. A poem such as Laurence Binyon's " Inheritance ", which forms the prologue to this anthology, is a distinctively English poem, and one which would not have been written by a foreign or an ancient poet in exactly the same way :

" O English earth
'Mid the blown seas lying
Green, green,
When the birds come flying

" Out of the empty south
To the old willow,
Ash, thorn, chestnut—
Boughs that they know . . ."

It is this sense of mystic harmony between Man and Nature which forms the main theme of Wordsworth, who was perhaps the most English of all our poets :

" that blessed mood,
In which the burthen of the mystery,
In which the heavy and the weary weight
Of all this unintelligible world
Is lightened :— that serene and blessed mood,
In which the affections gently lead us on,
Until, the breath of this corporeal frame
And even the motion of our human blood
Almost suspended, we are laid asleep
In body, and become a living soul :
While with an eye made quiet by the power
Of harmony, and the deep power of joy,
We see into the life of things. . . ."

A foreigner would notice also, on reading this anthology, that our treatment of Nature tends to be intimate rather than general, and that we deal frequently, not with the wide prospect of plain or mountain, but with small hedgerow events. It is interesting, for instance, to observe how our poets, when they treat of landscape, are apt to concentrate upon some sharp-lit incident, such as the church-spire which is caught by Tennyson's " wildly dashed sunbeam " or by Binyon's " shower-light ". The intimacy of our love of Nature is thus emphasised, and differentiated from other forms of Nature-worship, by our constant preoccupation with tiny things. No other body of poetry can show such understanding of and interest in the smaller manifestations of Nature; in wild-flowers, or in ordinary little birds. Robert Bridges' "The Idle Flowers", with its careful hedgerow catalogue, is a distinctively English poem; nor could a stanza such as the following from Matthew Arnold's "Thyrsis" have arisen from any tradition other than our English tradition:

"Too quick despairer, wherefore wilt thou go?
  Soon will the high Midsummer pomps come on,
    Soon will the musk carnations break and swell,
  Soon shall we have gold-dusted snapdragon,
    Sweet-William with his homely cottage-smell,
      And stocks in fragrant blow;
Roses that down the alleys shine afar,
    And open, jasmine-muffled lattices,
    And groups under the dreaming garden-trees,
And the full moon, and the white evening star."

This, I suggest, is the first lesson that can be learnt from these pages, namely, the amazing continuity throughout all these centuries of a specific attitude towards Nature—an attitude which is more natural, more intimate, more mystical than can be found in the poetry of any other race.

There are other specific and continuous characteristics which the reader will notice. Our poetry is both the product and the creator of our national character. "What lay behind", writes our present Poet Laureate,

"Was English character and mind,
Great kindness, delicate sweet feeling
(Most shy—most clever in concealing
Its depth) for beauty of all sorts,
Great manliness and love of sports,
A grave, wise thoughtfulness and truth,
A merry fun outlasting youth,
A courage terrible to see,
And mercy for his enemy."

The innate conservatism of the English temperament is fully represented. At moments it is perfectly harmless as when Wilfrid Scawen Blunt exclaims—

> " I like the hunting of the hare ;
> New sports I hold in scorn.
> I like to be as my fathers were,
> In the days ere I was born."

At other moments it reflects that self-satisfaction which jars upon the nerves of foreign observers, as in the complacency of Tennyson's too familiar lines on " sober-suited freedom ". There are moments also when our patriotism and our pride may strike the foreign observer as savouring of arrogance. Nobody can really enjoy the more boastful stanzas of Henley's " England " :

> " Where shall the watchful Sun,
> England, my England !
> Match the master-work you've done,
> England, my own ?
> When shall he rejoice agen
> Such a breed of mighty men
> As come forward, one to ten,
> To the Song on your bugles blown,
> England—
> Down the years on your bugles blown ? "

Nor do I feel that Thomas Campbell's patriotic verses are likely to make a very direct appeal, either to the foreign reader or to those Englishmen who have experienced two German wars :

> " Men of England ! who inherit
> Rights that cost your sires their blood !
> Men whose undegenerate spirit
> Has been proved on land and flood
>
> By the foes ye've fought, uncounted,
> By the glorious deeds ye've done,
> Trophies captured—breaches mounted,
> Navies conquered—kingdoms won ! "

The sympathetic or the careful reader would admit, however, that these moods of overweening pride are not constant moods. He would recognise, in Kipling's "For all we have and are", that deep dread of boastfulness which seventeen years before had inspired his "Recessional". He would observe that our patriotism is not nationalistic but is mingled, as in Coleridge's magnificent lines, with

> "All sweet sensations, all ennobling thoughts,
> All adoration of the God in nature,
> All lovely and all honourable things,
> Whatever makes this mortal spirit feel
> The joy and greatness of his future being."

He would notice how constant is our sense of both the dangers and the protection of the surrounding sea; that moat which today, as in Shakespeare's time, preserves us "against the envy of less happier lands"; that element which Edmund Waller, in six curious lines, defined as the natural element of all the English:

> "Others may use the ocean as their road,
> Only the English make it their abode,
> Whose ready sails with ev'ry wind can fly,
> And make a cov'nant with the inconstant sky
> Our oaks secure, as if they there took root,
> We tread on billows with a steady foot."

The observant reader would notice other things. He would detect an underlying sense of moral purpose, a recurrent note of modesty, a frequent tendency to understatement. And again and again he would hear the deep voice of responsibility which "to the open sea of the world's praise from dark antiquity hath flowed"—responsibility for the freedom of other men:

> "We must be free or die, who speak the tongue
> That Shakespeare spake; the faith and morals hold
> Which Milton held."

It is fitting indeed that this collection of poems, so redolent of English happiness, so resonant with English pride, should be prefaced by the words uttered in 1942 by General Smuts : " Glory has not departed from this land. . . . I speak of that inward glory, that splendour of the spirit, which has shone over this land from the soul of its people, and has been a beacon light to the oppressed and downtrodden peoples in this new martyrdom of man."

HAROLD NICOLSON

ACKNOWLEDGMENTS

THE English Association is indebted to the following authors, authors' representatives, and publishers for permission to reprint the poems of which they control the copyright :

Mr. Richard Aldington and Messrs. Wm. Heinemann, Ltd. ; Messrs. George Allen & Unwin, Ltd., for the poem from the *Poetical Works* of Lionel Johnson; the Hon. Herbert Asquith and Messrs. Sidgwick & Jackson, Ltd. ; the Hon. Maurice Baring ; Mrs. George Bambridge, Messrs. Macmillan & Co., Ltd., Messrs. Methuen & Co., Ltd., and the Oxford University Press for poems from *Rewards and Fairies*, *The Years Between*, and *A History of England*, by the late Rudyard Kipling ; Messrs. Ernest Benn, Ltd., for the poem by the late Amy Levy ; Mrs. Binyon for poems by the late Laurence Binyon ; Mr. Edmund Blunden ; the Executors of W. S. Blunt ; Dr. F. S. Boas ; Mr. Guy Boas ; Mr. R. S. Clement Brown for the poem by Sir Owen Seaman ; Mr. Ivor Brown ; the Executors of T. E. Brown ; Messrs. Jonathan Cape, Ltd., for the poem by Mary Webb ; Sir Edmund K. Chambers ; the Executrix of the late G. K. Chesterton and Messrs. Methuen & Co., Ltd., for poems from *The Collected Poems of G. K. Chesterton* ; The Clarendon Press, Oxford, for poems from *The Shorter Poems of Robert Bridges* ; Mrs. Frances Cornford ; Miss Clemence Dane and Messrs. Wm. Heinemann, Ltd. ; Mr. Walter de la Mare ; Messrs. J. M. Dent & Sons, Ltd., for lines from Langland's *Piers Plowman*, modernised by Arthur Burrell ; Mr. Alban Dobson and the Oxford University Press for the poem by Austin Dobson ; the Early English Text Society for the text of their edition of *Hoccleve's Works* ; Dr. Arundell Esdaile, Messrs. Grafton & Co., and *The Times* ; Miss V. H. Friedlaender ; Mr. Wilfrid Gibson ; Mr. G. Rostrevor Hamilton ; the Trustees of the Hardy Estate for poems from *Collected Poems of Thomas Hardy* ; Messrs. Wm. Heinemann, Ltd., for poems by A. C. Swinburne ; the Author's Executors for poems by

W. E. Henley; Mr. A. P. Herbert; Mr. H. S. Vere Hodge; the Trustees of the Estate of the late A. E. Housman for permission to include two poems; Mr. E. V. Knox; Messrs. John Lane the Bodley Head Ltd. for the poem from *The Collected Poems of Margaret L. Woods*; Messrs. Longmans Green & Co., Ltd., for the poem from *The Poetical Works of Andrew Lang*; Mr. F. L. Lucas; Mrs. Sylvia Lynd; Messrs. Macmillan & Co., Ltd., for poems from *The Poetical Works of W. S. Blunt*, from *Collected Poems* by T. E. Brown, and by P. G. Hamerton; Miss Nancy McIntosh, for "Etiquette", from *The Bab Ballads*, by Sir W. S. Gilbert; Dr. L. Birkett Marshall for lines from Thomas Master's poem from *Rare Poems of the 17th Century*; Mr. John Masefield for extracts from *Right Royal* and *Reynard the Fox*, and for "Vagabond", from *Collected Poems of John Masefield* (Wm. Heinemann, Ltd.); Major George W. L. Meredith for poems by George Meredith; Messrs. Methuen & Co., Ltd., for the lines from *The White Cliffs*, by Alice Duer Miller; Mr. Wilfrid Meynell for poems by Alice Meynell and Francis Thompson; Mr. A. A. Milne and *The Times*; Mrs. Harold Monro and the Poetry Bookshop for the poem by Charlotte Mew; Mrs. F. W. H. Myers for the poem by F. W. H. Myers; Capt. Francis Newbolt for poems by the late Sir Henry Newbolt from *Poems New and Old*, published by Messrs. John Murray; Mr. Philip B. B. Nichols for the poem by the late J. Bowyer Nichols; Mr. Alfred Noyes and Messrs. Wm. Blackwood & Sons, Ltd.; the Oxford University Press and the poet's family for poems by Gerard Manley Hopkins; Professor V. de Sola Pinto and Messrs. Williams & Norgate, Ltd.; the Proprietors of *Punch*, for poems by Mr. Hilton Brown, John MacCrae, Sir Owen Seaman, Miss Jan Struther, and Miss D. M. Stuart, also for "Night Bombers" and "The Death of a Zeppelin", published anonymously; Messrs. Putnam & Co., Ltd., for the poem by John MacCrae; Miss Ruth Pitter and the Cresset Press; Sir Arthur Quiller-Couch; Miss Dorothy Una Ratcliffe and Country Life, Ltd.; the Hon. V. Sackville-West; Mr. Siegfried Sassoon; The Scottish Text Society for their text of Dunbar's "London"; Mr. Edward Shanks; Mrs. E. Sidgwick for the poem by the late A. H. Sidgwick;

Messrs. Sidgwick & Jackson, Ltd., for poems by Rupert Brooke, by John Drinkwater, and by E. Hilton Young ; Sir Osbert Sitwell and Messrs. Gerald Duckworth & Co., Ltd., ; the Society of Antiquaries for lines from *The Earthly Paradise* by William Morris ; Sir John Squire ; Mrs. M. H. Stephen for the lines from *Lapsus Calami* by J. K. Stephen ; Mr. James Walker ; Messrs. Frederick Warne & Co., Ltd., for the lines from *Preface to Nonsense Songs* by Edward Lear ; Mr. J. E. H. Wartnaby for the poem by the late E. V. Lucas ; Lady Watson for the poem by the late Sir William Watson ; Lt.-Comdr. Frederick B. Watt ; Mrs. G. M. P. Welby-Everard for the poem by the late Maurice Hewlett ; Mr. E. Hilton Young ; and Mr. Geoffrey Winthrop Young.

CONTENTS

PROLOGUE

COUNTRYSIDE

TOWN

SPORT

WAR

REFLECTION

HUMOUR

ART

Poets

Painting, Architecture, Sculpture

Music

CHARACTER

ENGLAND

EPILOGUE

Many of England's ancient monuments are damaged or gone for ever. The blitz has passed over cities, ports, churches, temples, humble homes and palaces, Houses of Parliament and Law Courts. Irreplaceable treasures of a thousand years of almost uninterrupted progress and culture and peaceful civilisation have disappeared for ever. Much is gone which is lost for ever.

But one thing is not lost—one thing, the most precious of all, remains and has rather increased. For what will it profit a nation if it wins the world and loses its soul? The soul remains, Glory has not departed from this land. I speak not of outward glory, of what your Gallic neighbours call "la Gloire". *I speak rather of that inward glory, that splendour of the spirit, which has shone over this land from the soul of its people, and has been a beacon light to the oppressed and downtrodden peoples in this new martyrdom of man.*

General Smuts

PROLOGUE

INHERITANCE

I

To a bare blue hill
Wings an old thought roaming,
At a random touch
Of memory homing.

The first of England
These eyes to fill
Was the lifted head
Of that proud hill.

As lion-fronted
Alone it warded
The vale, and the far
Bright West regarded.

Who knows what wells
Are a child's unthinking
Eyes ? What skies
Thro' the clear of them sinking

Have for ever coloured
A mind that springs
From buried hope, dumb prayer,
Prized small things

Precious to dust that once
Throbbed in hearts, now
Crumbled, where ignorant
Passes the plough ?

II

I have walked by streams
In shadowy places

Where wild-rose June
With the moon embraces,

And smelt the magic
Of dew-drenched herbs
In a hush that trances,
Delights, disturbs.

I have roamed in a frail mist's
Filtered gold
The Downs, so cleanly
And smooth and old.

I know how the shower-light
Touches gray spires
In the slumbrous bosom
Of the elmy shires ;

And lying on warm thyme
Watched at the sheer
Black cliff the grand wave
Lunge and rear,

When the whole Atlantic
Amassed recoils,
And in indolent thunder
Bursts and boils.

I have followed the Romans'
Wall that wound
Over lone moors, leaving
The Druid mound

In the secret hills
Where the lost race lies,
Dreaming the dream
That the world denies ;

A dream that the voices
Of England have sung,
That is born in the blood
And the eyes of the young.

III

O English earth
'Mid the blown seas lying
Green, green,
When the birds come flying

Out of the empty south
To the old willow,
Ash, thorn, chestnut—
Boughs that they know—

Sweet, sweet, sweet to be
Back in May bowers
When the grass grows tall
Round the English flowers.

O the light on tost clouds
As you take to your breast
Your stormy lover,
The strong South-West,

That breathes a wild whisper
In youth's thrilled ear,
Of strange things, of far things,
Of glory and fear !

But the things that are dearest
You have told them never ;
They are deep in our veins
For ever and ever ;

They come over the mind
When the world's noise is still
As to me comes the vision
Of one blue hill,

Beautiful, dark,
And solitary,
The first of England
That spoke to me.

Laurence Binyon

COUNTRYSIDE

A CHARM

TAKE of English earth as much
As either hand may rightly clutch.
In the taking of it breathe
Prayer for all who lie beneath—
Not the great nor well-bespoke,
But the mere uncounted folk
Of whose life and death is none
Report or lamentation.
  Lay that earth upon thy heart,
  And thy sickness shall depart !

It shall sweeten and make whole
Fevered breath and festered soul ;
It shall mightily restrain
Over-busied hand and brain ;
It shall ease thy mortal strife
'Gainst the immortal woe of life,
Till thyself restored shall prove
By what grace the Heavens do move.

Take of English flowers these—
Spring's full-facèd primroses,
Summer's wild wide-hearted rose,
Autumn's wallflower of the close,
And, thy darkness to illume,
Winter's bee-thronged ivy-bloom.
Seek and serve them where they bide
From Candlemas to Christmas-tide.
  For these simples used aright
  Can restore a failing sight.

These shall cleanse and purify
Webbed and inward-turning eye ;
These shall show thee treasure hid,
Thy familiar fields amid,

At thy threshold, on thy hearth,
Or about thy daily path ;
And reveal (which is thy need)
Every man a King indeed.

Rudyard Kipling

RETURN OF SPRING

Now fades the last long streak of snow,
  Now burgeons every maze of quick
  About the flowering squares, and thick
By ashen roots the violets blow.

Now rings the woodland loud and long,
  The distance takes a lovelier hue,
  And drown'd in yonder living blue
The lark becomes a sightless song.

Now dance the lights on lawn and lea,
  The flocks are whiter down the vale,
  And milkier every milky sail
On winding stream or distant sea ;

Where now the seamew pipes, or dives
  In yonder greening gleam, and fly
  The happy birds, that change their sky
To build and brood ; that live their lives

From land to land ; and in my breast
  Spring wakens too ; and my regret
  Becomes an April violet,
And buds and blossoms like the rest.

Lord Tennyson

TARDY SPRING

Now hill to hill has made the stride,
And distance waves the without end :
Now in the breast a door flings wide ;
Our farthest smiles, our next is friend.

And song of England's rush of flowers
Is this full breeze with mellow stops,
That spins the lark for shine, for showers ;
He drinks his hurried flight, and drops.
The stir in memory seem these things,
Which out of moistened turf and clay,
Astrain for light push patient rings,
Or leap to find the waterway.
'T is equal to a wonder done,
Whatever simple lives renew
Their tricks beneath the father sun,
As though they caught a broken clue :
So hard was earth an eyewink back ;
But now the common life has come,
The blotting cloud a dappled pack,
The grasses one vast underhum. . . .

George Meredith

JOLLY WAT

Can I not sing but " Hoy ",
Whan the joly shepard made so much joy?

The shepard upon a hill he sat ;
He had on him his tabard [1] and his hat,
His tarbox,[2] his pipe and his flagat ; [3]
His name was callèd Joly Joly Wat,
For he was a gud herdes boy.
Ut hoy !
For in his pipe he made so much joy.

The shepard upon a hill was laid ;
His dog unto his girdell was taid ;
He had not slept but a litill braid,
But *Gloria in excelsis* was to him said.
Ut hoy !
For in his pipe he made so much joy.

[1] *tabard* : sleeveless coat.
[2] *tarbox* : box of salve for sheep.
[3] *flagat* : flask.

The shepard on a hill he stode ;
Round about him his shepe they yode ;[1]
He put his hand under his hode,
He saw a star as rede as blode.
Ut hoy !
For in his pipe he made so much joy.

The shepard said anon right,
" I will go see yon ferly[2] sight,
Whereas the angel singeth on hight,
And the star that shineth so bright."
Ut hoy !
For in his pipe he made so much joy.

" Now farewell, Mall, and also Will !
For my love go ye all still
Unto I cum again you till,
And evermore, Will, ring well thy bell."
Ut hoy !
For in his pipe he made so much joy.

" Now must I go there Crist was born ;
Farewell ! I cum again to-morn.
Dog, kepe well my shepe fro the corn,
And warn well 'Warroke' when I blow my horn ! "
Ut hoy !
For in his pipe he made so much joy.

When Wat to Bedlem cumen was,
He swet, he had gone faster than a pace ;
He found Jesu in a simpell place,
Between an ox but and an asse.
Ut hoy !
For in his pipe he made so much joy.

" Jesu, I offer to thee here my pipe,
My skirt, my tarbox, and my scrip ;
Home to my felowes now will I skip,
And also look unto my shepe."
Ut hoy !
For in his pipe he made so much joy.

[1] *yode* : went. [2] *ferly* : wonderful.

"Now farewell, mine owne herdesman Wat!"—
"Yea, for God, lady, even so I hat;[1]
Lull well Jesu in thy lap,
And farewell, Joseph, with thy round cap!"
Ut hoy!
For in his pipe he made so much joy.

"Now may I well both hope and sing,
For I have been at Cristes bering;
Home to my felowes now will I fling.
Crist of heven to his bliss us bring!"
Ut hoy!
For in his pipe he made so much joy.

Anonymous (*c.* 1500)

SWEET SPRING

Spring, the sweet spring, is the year's pleasant king;
Then blooms each thing, then maids dance in a ring,
Cold doth not sting, the pretty birds do sing:
Cuckoo, jug-jug, pu-we, to-witta-woo!

The palm and may make country houses gay,
Lambs frisk and play, the shepherds pipe all day,
And we hear aye birds tune this merry lay:
Cuckoo, jug-jug, pu-we, to-witta-woo!

The fields breathe sweet, the daisies kiss our feet,
Young lovers meet, old wives a-sunning sit;
In every street these tunes our ears do greet:
Cuckoo, jug-jug, pu-we, to-witta-woo!
Spring, the sweet spring!

Thomas Nashe

THE MILKMAID'S LIFE

You rural goddesses,
That woods and fields possess,
Assist me with your skill
That may direct my quill

[1] *hat*: am called.

More jocundly to express
  The mirth and delight,
  Both morning and night,
On mountain or in dale,
  Of those who choose
  This trade to use,
  And through cold dews
  Do never refuse
To carry the milking pail.

The bravest lasses gay
Live not so merry as they ;
  In honest civil sort
  They make each other sport,
As they trudge on their way,
  Come fair or foul weather,
  They're fearful of neither—
Their courages never quail ;
  In wet and dry,
  Though winds be high
  And dark's the sky,
  They ne'er deny
To carry the milking pail.

Their hearts are free from care,
They never will despair ;
  Whatever may befall,
  They bravely bear out all,
And Fortune's frowns outdare.
  They pleasantly sing
  To welcome the spring—
'Gainst Heaven they never rail ;
  If grass will grow,
  Their thanks they show ;
  And, frost or snow,
  They merrily go
Along with the milking pail.

But idleness they do scorn,
They rise very early i' th' morn

And walk into the field,
Where pretty birds do yield
Brave music on every thorn ;
The linnet and thrush
Do sing on each bush,
And the dulcet nightingale
Her note doth strain
In a jocund vein
To entertain
That worthy train
Which carry the milking pail

. . . .

Upon the first of May,
With garlands fresh and gay,
With mirth and music sweet,
For such a season meet,
They pass their time away ;
They dance away sorrow
And all the day thorow
Their legs do never fail ;
They nimblely
Their feet do ply
And bravely try
The victory
In honour o' th' milking pail.

Martin Parker

PLAYMATES

When Herbert's Mama was a slim little Maid,
And lived among Waterfalls, Mountains and Lakes,
With Edith her cousin, she rambled and played
And both of them gardened with spades and with rakes.
Sweet Edith was fair as the lilies and pearls,
And swift as the tender Gazelle's were her feet,
And over her forehead the small silken curls
Waved yellow and light as the clusters of wheat.

A wood full of harebells was close to their home,
It led to a river all broken with rocks :

They lov'd o'er the thyme and the heather to roam,
'Mid bracken and brambles they ruined their frocks ;
They tucked up their trowsers to paddle and wade,
And washed their dolls' clothes in the water so cold ;
They wove pretty garlands within the cool shade—
Their May-Pole was beauteous indeed to behold.

In winter they put on their great wooden clogs,
And down to the lake with young Derwent they ran ;
The sun having chased all the vapours and fogs,
Their sport on the ice in high glee they began.
In summer they gathered the primroses pale,
And filled little baskets with fruit and with flowers ;
To make primrose wine and their friends to regale
Was one of their pleasures in summer's gay hours.

With Dora and Mary they went to the grove
And picked purple bilberries near the bright lake ;
They oft with each other in gathering strove—
An excellent pie did their bilberries make.
They frequently sat on the bough of a tree,
And climbed to the top of a very high beech ;
They sought for the foxgloves and O with what glee
They gathered the globe-flowers that grow within reach.

Sara Coleridge

YORKSHIRE'S FIVE

(Aire, Wharfe, Nidd, Ure, and Swale)

When I'se been by Tiber an' when I'se been by Seine,
Hearkenin' theer messages, I lang to hear again
Secrets of home watters, born amang moor-sedges,
Fallin' doon like sparklin' ale ower steean ridges.

When I'se been by Danube, an' when I'se been by Rhine,
A-listenin' theer tidings, my homin' heart would pine
For music of my own becks at spring 'mang boggy peat,
Wheer lapwing cry and moorlark lift prayers so pure an'
sweet.

Missouri an' St. Lawrence, Volga an' Thames an' Dee,
All on' em are varra fine, but nivver t'same to me
As rivers 'at are singin' wheer my father's tongue prevails,
A-crinklin' an' a-cranklin' doon my forsaken dales.

Dorothy Una Ratcliffe

CORINNA'S GOING A-MAYING

Get up, get up for shame ! The blooming morn
Upon her wings presents the god unshorn :
    See how Aurora throws her fair
    Fresh-quilted colours through the air :
    Get up, sweet slug-a-bed, and see
    The dew bespangling herb and tree !
Each flower has wept and bowed toward the east,
Above an hour since, yet you not drest,
    Nay, not so much as out of bed ?
    When all the birds have matins said,
    And sung their thankful hymns, 'tis sin,
    Nay, profanation, to keep in,
Whenas a thousand virgins on this day
Spring sooner than the lark to fetch in May.

Rise, and put on your foliage, and be seen
To come forth like the spring-time fresh and green,
    And sweet as Flora. Take no care
    For jewels for your gown or hair :
    Fear not ; the leaves will strew
    Gems in abundance upon you :
Besides, the childhood of the day has kept,
Against you come, some orient pearls unwept.
    Come, and receive them while the light
    Hangs on the dew-locks of the night,
    And Titan on the eastern hill
    Retires himself, or else stands still
Till you come forth ! Wash, dress, be brief in praying :
Few beads are best when once we go a-Maying.

Come, my Corinna, come ; and coming, mark
How each field turns a street, each street a park,
    Made green and trimmed with trees ! see how
    Devotion gives each house a bough

Or branch ! each porch, each door, ere this,
An ark, a tabernacle is,
Made up of white-thorn neatly interwove,
As if here were those cooler shades of love.
Can such delights be in the street
And open fields, and we not see't ?
Come, we'll abroad : and let's obey
The proclamation made for May,
And sin no more, as we have done, by staying,
But, my Corinna, come, let's go a-Maying.

There's not a budding boy or girl this day,
But is got up and gone to bring in May.
A deal of youth ere this is come
Back and with white-thorn laden home.
Some have despatched their cakes and cream,
Before that we have left to dream :
And some have wept and wooed, and plighted troth,
And chose their priest, ere we can cast off sloth :
Many a green-gown has been given,
Many a kiss, both odd and even :
Many a glance too has been sent
From out the eye, love's firmament :
Many a jest told of the keys betraying
This night, and locks picked : yet we're not a-Maying.

Come, let us go, while we are in our prime,
And take the harmless folly of the time !
We shall grow old apace, and die
Before we know our liberty.
Our life is short, and our days run
As fast away as does the sun :
And as a vapour, or a drop of rain
Once lost, can ne'er be found again,
So when or you or I are made
A fable, song, or fleeting shade,
All love, all liking, all delight,
Lies drowned with us in endless night.
Then, while time serves, and we are but decaying,
Come, my Corinna, come, let's go a-Maying.

Robert Herrick

SUMMER RAIN

Now be you thankful, who in England dwell,
That to the starving trees and thirsty grass
Even at summer's height come cloudy fleets
Moist from the wastes of the Atlantic swell,
To spill their rain, and pass,
While fields renew their sweets.
Not as the Arab watches in despair
The scrannel promise of his harvest parch
Even before the sun climbs high in March
And only dust-motes dim the scorching air.
Such arid months as only exiles know,
With longing for the smell of English rains,
Some drops to lay the dust, some shower to stir
The earthy redolence of soaking loam,
Some saddening of the sky before the shower,
Some dew to hold a footprint for an hour ;
When through the stones the lizard and the snake
Rustle their brittle length, and crickets chirr
Day after day, and broom-pods crackling break,
Scavenger kites hang waiting for the dead
Over the old and solitary ram,
And the mule picks his way up the dried river-bed,—
This know, and know then how the heart can ache
With pining for the woods and clouds of home.

V. Sackville-West

THE IDLE FLOWERS

I HAVE sown upon the fields
Eyebright and Pimpernel
And Pansy and Poppy-seed
Ripen'd and scatter'd well,

And silver Lady-smock
The meads with light to fill,
Cowslip and Buttercup,
Daisy and Daffodil ;

Kingcup and Fleur-de-lys
Upon the marsh to meet
With Comfrey, Watermint
Loose-strife and Meadowsweet

And all along the stream
My care hath not forgot
Crowfoot's white galaxy
And love's Forget-me-not :

And where high grasses wave
Shall great Moon-daisies blink,
With Rattle and Sorrel sharp
And Robin's ragged pink.

Thick on the woodland floor
Gay company shall be,
Primrose and Hyacinth
And frail Anemone,

Perennial Strawberry-bloom,
Woodsorrel's pencilled veil,
Dishevel'd Willow-weed
And Orchis purple and pale,

Bugle, that blushes blue,
And Woodruff's snowy gem,
Proud Foxglove's finger-bells
And Spurge with milky stem.

High on the Downs so bare,
Where thou dost love to climb,
Pink Thrift and Milkwort are,
Lotus and scented Thyme ;

And in the shady lanes
Bold Arum's hood of green,
Herb Robert, Violet,
Starwort and Celandine ;

And by the dusty road
Bedstraw and Mullein tall,

With red Valerian
And Toadflax on the wall.

Yarrow and Chicory,
That hath for hue no like,
Silene and Mallow mild
And Agrimony's spike,

Blue-eyed Veronicas
And grey-faced Scabious
And downy Silverweed
And striped Convolvulus :

Harebell shall haunt the banks,
And thro' the hedgerow peer
Withwind and Snapdragon
And Nightshade's flower of fear.

And where men never sow,
Have I my Thistles set,
Ragwort and stiff Wormwood,
And straggling Mignonette,

Bugloss and Burdock rank
And prickly Teasel high,
With Umbels yellow and white,
That come to kexes dry.

Pale Chlora shalt thou find,
Sun-loving Centaury,
Cranesbill and Sinjunwort,
Cinquefoil and Betony :

Shock-headed Dandelion,
That drank the fire of the Sun ;
Hawkweed and Marigold,
Cornflower and Campion.

Let Oak and Ash grow strong,
Let Beech her branches spread,

Let Grass and Barley throng
And waving Wheat for bread ;

Be share and sickle bright
To labour at all hours ;
For thee and thy delight
I have made the idle flowers.

Robert Bridges

NURSE'S SONG

When the voices of children are heard on the green,
  And laughing is heard on the hill,
My heart is at rest within my breast,
  And everything else is still.

" Then come home, my children, the sun is gone down,
  And the dews of night arise ;
Come, come, leave off play, and let us away
  Till the morning appears in the skies."

" No, no, let us play, for it is yet day,
  And we cannot go to sleep ;
Besides, in the sky the little birds fly,
  And the hills are all covered with sheep."

" Well, well, go and play till the light fades away,
  And then go home to bed."
The little ones leapèd and shoutèd and laugh'd
  And all the hills echoèd.

William Blake

JACK AND JOAN

Jack and Joan they think no ill,
But loving live and merry still ;
Do their week-days' work and pray
Devoutly on the holy day ;

Skip and trip it on the green,
And help to choose the Summer Queen ;
Lash out at a country feast
Their silver penny with the best.

Well can they judge of nappy ale,
And tell at large a winter tale ;
Climb up to the apple loft
And turn the crabs till they be soft.
Tib is all the father's joy,
And little Tom the mother's boy.
All their pleasure is Content ;
And care to pay their yearly rent.

Joan can call by name her cows,
And deck her windows with green boughs ;
She can wreaths and tuttyes [1] make,
And trim with plums a bridal cake.
Jack knows what brings gain or loss,
And his long flail can stoutly toss ;
Makes the hedge which others break,
And ever thinks what he doth speak.

Now you courtly dames and knights,
That study only strange delights,
Though you scorn the home-spun gray
And revel in your rich array,
Though your tongues dissemble deep
And can your heads from danger keep,
Yet, for all your pomp and train,
Securer lives the silly swain.

Thomas Campion

HELP, GOOD SHEPHERD

Turn not aside, Shepherd, to see
How bright the constellations are,
Hanging in heaven, or on the tree ;
The sky-born or terrestrial star

[1] *tuttyes* : nosegays.

Brood not upon ; the waters fleet,
Willows, or thy crown-destined thorn,
Full of her rubies, as is meet,
Or whitening in the eye of morn,

Pause not beside : shepherds' delight,
The pipe and tabor in the vale,
And mirthful watchfires of a night,
And herdsman's rest in wattled pale,

Forsake, though dearly earned : and still
Sound with thy crook the darkling flood,
Still range the sides of shelvy hill
And call about in underwood :

For on the hill are many strayed,
Some held in thickets plunge and cry,
And the deep waters make us afraid.
Come then and help us, or we die.

Ruth Pitter

TO MEADOWS

Ye have been fresh and green,
  Ye have been filled with flowers.
And ye the walks have been
  Where maids have spent their hours.

You have beheld how they
  With wicker arks did come
To kiss and bear away
  The richer cowslips home.

You've heard them sweetly sing,
  And seen them in a round :
Each virgin like a spring,
  With honeysuckles crowned.

But now we see none here
  Whose silvery feet did tread
And with dishevelled hair
  Adorned this smoother mead.

Like unthrifts, having spent
  Your stock and needy grown,
You're left here to lament
  Your poor estates, alone.

Robert Herrick

REST

  To spend the long warm days
Silent beside the silent-stealing streams,
  To see, not gaze,
To hear, not listen, thoughts exchanged for dreams :

  See clouds that slowly pass
Trailing their shadows o'er the far faint down,
  And ripening grass,
While yet the meadows wear their starry crown.

  To hear the breezes sigh
Cool in the silver leaves like falling rain,
  Pause and go by,
Tired wanderers o'er the solitary plain :

  See far from all affright
Shy river creatures play hour after hour,
  And night by night
Low in the West the white moon's folding flower.

  Thus lost to human things,
To blend at last with Nature and to hear
  What song she sings
Low to herself when there is no one near.

Margaret L. Woods

THE UPPER THAMES

How changed is here each spot man makes or fills !
In the two Hinkseys nothing keeps the same ;
The village street its haunted mansion lacks,
And from the sign is gone Sibylla's name,
And from the roofs the twisted chimney-stacks—
Are ye too changed, ye hills ?
See, 'tis no foot of unfamiliar men
Tonight from Oxford up your pathway strays !
Here came I often, often, in old days—
Thyrsis and I ; we still had Thyrsis then.

Runs it not here, the track by Childsworth Farm,
Past the high wood, to where the elm tree crowns
The hill behind whose ridge the sunset flames ?
The signal-elm, that looks on Ilsley Downs,
The Vale, the three lone weirs, the youthful Thames ?
This winter-eve is warm,
Humid the air ! leafless, yet soft as spring,
The tender purple spray on copse and briers !
And that sweet city with her dreaming spires,
She needs not June for beauty's heightening.

. . . . . .

Too rare, too rare, grow now my visits here;
But once I knew each field, each flower, each stick ;
And with the country-folk acquaintance made
By barn in threshing-time, by new-built rick.
Here, too, our shepherd pipes we first assayed.
Ah me ! this many a year
My pipe is lost, my shepherd's-holiday !
Needs must I lose them, needs with heavy heart
Into the world and wave of men depart ;
But Thyrsis of his own will went away.

. . . . . .

So, some tempestuous morn in early June,
When the year's primal burst of bloom is o'er,
Before the roses and the longest day—
When garden-walks and all the grassy floor
With blossoms red and white of fallen May
And chestnut-flowers are strewn—

So have I heard the cuckoo's parting cry,
From the wet field, through the vext garden trees,
Come with the volleying rain and tossing breeze :
The bloom is gone, and with the bloom go I.

Too quick despairer, wherefore wilt thou go ?
Soon will the high midsummer pomps come on,
Soon will the musk carnations break and swell,
Soon shall we have gold-dusted snapdragon,
Sweet-William with his homely cottage-smell,
And stocks in fragrant blow ;
Roses that down the alleys shine afar,
And open, jasmine-muffled lattices,
And groups under the dreaming garden-trees,
And the full moon, and the white evening-star.

He hearkens not ! light comer, he is flown !
What matters it ? next year he will return,
And we shall have him in the sweet spring-days,
With whitening hedges and uncrumpling fern,
And blue-bells trembling by the forest-ways,
And scent of hay new-mown.
But Thyrsis never more we swains shall see ;
See him come back, and cut a smoother reed,
And blow a strain the world at last shall heed—
For Time, not Corydon, hath conquered thee !

. . . .

Well ! wind-dispersed and vain the words will be,
Yet, Thyrsis, let me give my grief its hour
In the old haunt, and find our tree-topped hill !
Who, if not I, for questing here hath power ?
I know the wood which hides the daffodil,
I know the Fyfield tree,
I know what white, what purple fritillaries
The grassy harvest of the river-fields,
Above by Ensham, down by Sandford, yields,
And what sedged brooks are Thames's tributaries ;

I know these slopes ; who knows them if not I ?—
But many a dingle on the loved hill-side,
With thorns once studded, old, white-blossomed trees,

Where thick the cowslips grew, and far descried
  High towered the spikes of purple orchises,
    Hath since our day put by
The coronals of that forgotten time ;
Down each green bank hath gone the ploughboy's
    team,
  And only in the hidden brookside gleam
Primroses, orphans of the flowery prime.

Where is the girl, who by the boatman's door,
  Above the locks, above the boating throng,
    Unmoored our skiff when through the Wytham flats,
  Red loosestrife and blond meadow-sweet among
    And darting swallows and light water-gnats,
      We tracked the shy Thames shore ?
  Where are the mowers, who, as the tiny swell
    Of our boat passing heaved the river-grass,
    Stood with suspended scythe to see us pass ?—
  They all are gone, and thou art gone as well !

Matthew Arnold

THE BEECH AND THE OAK

For the slender beech and the sapling oak,
  That grow by the shadowy rill,
You may cut down both at a single stroke,
  You may cut down which you will.

But this you must know, that as long as they grow,
  Whatever change may be,
You can never teach either oak or beech
  To be aught but a greenwood tree.

Thomas Love Peacock

CALPHER WOOD

Once more the grasses rippling
    Round Calpher Wood are mown :
An old horse, a stripling
    Mow there alone.

No more the merry chatter
    Of mowers scything clean ;
Only the iron clatter
    Of the machine.

Oh well for the brain's bright cunning,
    That has the strength of ten !
Do they lie at ease and sunning,
    Those nine men ?

Whither, from field and fallow,
    Mowers of olden time ?
" We live where streets are sallow,
    And skies are grime.

New tenements, longer alleys,
    Under a sickened sun,
While lonelier sleep the valleys
    Of Huntingdon.

Towns where no man has neighbours,
    Have seized us, flesh and soul.
Where no man needs our labours,
    We reap the dole.

Where our fathers' flocks were pastured,
    White-fleeced the thistle runs :
Thorns claw the fields they mastered,
    And crown their sons.

The silverweed has settled
    Where gold their wheat would be :
Lanes where they loved are nettled,
    And weeds are we."

F. L. Lucas

LOVELIEST VILLAGE

SWEET Auburn, loveliest village of the plain,
Where health and plenty cheered the labouring swain,
Where smiling spring its earliest visit paid,
And parting summer's lingering blooms delayed.

Dear lovely bowers of innocence and ease,
Seats of my youth, when every sport could please,
How often have I loitered o'er thy green,
Where humble happiness endeared each scene !
How often have I paused on every charm,
The sheltered cot, the cultivated farm,
The never-failing brook, the busy mill,
The decent church that topped the neighbouring hill,
The hawthorn bush, with seats beneath the shade,
For talking age and whispering lovers made !
How often have I blessed the coming day,
When toil remitting lent its turn to play,
And all the village train, from labour free,
Led up their sports beneath the spreading tree,
While many a pastime circled in the shade,
The young contending as the old surveyed ;
And many a gambol frolicked o'er the ground,
And sleights of art and feats of strength went round ;
And still as each repeated pleasure tired,
Succeeding sports the mirthful band inspired :
The dancing pair that simply sought renown,
By holding out, to tire each other down.

. . . . . .

Sweet was the sound, when oft, at evening's close,
Up yonder hill the village murmur rose ;
There, as I passed with careless steps and slow,
The mingling notes came softened from below :
The swain responsive as the milk-maid sung,
The sober herd that lowed to meet their young :
The noisy geese that gabbled o'er the pool,
The playful children just let loose from school ;
The watchdog's voice that bayed the whispering wind,
And the loud laugh that spoke the vacant mind.

Oliver Goldsmith

THE REAL VILLAGE

I GRANT indeed that fields and flocks have charms
For him that grazes or for him that farms ;
But when amid such pleasing scenes I trace
The poor laborious natives of the place,

And see the midday sun, with fervid ray,
On their bare heads and dewy temples play,
While some, with feebler heads and fainter hearts,
Deplore their fortune, yet sustain their parts—
Then shall I dare these real ills to hide
In tinsel trappings of poetic pride ?

. . . . . .

Lo ! where the heath, with withering brake grown o'er,
Lends the light turf that warms the neighbouring poor ;
From thence a length of burning sand appears,
Where the thin harvest waves its withered ears ;
Rank weeds, that every art and care defy,
Reign o'er the land and rob the blighted rye ;
There thistles stretch their prickly arms afar,
And to the ragged infant threaten war ;
There poppies, nodding, mock the hope of toil ;
There the blue bugloss paints the sterile soil ;
Hardy and high, above the slender sheaf,
The slimy mallow waves her silky leaf ;
O'er the young shoot the charlock throws a shade,
And clasping tares cling round the sickly blade ;
With mingled tints the rocky coasts abound,
And a sad splendour vainly shines around.

. . . . . .

No longer truth, though shown in verse, disdain,
But own the Village Life a life of pain :
I too must yield, that oft amid those woes
Are gleams of transient mirth and hours of sweet repose,
Such as you find on yonder sportive Green,
The squire's tall gate and churchway-walk between ;
Where loitering stray a little tribe of friends
On a fair Sunday when the sermon ends :
Then rural beaux their best attire put on,
To win their nymphs, as other nymphs are won ;
While those long wed go plain, and by degrees,
Like other husbands, quit their care to please.
Some of the sermon talk, a sober crowd,
And loudly praise, if it were preached aloud ;
Some on the labours of the week look round,
Tell their own worth, and think their toil renown'd ;
While some, whose hopes to no renown extend,

Are only pleased to find their labours end.
  Thus, as their hours glide on, with pleasure fraught,
Their careful masters brood the painful thought ;
Much in their mind they murmur and lament
That one fair day should be so idly spent ;
And think that Heaven deals hard, to tithe their store
And tax their time for preachers and the poor.

George Crabbe

OUR VILLAGE

Our village, that's to say not Miss Mitford's village, but our village of Bullock Smithy,
Is come into by an avenue of trees, three oak pollards, two elders, and a withy ;
And in the middle, there's a green of about not exceeding an acre and a half ;
It's common to all, and fed off by nineteen cows, six ponies, three horses, five asses, two foals, seven pigs, and a calf !
Besides a pond in the middle, as is held by a similar sort of common law lease,
And contains twenty ducks, six drakes, three ganders, two dead dogs, four drowned kittens, and twelve geese.
Of course the green's cropt very close, and does famous for bowling when the little village boys play at cricket ;
Only some horse, or pig, or cow, or great jackass, is sure to come and stand right before the wicket.
There's fifty-five private houses, let alone barns and workshops, and pigstyes, and poultry huts, and such-like sheds ;
With plenty of public-houses—two Foxes, one Green Man, three Bunch of Grapes, one Crown, and six King's Heads.
The Green Man is reckoned the best, as the only one that for love or money can raise
A postilion, a blue jacket, two deplorable lame white horses, and a ramshackled " neat postchaise ".
There's one parish church for all the people, whatsoever may be their ranks in life or their degrees,

Except one very damp, small, dark, freezing-cold, little
Methodist chapel of Ease ;
And close by the church-yard there's a stone-mason's yard,
that, when the time is seasonable,
Will furnish with afflictions sore and marble urns and
cherubims very low and reasonable.
There's a cage, comfortable enough ; I've been in it with
old Jack Jeffrey and Tom Pike ;
For the Green Man next door will send you in ale, gin, or
anything else you like.
I can't speak of the stocks, as nothing remains of them but
the upright post ;
But the pound is kept in repairs for the sake of Cob's horse,
as is always there almost.
There's a smithy of course, where that queer sort of a chap
in his way, Old Joe Bradley,
Perpetually hammers and stammers, for he stutters and
shoes horses very badly.
There's a shop of all sorts, that sells everything, kept by
the widow of Mr. Task ;
But when you go there, it's ten to one she's out of everything you ask.
You'll know her house by the swarm of boys, like flies,
about the old sugary cask ;
There are six empty houses, and not so well papered inside
as out.
For bill-stickers won't beware, but stick notices of sales
and election placards all about.
That's the Doctor's with a green door, where the garden
pots in the window is seen ;
A weakly monthly rose that don't blow, and a dead
geranium, and a tea-plant with five black leaves and
one green.
As for hollyoaks at the cottage doors, and honeysuckles
and jasmines, you may go and whistle ;
But the Tailor's front garden grows two cabbages, a dock,
a ha'porth of pennyroyal, two dandelions, and a thistle.
There are three small orchards—Mr. Busby's the school-
master's is the chief—
With two pear-trees that don't bear ; one plum and an
apple, that every year is stripped by a thief.

There's another small day-school too, kept by the respectable Mrs. Gaby;
A select establishment, for six little boys and one big, and four little girls and a baby.
There's a rectory, with pointed gables and strange odd chimneys that never smokes,
For the rector don't live on his living like other Christian sort of folks;
There's a barber's, once a week well filled with rough black-bearded, shock-headed churls,
And a window with two feminine men's heads, and two masculine ladies in false curls;
There's a butcher's, and a carpenter's, and a plumber's, and a small greengrocer's and a baker,
But he won't bake on a Sunday, and there's a sexton that's a coal-merchant besides, and an undertaker;
And a toyshop, but not a whole one, for a village can't compare with the London shops;
One window sells drums, dolls, kites, carts, bats, Clout's balls, and the other sells malt and hops.
And Mrs. Brown, in domestic economy not to be a bit behind her betters,
Lets her house to a milliner, a watchmaker, a rat-catcher, a cobbler, lives in it herself, and it's the post-office for letters.
Now I've gone through all the village—aye, from end to end, save and except one more house,
But I haven't come to that—and I hope I never shall—and that's the Village Poor House!

Thomas Hood

SOUTH-WEST WIND IN AUTUMN

All day up from the Channel clouds have been flowing,
Dove-brown, dark with rain;
But look now! Speedwell-blue, sky-spaces open—
Shall I see just this again?

Shall I walk another year, as when all was new to me,
See what, a boy, I saw,

The eternal twelve-faced wheel of wonder and beauty
  Follow its ancient law ?

See earth's high triumph, in what sure succession,
  Million-bannered, it goes,
From February's van to July's rearguard,
  Dog-mercury to dog-rose ?

But most, on a day like this another autumn,
  When the oak-woods are thinned,
Shall I smell the smell of the oak-leaves dead and fallen,
  Shall I taste the south-west wind,

The wind of the Downs and the Weald that, when rain is
    lifting,
  Sets all the world ashine,
This hurrying, living air, sweet as new milk is
  And noble as old wine ?

If I see, smell, taste them never again, so be it !
  I shall have made my own,
Part of me, long as I live, immortal sweetness,
  That is no man's alone,

No man's, nor mine alone, for to those before me,
  From whom I had my birth,
And to sons and daughters of mine, and their sons and
    daughters,
  All this glory of earth

Was, is, shall be, as to me today. Be it mine then,
  Life and its worship spent,
To hear strike the hour that shall bid me say good-bye to
    them,
  And be content.

Arundell Esdaile

CAMBRIDGESHIRE

THE stacks, like blunt impassive temples, rise
Across flat fields against the autumnal skies,
The hairy-hoovèd horses plough the land,
Or as in prayer and meditation stand

Upholding square, primeval, dung-stained carts,
With an unending patience in their hearts.

Nothing is changed. The farmer's gig goes by
Against the horizon. Surely, the same sky,
So vast and yet familiar, grey and mild,
And streaked with light like music, I, a child,
Lifted my face from leaf-edged lanes to see,
Late-coming home, to bread-and-butter tea.

Frances Cornford

ST. BEE'S HEAD

I HAVE seen cliffs that met the ocean foe
  As a black bison, with his crouching front
  And neck back-coiled, awaits the yelping hunt,
That reck not of his horns protruding low.

And others I have seen with calm disdain
  O'erlook the immediate strife, and gaze afar :
  Eternity was in that gaze ; the jar
Of temporal broil assailed not its domain.

Some cliffs are full of pity : in the sweep
  Of their bluff brows a kindly tolerance waits,
  And smiles upon the petulant sea, that rates,
And fumes, and scolds, against the patient steep.

And some are joyous with a hearty joy,
  And in mock-earnest wage the busy fight :
  So may you see a giant with delight
Parrying the buffets of a saucy boy !

Remonstrant others stand—a wild surprise
  Glares from their crests against the insolent throng ;
  Half frightened, half indignant at the wrong,
They look appealing at those heedless skies.

And other some are of a sleepy mood,
  Who care not if the tempest does its worst :

What is't to them if bounding billows burst,
Or winds assail them with their jeerings rude?

But like not unto any one of these
Is that tall crag, that northward guards the bay,
And stands, a watchful sentry, night and day
Above the pleasant downs of old St. Bee's.

Straight-levelled as the bayonet's dread array,
His shelves abide the charge. Come one, come all!
The blustering surges at his feet shall fall
And writhe and sob their puny lives away!

T. E. Brown

REMEMBRANCES

SUMMER's pleasures they are gone like to visions every one,
And the cloudy days of autumn and of winter cometh on.
I tried to call them back, but unbidden they are gone
Far away from heart and eye and for ever far away.
Dear heart, and can it be that such raptures meet decay?
I thought them all eternal when by Langley Bush I lay,
I thought them joys eternal when I used to shout and play
On its bank at "clink and bandy", "chock", and "taw" and "ducking-stone",
Where silence sitteth now on the wild heath as her own,
Like a ruin of the past all alone.

When I used to lie and sing by old Eastwell's boiling spring,
When I used to tie the willow boughs together for a swing,
And fish with crooked pins and thread, and never catch a thing,
With heart just like a feather, now as heavy as a stone;
When beneath old Lea Close Oak I the bottom branches broke
To make our harvest cart like so many working folk,
And then to cut a straw at the brook to have a soak;
Oh! I never dreamed of parting or that trouble had a sting,

Or that pleasures like a flock of birds would ever take to
wing,
Leaving nothing but a little naked spring.

When jumping time away on old Crossberry Way,
And eating haws like sugarplums ere they had lost the
may,
And skipping like a leveret before the peep of day
On the roly-poly up-and-downs of pleasant Swordy Well,
When in Round Oak's narrow lane as the south got black
again
We sought the hollow ash that was shelter from the rain,
With our pockets full of peas we had stolen from the
grain ;
How delicious was the dinner-time on such a showery day !
Oh, words are poor receipts for what time hath stole away,
The ancient pulpit trees and the play.

. . . .

Oh, I never thought that joys would run away from boys,
Or that boys would change their minds and forsake such
summer joys ;
But alack, I never dreamed that the world had other toys
To petrify first feelings like the fable into stone,
Till I found the pleasure past and a winter come at last.
Then the fields were sudden bare and the sky got overcast,
And boyhood's pleasing haunt, like a blossom in the
blast,
Was shrivelled to a withered weed and trampled down
and done,
Till vanished was the morning spring and set the summer
sun,
And winter fought her battle strife and won.

By Langley Bush I roam, but the bush hath left its hill,
On Cowper Green I stray, 'tis a desert strange and chill,
And the spreading Lea Close Oak, ere decay had penned
its will,
To the axe of the spoiler and self-interest fell a prey,
And Crossberry Way and old Round Oak's narrow lane
With its hollow trees like pulpits I shall never see again,
Enclosure like a Buonaparte let not a thing remain ;

It levelled every bush and tree, and levelled every hill,
And hung the moles for traitors—though the brook is
running still,
It runs a naked stream, cold and chill.

Oh ! had I known as then joy had left the paths of men,
I had watched her night and day, be sure, and never slept
agen.
And when she turned to go, oh, I'd caught her mantle
then,
And wooed her like a lover by my lonely side to stay ;
Ay, knelt and worshipped on, as Love in beauty's bower,
And clung upon her smiles as a bee upon a flower,
And gave her heart my posies, all cropt in a sunny hour,
As keepsakes and pledges all to never fade away ;
But love never heeded to treasure up the may,
So it went the common road to decay.

John Clare

THE WINTER WALK AT NOON

How soft the music of those village bells
Falling at intervals upon the ear
In cadence sweet, now dying all away,
Now pealing loud again, and louder still,
Clear and sonorous, as the gale comes on ! . . .
The night was winter in his roughest mood ;
The morning sharp and clear. But now at noon
Upon the southern side of the slant hills,
And where the woods fence off the northern blast,
The season smiles, resigning all its rage,
And has the warmth of May. The vault is blue
Without a cloud, and white without a speck
The dazzling splendour of the scene below.
Again the harmony comes o'er the vale ;
And through the trees I view the embattled tower
Whence all the music. I again perceive
The soothing influence of the wafted strains,
And settle in soft musings as I tread
The walk, still verdant, under oaks and elms,

Whose outspread branches overarch the glade.
The roof, though movable through all its length
As the wind sways it, has yet well sufficed,
And, intercepting in their silent fall
The frequent flakes, has kept a path for me.
No noise is here, or none that hinders thought.
The redbreast warbles still, but is content
With slender notes, and more than half suppress'd ;
Pleased with his solitude, and flitting light
From spray to spray, where'er he rests he shakes
From many a twig the pendent drops of ice,
That tinkle in the withered leaves below. . . .
  Here, unmolested, through whatever sign
The sun proceeds, I wander ; neither mist,
Nor freezing sky nor sultry, checking me,
Nor stranger intermeddling with my joy.
Even in the spring and playtime of the year,
That calls the unwonted villager abroad
With all her little ones, a sportive train,
To gather kingcups in the yellow mead,
And prink their hair with daisies, or to pick
A cheap but wholesome salad from the brook.
These shades are all my own. The timorous hare,
Grown so familiar with her frequent guest,
Scarce shuns me ; and the stockdove unalarmed
Sits cooing in the pine-tree, nor suspends
His long love-ditty for my near approach.

William Cowper

THE DARKLING THRUSH

I LEANT upon a coppice gate
  When Frost was spectre-grey,
And Winter's dregs made desolate
  The weakening eye of day.
The tangled bine-stems scored the sky
  Like strings of broken lyres,
And all mankind that haunted nigh
  Had sought their household fires.

The land's sharp features seemed to be
  The Century's corpse outleant,
His crypt the cloudy canopy,
  The wind his death-lament.
The ancient pulse of germ and birth
  Was shrunken hard and dry,
And every spirit upon earth
  Seemed fervourless as I.

At once a voice burst forth among
  The bleak twigs overhead
In a full-hearted evensong
  Of joy illimited ;
An aged thrush, frail, gaunt and small,
  In blast-beruffled plume,
Had chosen thus to fling his soul
  Upon the growing gloom.

So little cause for carolings
  Of such ecstatic sound
Was written on terrestrial things
  Afar or nigh around,
That I could think there trembled through
  His happy good-night air
Some blessed hope, whereof he knew
  And I was unaware.

Thomas Hardy

WEEPING DAWN

A DRIPPING day is two hours old,
  Unseen save by the matin cock ;
  The world is sodden, dark and cold ;
The fogger,[1] fumbling with the lock,
  Must hold his lanthorn to the bin
  Ere he can ease the lowing stock.
Laggard the morn comes weeping in,
  The drops fall heavy from the tree ;
  A shrouded candle shows within

[1] *fogger* : farm-hand chiefly engaged in feeding cattle.

The house, where Cicely girds her knee,
  And yawning gives her hair a twist,
  Or pins her shift and lets it be,
Scant guardian of her tumbled breast ;
  Then slippers down to blow the ash
  And blaze the chilblain on her wrist.
She hears the great slow oxen plash
  Their way thro' puddles in the lane ;
  The wet wind whistles in the sash
Or spatters hasty on the pane—
  A hopeless dawn ! Nay, in the West,
  Beyond the fringes of the rain,
See like an opening palimpsest,
  Watchful and steadfast, Heaven's blue eye !
  Read there, O man, your gospell'd rest.

Maurice Hewlett

TOUGH GUY

THE shouts of ousel blackamoors
Are vocal as the gales ;
When winds are fanged and trees are bones.
Their lustihood prevails.

Later the scarce and tender thrush
More silverly will sing ;
But winter frets him ; mute he lurks
And stirs nor throat nor wing.

The rowdy ousel flashes by
With bill, and heart, of gold.
A blackshirt bird ? no bully he,
But freeman of the wold.

This is a time for gay and grim,
For those who soar and dare.
On, blackamoor, the hour is yours,
My tough guy of the air.

Ivor Brown

UPON ECKINGTON BRIDGE, RIVER AVON

O Pastoral heart of England ! like a psalm
  Of green days telling with a quiet beat—
O wave into the sunset flowing calm !
  O tirèd lark descending on the wheat !
Lies it all peace beyond that western fold
  Where now the lingering shepherd sees his star
Rise upon Malvern ? Paints an Age of Gold
  Yon cloud with prophecies of linkèd ease—
  Lulling this Land, with hills drawn up like knees,
To drowse beside her implements of war ?

Man shall outlast his battles. They have swept
  Avon from Naseby Field to Severn Ham ;
And Evesham's dedicated stones have stepp'd
  Down to the dust with Montfort's oriflamme.
Nor the red tear nor the reflected tower
  Abides ; but yet these eloquent grooves remain,
Worn in the sandstone parapet hour by hour
  By labouring bargemen where they shifted ropes.
  E'en so shall man turn back from violent hopes
To Adam's cheer, and toil with spade again.

Ay, and his mother Nature, to whose lap
  Like a repentant child at length he hies,
Not in the whirlwind or the thunder-clap
  Proclaims her more tremendous mysteries :
But when in winter's grave, bereft of light,
  With still, small voice divinelier whispering
—Lifting the green head of the aconite,
  Feeding with sap of hope the hazel-shoot—
  She feels God's finger active at the root,
Turns in her sleep, and murmurs of the Spring.

Sir Arthur Quiller-Couch

DISAPPOINTMENT

To a Young Lady on her leaving the Town after the Coronation

As some fond virgin, whom her mother's care
Drags from the town to wholesome country air,

Just when she learns to roll a melting eye,
And hear a spark, yet think no danger nigh ;
From the dear man unwilling she must sever,
Yet takes one kiss before she parts for ever :
Thus from the world fair Zephalinda flew,
Saw others happy, and with sighs withdrew ;
Not that their pleasures caused her discontent,
She sighed not that they stayed, but that she went.
  She went to plain-work, and to purling brooks,
Old-fashioned halls, dull aunts, and croaking rooks ;
She went from Opera, Park, Assembly, Play,
To morning walks, and prayers three hours a day ;
To part her time 'twixt reading and bohea,
To muse, and spill her solitary tea,
Or o'er cold coffee trifle with the spoon,
Count the slow clock, and dine exact at noon ;
Divert her eyes with pictures in the fire,
Hum half a tune, tell stories to the Squire ;
Up to her godly garret after seven,
There starve and pray, for that's the way to Heaven.
  Some Squire, perhaps, you take delight to rack,
Whose game is whisk,[1] whose treat a toast in sack ;
Who visits with a gun, presents you birds,
Then gives a smacking buss, and cries : " No words ! "
Or with his hound comes hallooing from the stable,
Makes love with nods and knees beneath a table ;
Whose laughs are hearty, though his jests are coarse,
And loves you best of all things—but his horse.
  In some fair evening, on your elbow laid,
You dream of triumphs in the rural shade ;
In pensive thought recall the fancied scene,
See coronations rise on every green ;
Before you pass the imaginary sights
Of lords, and earls, and dukes, and gartered knights,
While the spread fan o'ershades your closing eyes ;
Then give one flirt, and all the vision flies.
Thus vanish sceptres, coronets, and balls,
And leave you in lone woods or empty walls.

Alexander Pope

[1] *whisk* : whist.

TOWN

MY MOTHER CAMBRIDGE

NEXT these the plenteous Ouse came far from land,
  By many a city and by many a towne,
And many rivers taking under hand
  Into his waters as he passeth downe,
  The Cle, the Were, the Grant, the Sture, the Rowne,
Thence doth by Huntingdon and Cambridge flit,
  My mother Cambridge, whom as with a crowne
He doth adorne, and is adorned of it
With many a gentle Muse, and many a learned wit.

Edmund Spenser

DUNS SCOTUS'S OXFORD

TOWERY city and branchy between towers ;
Cuckoo-echoing, bell-swarmèd, lark-charmèd,
    rook-racked, river-rounded ;
The dapple-eared lily below thee ; that country and
    town did
Once encounter in, here coped and poisèd powers ;

Thou hast a base and brickish skirt there, sours
That neighbour-nature thy grey beauty is grounded
Best in ; graceless growth, thou hast confounded
Rural rural keeping—folk, flocks, and flowers.

Yet ah ! this air I gather and I release
He lived on ; these weeds and waters, these walls are
    what
He haunted who of all men most sways my spirits to
    peace ;

Of realty the rarest-veinèd traveller ; a not
Rivalled insight, be rival Italy or Greece ;
Who fired France for Mary without spot.

Gerard Manley Hopkins

LINCOLN

By this to Lincoln com'n, upon whose lofty site
Whilst wistly Wytham looks with wonderful delight
Enamoured of the state and beauty of the place
That her of all the rest especially doth grace.

Michael Drayton

INDUSTRY TRIUMPHANT

Take we now our eastward course
To the rich fields of Burstal. Wide around
Hillock and valley, farm and village, smile ;
And ruddy roofs and chimney-tops appear
Of busy Leeds, upwafting to the clouds
The incense of thanksgiving ; all is joy,
And trade and business guide the living scene,
Roll the full cars, adown the winding Aire
Load the slow-sailing barges, pile the pack
On the low-tinkling train of slow-pac'd steeds.
As when a sunny day invites abroad
The sedulous ants, they issue from their cells
In bands unnumber'd, eager for their work ;
O'er high, o'er low, they lift, they draw, they haste
With warm affection to each other's aid ;
Repeat their virtuous efforts and succeed.
Thus all is here in motion, all is life ;
The creaking wain brings copious store of corn ;
The grazier's sleeky kine obstruct the roads ;
The neat-dress'd housewives, for the festal board
Crown'd with full baskets, in the field-way paths
Come tripping on ; the echoing hills repeat
The stroke of axe and hammer ; scaffolds rise
And growing edifices ; heaps of stone
Beneath the chisel beauteous shapes assume
Of frieze and column. Some with even line
New streets are marking in the neighbouring fields,
And sacred domes of worship. Industry,
Which dignifies the artist, lifts the swain,

And the straw cottage to a palace turns,
Over the work presides. Such was the scene
Of hurrying Carthage, when the Trojan chief
First view'd her growing turrets. So appear
Th' increasing walls of busy Manchester,
Sheffield and Birmingham, whose reddening fields
Rise and enlarge their suburbs. Lo, in throngs
For every realm the careful factors meet
Whispering each other. In long ranks the bales,
Like war's bright files, beyond the sight extend.
Straight ere the sounding bell the signal strikes,
Which ends the hour of traffic, they conclude
The speedy compact ; and well-pleas'd transfer
With mutual benefit superior wealth
To many a kingdom's rent or tyrant's hoard.

John Dyer

A BALLAD OF BATH

Like a queen enchanted who may not laugh or weep,
Glad at heart and guarded from change and care like ours,
Girt about with beauty by days and nights that creep
Soft as breathless ripples that softly shoreward sweep,
Lies the lovely city whose grace no grief deflowers.
Age and grey forgetfulness, time that shifts and veers,
Touch not thee, our fairest, whose charm no rival nears,
Hailed as England's Florence of one whose praise gives grace,
Landor, once thy lover, a name that love reveres :
Dawn and noon and sunset are one before thy face.

Dawn whereof we know not, and noon whose fruit we reap,
Garnered up in record of years that fell like flowers,
Sunset liker sunrise along the shining steep
Whence thy fair face lightens, and where thy soft springs leap,
Crown at once and gird thee with grace of guardian powers.

Loved of men beloved of us, souls that fame inspheres,
All thine air hath music for him who dreams and hears ;
  Voices mixed of multitudes, feet of friends that pace,
Witness why for ever, if heaven's face clouds or clears,
  Dawn and noon and sunset are one before thy face.

Peace hath here found harbourage mild as very sleep :
  Not the hills and waters, the fields and wildwood bowers,
Smile or speak more tenderly, clothed with peace more
    deep,
Here than memory whispers of days our memories keep
  Fast with love and laughter and dreams of withered
    hours.
Bright were these as blossom of old, and thought endears
Still the fair soft phantoms that pass with smiles or tears,
  Sweet as roseleaves hoarded and dried wherein we
    trace
Still the soul and spirit of sense that lives and cheers :
  Dawn and noon and sunset are one before thy face.

City lulled asleep by the chime of passing years,
Sweeter smiles thy rest than the radiance round thy peers ;
  Only love and lovely remembrance here have place.
Time on thee lies lighter than music on men's ears ;
  Dawn and noon and sunset are one before thy face.

Algernon Charles Swinburne

BRIGHTON

HER brave sea-bulwarks builded strong
  No tides uproot, no storms appal ;
By sea-blown tamarisks the throng
  Of idlers pace her broad sea-wall ;
Rain-plashed the long-lit pavements gleam ;
  Still press the gay groups to and fro ;
Dark midnight deepens ; on they stream ;
  The wheels, the clattering horses go.

But that wave-limit close anear,
  Which kissed at morn the children's play,
With dusk becomes a phantom fear,
  Throws in the night a ghostly spray :—
O starless waste ! remote despair !
  Deep-weltering wildness, pulsing gloom !
As tho' the whole world's heart was there,
  And all the whole world's heart a tomb.

Eternal sounds the waves' refrain ;
  " Eternal night ",—they moan and say,—
" Eternal peace, eternal pain,
  Press close upon your dying day.
Who, who at once beyond the bound,
  What world-worn soul will rise and flee,—
Leave the crude lights and clamorous sound,
  And trust the darkness and the sea ? "

F. W. H. Myers

THE RIVER'S TALE

(Prehistoric)

Twenty bridges from Tower to Kew—
(Twenty bridges or twenty-two)—
Wanted to know what the River knew,
For they were young and the Thames was old,
And this is the tale that the River told :—

" I walk my beat before London Town,
Five hours up and seven down.
Up I go till I end my run
At Tide-end-town, which is Teddington.
Down I come with the mud in my hands
And plaster it over the Maplin Sands.
But I'd have you know that these waters of mine
Were once a branch of the River Rhine,
When hundreds of miles to the East I went
And England was joined to the Continent.

I remember the bat-winged lizard-birds,
The Age of Ice and the mammoth herds,

And the giant tigers that stalked them down
Through Regent's Park into Camden Town.
And I remember like yesterday
The earliest Cockney who came my way,
When he pushed through the forest that lined the
    Strand,
With paint on his face and a club in his hand.
He was death to feather and fin and fur,
He trapped my beavers at Westminster.
He netted my salmon, he hunted my deer,
He killed my herons off Lambeth Pier.
He fought his neighbour with axes and swords,
Flint or bronze, at my upper fords,
While down at Greenwich, for slaves and tin,
The tall Phoenician ships stole in,
And North-Sea war-boats, painted and gay,
Flashed like dragon-flies, Erith way;
And Norseman and Negro and Gaul and Greek
Drank with the Britons in Barking Creek,
And life was gay, and the world was new,
And I was a mile across at Kew!
But the Roman came with a heavy hand,
And bridged and roaded and ruled the land,
And the Roman left and the Danes blew in—
And that's where your history-books begin!"

Rudyard Kipling

LONDON

LONDON, thou art of townès A per se.[1]
  Sovereign of cities, semeliest in sight,
Of high renoun, riches, and royaltie;
  Of Lordis, barons, and many a goodly knyght;
  Of most delectable lusty[2] ladies bright;
Of famous prelatis, in habitis clerical;
  Of merchauntis full of substaunce and of might:
London, thou art the flour of cities all.

[1] *A per se*: unique. [2] *lusty*: pleasing.

Gladdith[1] anon, thou lusty Troynovaunt,[2]
  Citie that sometyme clepèd[3] was New Troy,
In all the erth, imperiall as thou stant,[4]
  Prynsess of townes, of pleasure and of joy,
  A richer resteth under no Christen roy ;[5]
For manly power, with craftis naturall,
  Fourmeth[6] none fairer, sith[7] the flode of Noy :[8]
London, thou art the flour of cities all.

Gemme of all joy, jasper of jocunditie,
  Most myghty carbuncle of vertue and valour ;
Strong Troy in vigour and in strenuyty ;
  Of royall cities rose and geraflour ;[9]
  Empresse of townès, exalt in honour ;
In beawtie bering the crone imperiall ;
  Swete paradise precelling[10] in pleasure :
London, thou art the flour of cities all.

Above all ryvers thy Ryver hath renowne,
  Whose beryall[11] stremys, pleasaunt and preclare,[12]
Under thy lusty wallys renneth down,
  Where many a swanne doth swymme with wyngès faire;
  Where many a barge doth saile, and row with are,[13]
Where many a ship doth rest with toppe-royall.
  O ! towne of townes, patrone and not compare ;[14]
London, thou art the flour of cities all.

Upon thy lusty Brigge of pylers white
  Been merchaunts full royall to behold ;
Upon thy streetis goth many a semely knyght
  In velvet gownès and in cheynès of gold.
  By Julyus Cesar thy Touer founded of old
May be the hous of Mars victoryall,
  Whose artillary with tonge may not be told :
London, thou art the flour of cities all.

[1] *Gladdith* : be glad.
[2] *Troynovaunt* : new Troy.
[3] *clepèd* : called.
[4] *stant* : standest.
[5] *roy* : king.
[6] *Fourmeth* : appears.
[7] *sith* : since.
[8] *Noy* : Noah.
[9] *geraflour* : gillyflower.
[10] *precelling* : excelling.
[11] *beryall* : shining like a beryl stone.
[12] *preclare* : famous.
[13] *are* : oar.
[14] *compare* : equal.

Strong be thy wallis that about thee standis ;
  Wise be the people that within thee dwellis ;
Fresh is thy ryver with his lusty strandis ;
  Blith be thy chirches, wele sownyng be thy bellis,
  Rich be thy merchauntis in substaunce that excellis ;
Fair be their wives, right lovesom, white and small ;[1]
  Clere[2] be thy virgyns, lusty under kellis :[3]
London, thou are the flour of cities all.

Thy famous Maire, by pryncely governaunce,
  With swerd of justice, thee rulith prudently.
No Lord of Parys, Venyce, or Floraunce
  In dignytie or honoure goeth to hym nye.
  He is exampler, loodè-ster and guye ;[4]
Pryncipall patrone and roose orygynalle,
  Above all Maires as maister moost worthy :
London, thou art the flour of cities all.

William Dunbar

HIS RETURN TO LONDON

FROM the dull confines of the drooping west,
To see the day spring from the pregnant east,
Ravished in spirit, I come, nay more, I fly
To thee, blest place of my nativity.
Thus, thus with hallowed foot I touch the ground,
With thousand blessings by thy fortune crowned.
O fruitful genius ! that bestowest here
An everlasting plenty, year by year.
O place ! O people ! Manners ! framed to please
All nations, customs, kindreds, languages !
I am a free-born Roman ; suffer then,
That I amongst you live a citizen.
London my home is ; though by hard fate sent
Into a long and irksome banishment ;
Yet since called back ; henceforward let me be,
O native country, repossessed by thee !

[1] *small* : slender. [2] *clere* : pure.
[3] *kellis* : head-dresses. [4] *guye* : guide.

For, rather than I'll to the west return,
I'll beg of thee first here to have mine urn.
Weak I am grown, and must in short time fall ;
Give thou my sacred relics burial.

Robert Herrick

DESCRIPTION OF A CITY SHOWER

Careful observers may foretell the hour
(By sure prognostics) when to dread a shower.
While rain depends, the pensive cat gives o'er
Her frolics, and pursues her tail no more.
Returning home at night, you'll find the sink
Strike your offended sense with double stink.
If you be wise, then go not far to dine ;
You'll spend in coach-hire more than save in wine.
A coming shower your shooting corns presage,
Old aches will throb, your hollow tooth will rage.
Sauntering in coffee-house is Dulman seen ;
He damns the climate, and complains of spleen.
Meanwhile the south, rising with dabbled wings,
A sable cloud athwart the welkin flings,
That swilled more liquor than it could contain,
And, like a drunkard, gives it up again.
Brisk Susan whips her linen from the rope,
While the first drizzling shower is borne aslope ;
Such is that sprinkling which some careless quean [1]
Flirts on you from her mop, but not so clean :
You fly, invoke the gods ; then, turning, stop
To rail ; she, singing, still whirls on her mop.
Not yet the dust had shunned the unequal strife,
But aided by the wind fought still for life ;
And, wafted with its foe by violent gust,
'Twas doubtful which was rain, and which was dust.
Ah ! where must needy poet seek for aid,
When dust and rain at once his coat invade ?
Sole coat ! where dust cemented by the rain
Erects the nap, and leaves a cloudy stain !

[1] *quean* : hussy.

Now in contiguous drops the flood comes down,
Threatening with deluge this devoted town.
To shops in crowds the daggled [1] females fly,
Pretend to cheapen [2] goods, but nothing buy.
The templar spruce, while every spout's abroach,[3]
Stays till 'tis fair, yet seems to call a coach.
The tucked-up seamstress walks with hasty strides,
While streams run down her oiled umbrella's sides.
Here various kinds, by various fortunes led,
Commence acquaintance underneath a shed.
Triumphant Tories and desponding Whigs
Forget their feuds, and join to save their wigs.
Boxed in a chair, the beau impatient sits,
While spouts run clattering o'er the roof by fits,
And ever and anon with frightful din
The leather sounds; he trembles from within.
So when Troy chairmen bore the wooden steed,
Pregnant with Greeks impatient to be freed
(Those bully Greeks, who, as the moderns do,
Instead of paying chairmen, ran them through),
Laocoon struck the outside with his spear,
And each imprisoned hero quaked for fear.
Now from all parts the swelling kennels flow,
And bear their trophies with them as they go:
Filths of all hues and odour seem to tell
What street they sailed from by their sight and smell.
They, as each torrent drives, with rapid force,
From Smithfield or St. 'Pulchre's shape their course,
And in huge confluence joined at Snowhill ridge,
Fall from the conduit prone to Holborn bridge.

Jonathan Swift

TO WHOM TO GIVE THE WALL

LET due civilities be strictly paid:
The wall surrender to the hooded maid;
Nor let thy sturdy elbow's hasty rage
Jostle the feeble steps of trembling age;

[1] *daggled*: bespattered. [2] *cheapen*: bid for.
[3] *abroach*: running over.

And when the porter bends beneath his load,
And pants for breath, clear thou the crowded road.
But, above all, the groping blind direct,
And from the passing throng the lame protect.
  You'll sometimes meet a fop, of nicest tread,
Whose mantling peruke veils his empty head ;
At every step he dreads the wall to lose,
And risks, to save a coach, his red-heeled shoes ;
Him, like the miller, pass with caution by,
Lest from his shoulder clouds of powder fly.
But when the bully, with assuming pace,
Cocks his broad hat, edged round with tarnished lace,
Yield not the way, defy his strutting pride,
And thrust him to the muddy kennel's side ;
He never turns again, nor dares oppose,
But mutters coward curses as he goes.

John Gay

HAMPTON COURT

Close by those meads, for ever crowned with flowers,
Where Thames with pride surveys his rising towers,
There stands a structure of majestic frame,
Which from the neighb'ring Hampton takes its name.
Here Britain's statesmen oft the fall foredoom
Of foreign tyrants and of nymphs at home ;
Here thou, great Anna ! whom three realms obey,
Dost sometimes counsel take—and sometimes tea.
Hither the heroes and the nymphs resort,
To taste awhile the pleasures of a court ;
In various talk the instructive hours they passed,
Who gave the ball, or paid the visit last ;
One speaks the glory of the British Queen,
And one describes a charming Indian screen ;
A third interprets motions, looks, and eyes ;
At every word a reputation dies.
Snuff, or the fan, supply each pause of chat,
With singing, laughing, ogling, and all that.
Meanwhile, declining from the noon of day,
The sun obliquely shoots his burning ray ;

The hungry judges soon the sentence sign,
And wretches hang that jury-men may dine ;
The merchant from the Exchange returns in peace,
And the long labours of the toilet cease.

Alexander Pope

STRAWBERRY HILL

Some cry up Gunnersbury !
For Sion some declare !
Some say, with Chiswick House
No Villa can compare !

But ask the Beaus of Middlesex,
Who know the country well,
If Strawberry Hill, if Strawberry Hill
Don't bear away the bell ?

. . . . .

Great William dwells at Windsor,
As Edward did of old ;
And many a Gaul, and many a Scot,
Have found him full as bold !

On lofty hills like Windsor,
Such Heroes ought to dwell ;
Yet the little folks on Strawberry Hill
Like Strawberry Hill as well !

William Pulteney, Earl of Bath

WESTMINSTER BRIDGE

(September 1802)

Earth has not anything to show more fair :
Dull would he be of soul who could pass by
A sight so touching in its majesty :
This City now doth, like a garment, wear
The beauty of the morning ; silent, bare,

Ships, towers, domes, theatres, and temples lie
Open unto the fields, and to the sky ;
All bright and glittering in the smokeless air.
Never did sun more beautifully steep
In his first splendour, valley, rock, or hill ;
Ne'er saw I, never felt, a calm so deep !
The river glideth at his own sweet will :
Dear God ! the very houses seem asleep ;
And all that mighty heart is lying still !

William Wordsworth

WHEREVER MEN ARE GATHERED

Wherever men are gathered, all the air
Is charged with human feeling, human thought ;
Each shout and cry and laugh, each curse and prayer,
Are into its vibrations surely wrought ;
Unspoken passion, wordless meditation,
Are breathed into it with our respiration ;
It is with our life fraught and overfraught.

So that no man there breathes earth's simple breath,
As if alone on mountains or wide seas ;
But nourishes warm life or hastens death
With joys and sorrows, health and foul disease,
Wisdom and folly, good and evil labours,
Incessant of his multitudinous neighbours ;
He in his turn affecting all of these.

That City's atmosphere is dark and dense,
Although not many exiles wander there,
With many a potent evil influence,
Each adding poison to the poisoned air ;
Infections of unutterable sadness,
Infections of incalculable madness,
Infections of incurable despair.

James Thomson (" B.V.")

A LONDON PLANE TREE

GREEN is the plane tree in the square,
  The other trees are brown ;
They droop and pine for country air ;
  The plane tree loves the town.

Here from my garret-pane I mark
  The plane tree bud and blow,
Shed her recuperative bark,
  And spread her shade below.

Among her branches, in and out,
  The city breezes play ;
The dull fog wraps her round about ;
  Above, the smoke curls grey.

Others the country take for choice,
  And hold the town in scorn ;
But she has listen'd to the voice
  On city breezes borne.

Amy Levy

CHAUCER'S THAMES

FORGET six counties overhung with smoke,
Forget the snorting steam and piston stroke,
Forget the spreading of the hideous town ;
Think rather of the pack-horse on the down,
And dream of London, small and white and clean,
The clear Thames bordered by its gardens green ;
Think, that below bridge, the green lapping waves
Smite some few keels that bear Levantine staves,
Cut from the yew-wood on the burnt-up hill,
And pointed jars that Greek hands toiled to fill,
And treasured scanty spice from some far sea,
Florence gold cloth, and Ypres napery,

And cloth of Bruges, and hogsheads of Guienne ;
While nigh the thronged wharf Geoffrey Chaucer's pen
Moves over bills of lading—mid such times
Shall dwell the hollow puppets of my rhymes.

William Morris

THE LADIES OF ST. JAMES'S

The ladies of St. James's
  Go swinging to the play ;
Their footmen run before them,
  With a " Stand by ! Clear the way ! "
But Phyllida, my Phyllida !
  She takes her buckled shoon,
When we go out a-courting
  Beneath the harvest moon.

The ladies of St. James's
  Wear satin on their backs ;
They sit all night at *Ombre*,
  With candles all of wax :
But Phyllida, my Phyllida !
  She dons her russet gown,
And hastes to gather May dew
  Before the world is down.

The ladies of St. James's !
  They are so fine and fair,
You'd think a box of essences
  Was broken in the air :
But Phyllida, my Phyllida !
  The breath of heath and furze,
When breezes blow at morning,
  Is not so fresh as hers.

The ladies of St. James's !
  They're painted to the eyes ;
Their white it stays for ever,
  Their red it never dies :

But Phyllida, my Phyllida !
  Her colour comes and goes ;
It trembles to a lily—
  It wavers to a rose.

The ladies of St. James's !
  You scarce can understand
The half of all their speeches,
  Their phrases are so grand :
But Phyllida, my Phyllida !
  Her shy and simple words
Are clear as after rain-drops
  The music of the birds.

The ladies of St. James's !
  They have their fits and freaks ;
They smile on you—for seconds ;
  They frown on you—for weeks :
But Phyllida, my Phyllida !
  Come either storm or shine,
From Shrove-tide unto Shrove-tide,
  Is always true—and mine.

My Phyllida ! my Phyllida !
  I care not though they heap
The hearts of all St. James's,
  And give me all to keep ;
I care not whose the beauties
  Of all the world may be,
For Phyllida—for Phyllida,
  Is all the world to me !

Austin Dobson

LONDON SNOW

WHEN men were all asleep the snow came flying,
In large white flakes falling on the city brown,
Stealthily and perpetually settling and loosely lying,
  Hushing the latest traffic of the drowsy town ;

Deadening, muffling, stifling its murmurs failing ;
Lazily and incessantly floating down and down :
  Silently sifting and veiling road, roof and railing ;
Hiding difference, making unevenness even,
Into angles and crevices softly drifting and sailing.
  All night it fell, and when full inches seven
It lay in the depth of its uncompacted lightness,
The clouds blew off from a high and frosty heaven ;
  And all woke earlier for the unaccustomed brightness
Of the winter dawning, the strange unheavenly glare :
The eye marvelled—marvelled at the dazzling whiteness ;
  The ear hearkened to the stillness of the solemn air ;
No sound of wheel rumbling nor of foot falling,
And the busy morning cries came thin and spare.
  Then boys I heard, as they went to school, calling,
They gathered up the crystal manna to freeze
Their tongues with tasting, their hands with snowballing ;
  Or rioted in a drift, plunging up to the knees ;
Or peering up from under the white-mossed wonder,
" O look at the trees ! " they cried, " O look at the trees ! "
  With lessened load a few carts creak and blunder,
Following along the white deserted way,
A country company long dispersed asunder :
  When now already the sun, in pale display
Standing by Paul's high dome, spread forth below
His sparkling beams, and awoke the stir of the day.
  For now doors open, and war is waged with the snow ;
And trains of sombre men, past tale of number,
Tread long brown paths, as toward their toil they go :
  But even for them awhile no cares encumber
Their minds diverted ; the daily word is unspoken,
The daily thoughts of labour and sorrow slumber
At the sight of the beauty that greets them, for the charm
  they have broken.

Robert Bridges

DOWN THROUGH THE ANCIENT STRAND

Down through the ancient Strand
The spirit of October, mild and boon

And sauntering, takes his way
This golden end of afternoon,
As though the corn stood yellow in all the land,
And the ripe apples dropped to the harvest-moon.

Lo ! the round sun, half down the western slope—
Seen as along an unglazed telescope—
Lingers and lolls, loth to be done with day :
Gifting the long, lean, lanky street
And its abounding confluences of being
With aspects generous and bland ;
Making a thousand harnesses to shine
As with new ore from some enchanted mine,
And every horse's coat so full of sheen
He looks new-tailored, and every bus feels clean,
And never a hansom but is worth the feeing ;
And every jeweller within the pale
Offers a real Arabian Night for sale ;
And even the roar
Of the strong streams of toil, that pause and pour
Eastward and westward, sounds suffused—
Seems as it were bemused
And blurred, and like the speech
Of lazy seas upon a lotus-haunted beach—
With this enchanted lustrousness,
This mellow magic, that (as a man's caress
Brings back to some faded face, beloved before,
A heavenly shadow of the grace it wore
Ere the poor eyes were minded to beseech)
Old things transfigures, and you hail and bless
Their looks of long-lapsed loveliness once more ;
Till the sedate and mannered elegance
Of Clement's, angular and cold and staid,—
Gleams forth in glamour's very stuffs arrayed ;
And Bride's, her aëry, unsubstantial charm
Through flight on flight of springing, soaring stone
Grown flushed and warm,
Laughs into life, full-mooded and fresh-blown ;
And the high majesty of Paul's
Uplifts a voice of living light, and calls—

Calls to his millions to behold and see
How goodly this his London Town can be !

For earth and sky and air
Are golden everywhere,
And golden with a gold so suave and fine,
The looking on it lifts the heart like wine.
Trafalgar Square
(The fountains volleying golden glaze)
Shines like an angel-market. High aloft
Over his couchant Lions, in a haze
Shimmering and bland and soft,
A dust of chrysoprase,
Our Sailor takes the golden gaze
Of the saluting sun, and flames superb,
As once he flamed it on his ocean round.

The dingy dreariness of the picture-place,
Turned very nearly bright,
Takes on a luminous transiency of grace,
And shows no more a scandal to the ground.
The very blind man pottering on the kerb,
Among the posies and the ostrich feathers
And the rude voices touched with all the weathers
Of the long, varying year,
Shares in the universal alms of light.
The windows, with their fleeting, flickering fires,
The height and spread of frontage shining sheer,
The quiring signs, the rejoicing roofs and spires—
'Tis El Dorado—El Dorado plain,
The Golden City ! And when a girl goes by,
Look ! as she turns her glancing head,
A call of gold is floated from her ear !
Golden, all golden ! In a golden glory,
Long-lapsing down a golden-coasted sky,
The day, not dies but seems
Dispersed in wafts and drifts of gold, and shed
Upon a past of golden song and story
And memories of gold and golden dreams.

W. E. Henley

NOVEMBER BLUE

"The golden tint of the electric lights seems to give a complementary colour to the air in the early evening."—Essay on London.

O heavenly colour, London town
  Has blurred it from her skies ;
And, hooded in an earthly brown,
  Unheaven'd the city lies.
No longer, standard-like, this hue
  Above the broad road flies ;
Nor does the narrow street the blue
  Wear, slender pennon-wise.

But when the gold and silver lamps
  Colour the London dew,
And, misted by the winter damps,
  The shops shine bright anew—
Blue comes to earth, it walks the street,
  It dyes the wide air through ;
A mimic sky about their feet,
  The throng go crowned with blue.

Alice Meynel

ANTICIPATIONS

When still in the season
Of sunshine and leisure,
While blithe yet we wander
  O'er meadow and Down,
O say is it treason
To think of the treasure
Heaped up for us yonder
  In grey London town ?

We hunt the sweet berry
With purple-stained ardour ;
Each bramble one hooks in
  Is bent 'neath its load :

It's free and it's merry
In nature's rich larder—
But O to hunt books in
   The Charing Cross Road !

As daylight expires in
This best of Septembers,
A coolness comes blowing—
   A chill wintry hint !
But think ! it blows fires in,
And dream-kindling embers,
And candle-light glowing
   On time-mellowed print !

This glory of Summer
One's being rejoices ;
Yet hail to this flavour
   Of Summer's decay !
It's bringing the glamour,
The lights and the voices,
The dear homely savour
   Of London this way !

E. V. Lucas

SEAGULLS ON THE SERPENTINE

Memory, out of the mist, in a long slow ripple
   Breaks, blindly, against the shore.
The mist has buried the town in its own oblivion.
   This, this is the sea once more.

Mist—mist—brown mist ; but a sense in the air of
      snowflakes !
   I stand where the ripples die,
Lift up an arm and wait, till my lost ones know me,
   Wheel overhead, and cry.

Salt in the eyes, and the seagulls, mewing and swooping,
   Snatching the bread from my hand ;
Brushing my hand with their breasts, in swift caresses
   To show that they understand.

Oh, why are you so afraid ? We are all of us exiles !
  Wheel back in your clamorous rings !
We have all of us lost the sea, and we all remember.
  But you—have wings.

Alfred Noyes

PASTEL

The lowering sooty London sky
  Flushes with roses manifold ;
The spattered feet of the passers-by
  Slip and slide in silver and gold.

Lilac and violet and blue
  The lines of chimney-pots and bricks ;
The omnibus with its spectre crew
  Fades like the purple barque of Styx.

John Bowyer Nichols

LONDON

(1940)

Beloved London's ancient walls,
  Battered by hail of steel and fire,
  Look down with proud and scornful ire
On all the ruin of its halls.

So with disdain the pillared rock,
  Deep-rooted in mid-ocean's bed,
  Undaunted proudly lifts its head
Scorning the waves' imperious shock.

So too the oak, that bows before
  The furious raging of the blast,
  The tyranny now overpast,
Unconquered rears itself once more.

In vain upon our stricken lands
  The flying hordes rain death and fear ;
  Fighting for all we hold most dear
Old London's spirit firmly stands.

A. A. Milne

WESTMINSTER

(May 1941)

" EARTH has not anything to show more fair " :
So Wordsworth sang, enraptured with the sight
Of Westminster clad in its morning light
Of beauty, radiant and beyond compare ;
Its towers, domes, temples glittering in the air,
And nought above them but the birds in flight.
But now the sky-borne engines of the night
Have rained their bolts with thundering and flare.
Ah ! could the singer take his stand again
Upon the Bridge, how measureless his pain
To see the lovely vision maimed and marred—
But he would hear the " mighty heart " still beat
Undaunted, undismayed, and smiling greet
A Westminster whose soul could not be scarred.

F. S. Boas

LONDONER

" WHY? " you said, as the evening sirens blew
(And one knew there were fourteen weary hours till day),
" Why do you stay in this awful hullaballoo ?
" Why don't you get away ? "

I didn't reply, I was thinking of other things
(You were looking extremely sweet), and besides, you know,
There are thoughts that won't come out till the words find wings. . . .
But at half past twelve or so—

A Jerry droning dismally high above,
A lone bomb whistling down in N.W.3.—
I thought of the answer : " I live in London, love,
Because that's where I like to be."

I always did. And when Hitler started in style,
  I thought to myself, in the way that people do,
" London and I, we've been together awhile ;
    Together let's see this through."

For I have been London's lover for thirty years,
  And how I've enjoyed it ! Never has London hid
Her laughter from me. Now I like her in tears
    As well as ever I did.

She's lost her looks a little ? She isn't dressed
  With the splendour of yore ? Well, nobody cares a damn ;
She's still herself, she's London, she's still the best—
    And anyway, here I am.

Hellish, these last three months, and hard to face,
  And they haven't done anyone any manner of good ;
But would I have passed them in any other place ?
    Not on your life I would !

Hilton Brown

SPORT

AS I CAME BY

As I came by a grene forest side,
I met with a forster [1] that hadde me abide,
  With " *Hey go bet, hey go bet, hey go howe !* "

Underneath a tree I did me set,
And with a grete herte anone I met ;
I badde let slippe, and said " *Hey go bet !* "
  With " *Hey go bet, hey go bet, howe !* "

I had not stande there but a while,
For the mountenance [2] of a mile,
There came a grete herte, without gile.
  " *There he gothe, there he gothe, hey go howe !*
  We shall have sporte and game enowe."

Talbot my hounde with a mery nose
All about the grene wode he gan cast,
I toke my horne and blew him a blast,
  With " *Tro-ro-ro-ro, tro-ro-ro-ro !* "
  With " *Hey go bet, hey go bet, hey go howe !*
  There he gothe, there he gothe, hey go howe !
  We shall have sport and game enowe."

Anonymous (*c.* 1500)

THE KING'S HUNT

THE hunt is up, the hunt is up,
  And it is wellnigh day,
And Harry our King is gone hunting,
  To bring his deer to bay.

[1] *forster* : forester. [2] *mountenance* : amount.

The East is bright with morning light,
  And darkness it is fled,
And the merry horn wakes up the morn
  To leave his idle bed.

Behold the skies with golden dyes
  Are glowing all around,
The grass is green, and so are the treen,
  All laughing at the sound.

The horses snort to be at the sport,
  The dogs are running free,
The woods rejoice at the merry noise
  Of *hey tantarà tee ree !*

The sun is glad to see us clad
  All in our lusty green,
And smiles in the sky as he riseth high
  To see and to be seen.

Awake, all men, I say again,
  Be merry as you may,
For Harry our King is gone hunting
  To bring his deer to bay.

Anonymous (*c.* 1520)

ARSCOTT OF TETCOTT

On the ninth of November, in the year fifty-two,
Three jolly fox-hunters, all sons of true blue,
They rode from Pencarrow, not fearing a wet coat,
To take their diversion with Arscott of Tetcott.

He went to his kennel and took them within :
" On Monday," said Arscott, " our joys shall begin."
Both horses and hounds, how they pant to be gone !
How they'll follow afoot, not forgetting Black John !

When Monday was come, right early at morn
John Arscott arose, and he took down his horn ;
He gave it a flourish so loud, in the hall,
Each heard the glad summons and came at the call.

They heard it with pleasure, but Webb was first dressed,
Resolving to give a cold pig to the rest ; [1]
Bold Bob and the Briton, they hastened downstairs—
It was generally thought they neglected their prayers.

At breakfast they scrambled for butter and toast,
But Webb was impatient that time should be lost ;
So old Cheyney was ordered to bring to the door
Both horses and hounds, and away to the moor.

On Monday, says Arscott, as he mounted his nag,
" I took to Old Black Cap, for he'll hit the drag ! "
The drag it was hit, but they said it was old,
For a drag in the morning could not be so cold.

They pricked it along to Becket and Thorn,
And there the old dogs they set out, I'll be sworn ;
'Twas Ringwood and Rally, with capital scent,
Bold Princess and Madcap, good God, how they went !

" How far did they make it ? How far went they on ?
How far did they make it ? " said Simon the Son ;
" O'er the moors," said Joe Goodman, " hark to Bacchus, the word ! "
" Hark to Vulcan ! " cried Arscott, " that's it, by the Lord ! "

" Hark to Princess ! " says Arscott, " there's a fresh tally-ho ! "
The dogs they soon caught it, and how they did go !
'Twas Princess and Madcap, and Ringwood and Rally,
They charmed every hill and they echoed each valley.

From Becket, through Thorn, they went on their way,
To Swannacott Wood without break or delay ;

[1] Wake them with cold water, i.e. a cold sponge.

And when they came there, how they sounded again !
" What music it is ! " cried the glad Whitstone men.

In haste came up Arscott—" Oh, where are they gone ? "
" They are off to the cliffs," then said Simon the Son ;
Through Wike, and through Poundstock, St. Genys, they
went,
And when Reynard came there, he gave up by consent.

So when Reynard was dead, we broke up the field,
With joy in our hearts that we made him to yield ;
And when we came home we toasted the health
Of a man who ne'er varied for places or wealth !

When supper was ended we spent all the night
In gay flowing bumpers and social delight ;
With mirth and good humour did cheerfully sing,
A health to John Arscott, and God save the King !

R. S. Hawker

YOUNG REYNARD

GRACEFULLEST leaper, the dappled fox-cub
Curves over brambles with berries and buds,
Light as a bubble that flies from the tub,
Whisked by the laundry-wife out of her suds.
Wavy he comes, woolly, all at his ease,
Elegant, fashioned to foot with the deuce ;
Nature's own prince of the dance : then he sees
Me, and retires as if making excuse.

Never closed minuet courtlier ! Soon
Cubhunting troops were abroad, and a yelp
Told of sure scent : ere the stroke upon noon
Reynard the younger lay far beyond help.
Wild, my poor friend, has the fate to be chased ;
Civil will conquer : were 't other 't were worse.
Fair, by the flushed early morning embraced,
Haply you live a day longer in verse.

George Meredith

THE HUNTSMAN

THE huntsman, Robin Dawe, looked round.
He sometimes called a favourite hound,
Gently, to see the creature turn,
Look happy up and wag his stern.
He smiled and nodded and saluted
To those who hailed him, as it suited,
And patted Pip's, his hunter's neck.
His new pink was without a speck.
He was a red-faced smiling fellow,
His voice clear tenor, full and mellow,
His eyes, all fire, were black and small.
He had been smashed in many a fall.
His eyebrow had a white curved mark
Left by the bright shoe of The Lark.
Down in a ditch by Seven Springs
His coat had all been trod to strings,
His ribs laid bare and shoulder broken,
Being jumped on down at Water's Oaken
The time his horse came down and rolled.
His face was of the country mould
Such as the mason sometimes cutted
On English moulding-ends which jutted
Out of the church walls, centuries since.
And as you never know the quince,
How good he is, until you try,
So, in Dawe's face, what met the eye
Was only part ; what lay behind
Was English character and mind,
Great kindness, delicate sweet feeling
(Most shy, most clever in concealing
Its depth) for beauty of all sorts,
Great manliness and love of sports,
A grave, wise thoughtfulness and truth,
A merry fun outlasting youth,
A courage terrible to see,
And mercy for his enemy.

John Masefield

ST. VALENTINE'S DAY

Today, all day, I rode upon the down,
With hounds and horsemen, a brave company.
On this side in its glory lay the sea,
On that the Sussex weald, a sea of brown.
The wind was light, and brightly the sun shone,
And still we galloped on from gorse to gorse.
And once, when checked, a thrush sang, and my horse
Pricked his quick ears as to a sound unknown.
I knew the Spring was come—I knew it even
Better than all by this, that through my chase
In bush and stone and hill and sea and heaven
I seemed to see and follow still your face.
Your face my quarry was. For it I rode,
My horse a thing of wings, myself a god.

W. S. Blunt

THE CHASER'S CUP

The roads were filled with a drifting crowd,
Many mouth-organs droned aloud.

. . . . . .

Seven linked dancers singing a song
Bowed and kicked as they danced along,
The middleman thrust and pulled and squeezed
A concertina to tunes that pleased.
After them, honking, with Hey, Hey, Hey,
Came drivers thrusting to clear the way.

. . . . . .

Then came dog-carts and traps and wagons
With hampers of lunches, pies and flagons,
Bucks from city and flash young bloods
With vests " cut saucy " to show their studs.

. . . . . .

The costermongers as smart as sparrows
Brought their wives in their donkey-barrows.
The clean-legged donkeys, clever and cunning,
Their ears cocked forward, their neat feet running,

Their carts and harness flapping with flags,
Were bright as heralds and proud as stags.
And there in pride in the flapping banners
Were the costers' selves in blue bandannas,
And the costers' wives in feathers curling,
And their sons, with their sweet mouth-organs skirling.
  And from midst of the road to the roadside shifting
The crowd of the world on foot went drifting,
Standing aside on the trodden grass
To chaff as they let the traffic pass.
Then back they flooded, singing and cheering,
Plodding forward and disappearing,
Up to the course to take their places,
To lunch and gamble and see the races.

. . . . . .

  The March wind blew the smell of the crowd,
All men there seemed crying aloud,
But over the noise a louder roar
Broke, as the wave that bursts on shore
Drowns the roar of the wave that comes,
So this roar rose on the lesser hums,
" I back the Field ! I back the Field."
  Man who lives under sentence sealed,
Tragical man, who has but breath
For few brief years as he goes to death,
Tragical man by strange winds blown
To live in crowds ere he die alone,
Came in his jovial thousands massing
To see Life moving and beauty passing.
  They sucked their fruit in the wooden tiers
And flung the skins at the passers' ears ;
Drumming their heels on the planks below,
They sang of Dolly of Idaho.
Past, like a flash, the first race went.

The time drew by to the great event.

  At a quarter to three the big bell pealed ;
The horses trooped to the Saddling Field.
Covered in clothing, horse and mare
Pricked their ears at the people there ;

Some showed devil, and some composure,
As they trod their way to the great enclosure.
When the clock struck three and the men weighed out ;
Charles Cothill shook, though his heart was stout.
The thought of his bets, so gaily laid,
Seemed a stone the more when he sat and weighed.

. . . . . .

As he knotted the reins and took his stand
The horse's soul came into his hand,
And up from the mouth that held the steel
Came an innermost word, half thought, half feel,
" My day today, O master, O master ;
None shall jump cleaner, none shall go faster,
Call till you kill me, for I'll obey,
It's my day today, it's my day today."

John Masefield

THE OLD SQUIRE

I LIKE the hunting of the hare
Better than that of the fox ;
I like the joyous morning air
And the crowing of the cocks.

I like the calm of the early fields,
The ducks asleep by the lake,
The quiet hour which Nature yields,
Before mankind is awake.

I like the pheasants and feeding things
Of the unsuspicious morn ;
I like the flap of the wood-pigeon's wings
As she rises from the corn.

I like the blackbird's shriek, and his rush
From the turnips as I pass by,
And the partridge hiding her head in a bush,
For her young ones cannot fly.

I like these things, and I like to ride,
  When all the world is in bed,
To the top of the hill where the sky grows wide,
  And where the sun grows red.

The beagles at my horse-heels trot
  In silence after me ;
There's Ruby, Roger, Diamond, Dot,
  Old Slut and Margery,

A score of names well used and dear,
  The names my childhood knew ;
The horn with which I rouse their cheer
  Is the horn my father blew.

I like the hunting of the hare
  Better than that of the fox ;
The new world still is all less fair
  Than the old world it mocks.

I cover not a wider range
  Than these dear manors give ;
I take my pleasures without change,
  And as I lived I live.

I leave my neighbours to their thought,
  My choice it is, and pride,
On my own lands to find my sport,
  In my own fields to ride.

The hare herself no better loves
  The field where she was bred,
Than I the habit of these groves,
  My own inherited.

I know my quarries every one,
  The meuse [1] where she sits low ;
The road she chose today was run
  A hundred years ago.

[1] *meuse* : gap in a hedge.

The lags,[1] the gills,[2] the forest ways,
  The hedgerows one and all,
These are the kingdoms of my chase,
  And bounded by my wall ;

Nor has the world a better thing,
  Though one should search it round,
Than thus to live one's own sole king
  Upon one's own sole ground.

I like the hunting of the hare ;
  It brings me, day by day,
The memory of old days as fair,
  With dead men past away.

To these, as homeward still I ply
  And pass the churchyard gate,
Where all are laid as I must lie,
  I stop and raise my hat.

I like the hunting of the hare ;
  New sports I hold in scorn.
I like to be as my fathers were,
  In the days ere I was born.

W. S. Blunt

COURSING

Whilst Rockingham was heard with these reports to ring,
The Muse by making on tow'rds Welland's ominous spring,
With Kelmarsh there is caught, for Coursing of the Hare,
Which scorns that any place should with her plains
    compare :
Which in the proper terms the Muse doth thus report ;
The man whose vacant mind prepares him for the sport,
The Finder sendeth out, to seek out nimble Wat,
Which crosseth in the field, each furlong, every flat,
Till he this pretty beast upon the form hath found,

[1] *lags* : flat streamside meadows.
[2] *gills* : narrow wooded valleys.

Then viewing for the course, which is the fairest ground,
The greyhounds forth are brought, for coursing then in
case,
And choicely in the slip, one leading forth a brace ;
The Finder puts her up, and gives her coursers law :
And whilst the eager dogs upon the start do draw,
She riseth from her seat, as though on earth she flew,
Forc'd by some yelping cur to give the greyhounds view,
Which are at length let slip, when gunning out they go,[1]
As in respect of them the swiftest wind were slow.
When each man runs his horse, with fixèd eyes and notes
Which dog first turns the hare, which first the other
coats ;[2]
They wrench her once or twice, ere she a turn will take,
What's off'r'd by the first, the other good doth make ;
And turn for turn again with equal speed they ply,
Bestirring their swift feet with strange agility :
A hard'n'd ridge or way, when if the hare do win,
Then as shot from a bow, she from the dogs doth spin,
That strive to put her off, but when he cannot reach her,
This giving him a coat, about again doth fetch her
To him that comes behind, which seems the hare to fear ;
But with a nimble turn she casts them both arear
Till oft for want of breath, to fall to ground they make
her,
The greyhounds both so spent, that they want breath to
take her.
Here leave I whilst the Muse more serious things attends,
And with my course at hare, my Canto likewise ends.

Michael Drayton

HERON AND FALCON

The Heron mounted doth appear
On his own Peg'sus a Lanceer,
And seems on earth, when he doth hut,[3]
A proper halberdier on foot ;
Secure i' th' moor, about to sup,
The dogs have beat his quarters up.

[1] When the sportsmen give chase. [2] *coats*: outruns.
[3] *hut* : lodge.

And now he takes the open air,
Draws up his wings with tactic care ;
Whilst th' expert falcon swift doth climb
In subtle mazes serpentine ;
And to advantage closely twin'd
She gets the upper sky and wind,
Where she dissembles to invade,
And lies a pol'tic ambuscade.

The hedg'd-in heron, whom the foe
Awaits above, and dogs below,
In his fortification lies,
And makes him ready for surprise,
When rousèd with a shrill alarm,
Was shouted from beneath, they arm.

The falcon charges at first view
With her brigade of talons ; through
Whose shoots the wary heron beat,
With a well-counterwheel'd retreat.
But the bold gen'ral, never lost,
Hath won again her airy post ;
Who wild in this affront, now fries,[1]
Then gives a volley of her eyes.

The desp'rate Heron now contracts
In one design all former facts ;
Noble he is resolv'd to fall
His, and his en'my's funeral,
And (to be rid of her) to die
A public martyr of the sky.

When now he turns his last to wreak
The palisadoes of his beak ;
The raging foe impatient,
Wrack'd with revenge, and fury rent,
Swift as the thunderbolt he strikes,
Too sure upon the stand of pikes ;
There she his naked breast doth hit
And on the case of rapier's split.

[1] *fries* : burns with fury.

But ev'n in her expiring pangs
The heron's pounc'd within her fangs,
And so above she stoops to rise
A trophy and a sacrifice ;
Whilst her own bells in the sad fall
Ring out the double funeral.

Richard Lovelace

THE ANGLER'S WISH

I IN these flowery meads would be :
These crystal streams should solace me ;
To whose harmonious bubbling noise
I with my angle would rejoice :
  Sit here, and see the turtle-dove
  Court his chaste mate to acts of love ;

Or, on that bank, feel the west wind
Breathe health and plenty : please my mind,
To see sweet dewdrops kiss these flowers,
And then wash'd off by April showers ;
  Here, hear my Kenna [1] sing a song ;
  There, see a blackbird feed her young,

Or a leverock [2] build her nest ;
Here, give my weary spirits rest,
And raise my low-pitch'd thoughts above
Earth, or what poor mortals love :
  Thus, free from lawsuits and the noise
  Of Princes' Courts, I would rejoice :

Or, with my Bryan [3] and a book,
Loiter long days near Shawford brook ;
There sit by him, and eat my meat ;
There see the sun both rise and set ;
There bid good morning to next day ;
There meditate my time away ;
  And angle on, and beg to have
  A quiet passage to a welcome grave.

Izaak Walton

[1] *Kenna* : Walton's wife's maiden name was Ken.
[2] *leverock* : lark. [3] *Bryan* : perhaps his dog.

THE FISHER'S LIFE

Oh, the fisher's gentle life
  Happiest is of any ;
'Tis full of calmness, void of strife,
  And beloved of many :
    Other joys
    Are but toys,
    Only this
    Harmless is,
    For our skill
    Breeds no ill,
  But content and pleasure.

In a morning up we rise,
  Ere Aurora's peeping,
Drink a cup, to wash our eyes,
  Leave the sluggard sleeping :
    Then we go
    To and fro,
    With our knacks
    At our backs,
    To sweet streams,
    Lea or Thames,
  To enjoy our leisure.

When we please to walk abroad
  For our recreation,
In the fields is our abode
  Full of delectation :
    With a book
    By a brook,
    Or a lake,
    Sitting take
    With delight,
    Wait the bite
  Till we fish entangle.

We have gentles [1] in a horn,
  Flies and paste and worms too ;

[1] *gentles* : maggots used for bait.

We can watch both night and morn,
Suffer rain and storms too :
None are here
Used to swear,
Oaths will fray
Fish away,
We sit still,
Watch our quill,
Fishers must not wrangle.

If the sun's excessive heat
Make our bodies swelter,
To a fragrant hedge we get
For a friendly shelter ;
Where in a creek
Gudgeon, bleak,[1]
As we like,
Perch or pike,
Roach or dace
Pleased we chase,
With our sport contented.

Or we sometimes muse an hour
'Neath a trembling willow
That repels the soft sweet shower,
Making earth our pillow ;
There we may
Think and pray
Ere cold death
Seize our breath ;
Other joys
Are but toys,
And to be lamented.

John Chalkhill

THE LINCOLNSHIRE POACHER

When I was bound apprentice in famous Lincolnshire,
Full well I served my master for more than seven year,
Till I took up with poaching, as you shall quickly hear.
O 'tis my delight on a shining night in the season of the year.

[1] *bleak* : a small river fish.

As me and my companions were setting of a snare,
'Twas then we spied the game-keeper—for him we did not
care,
For we can wrestle and fight, my boys, and jump o'er anywhere.
O 'tis my delight on a shining night in the season of the
year.

As me and my companions were setting four or five,
And taking on 'em up again we caught a hare alive,
We took the hare alive, my boys, and through the woods
did steer.
O 'tis my delight on a shining night in the season of the
year.

We threw him over our shoulder, and then we trudgèd
home,
We took him to a neighbour's house and sold him for a
crown,
We sold him for a crown, my boys, but I do not tell you
where.
O 'tis my delight on a shining night in the season of the
year.

Success to every gentleman that lives in Lincolnshire,
Success to every poacher that wants to sell a hare,
Bad luck to every game-keeper that will not sell his deer.
O 'tis my delight on a shining night in the season of the
year.

Anonymous (18th century)

SKATING ON WINDERMERE

All shod with steel
We hissed along the polished ice in games
Confederate, imitative of the chase
And woodland pleasures,—the resounding horn,
The pack loud chiming, and the hunted hare.
So through the darkness and the cold we flew,
And not a voice was idle ; with the din
Smitten, the precipices rang aloud ;

The leafless trees and every icy crag
Tinkled like iron ; while far distant hills
Into the tumult sent an alien sound
Of melancholy not unnoticed, while the stars
Eastward were sparkling clear, and in the west
The orange sky of evening died away.

William Wordsworth

THE OLD HILL-CLIMBER

I HAVE not lost the magic of long days :
  I live them, dream them still.
Still am I master of the starry ways,
  And freeman of the hill.
Shattered my glass, ere half the sands had run,—
I hold the heights, I hold the heights I won.

Mine still the hope that hailed me from each height,
  Mine the unresting flame.
With dreams I charmed each doing to delight ;
  I charm my rest the same.
Severed my skein, ere half the strands were spun,—
I keep the dreams, I keep the dreams I won.

What if I live no more those kingly days ?
  Their night sleeps with me still.
I dream my feet upon the starry ways ;
  My heart rests in the hill.
I may not grudge the little left undone ;
I hold the heights, I keep the dreams I won.

Geoffrey Winthrop Young

EIGHTS

  LORD, how it all comes back !
That Wednesday evening, warm and bright,
With a wind from the westward falling light ;
The barge with its flags and frills and chatter,
Where racing seemed an extraneous matter ;

The room where we changed, with hearts like lead,
And the gay crowd trampling overhead ;
The trial trip, with a minute's burst,
When everyone managed to row his worst.
And I felt a ton's weight on my oar
Caused by the lateness of Two and Four ;
The dreary paddle down to the start,
When every stroke felt short and crabby ;
The dull resolve in every heart—
Victory or Westminster Abbey.

. . . .

The wait by the post, with the camera-stands
Mooning owlishly above,
As we doffed our sweaters and resined our hands
Awaiting the waterman's final shove ;
The minute-gun ; then " Touch her, Bow ! "
The silent thought, " We are in for it now."
The steady voice of the coach on the shore,
" Three quarters gone . . . ten seconds more . . .
Eight, seven, six, five, four, three, two, one. . . ."
A pause. A bang. The tension broke ;
We caught the first one well together,
Snatched at the second, and swung out
In the full sweep of the racing stroke ;
While behind us with rattle and shout,
Swift and bright in the evening sun,
Hard on the drive and neat on the feather,
Came the enemy, hell-for-leather.

O but they were a beautiful crew !
They settled down to their stroke, and drew
Steadily nearer, for all our straining,
Second by second, gaining, gaining.
At the Ferry we led by a yard ;
Jones quickened up ; we struggled hard ;
But on my shoulders lay the weight
Of Four, a tenth of a second late.
Nearer and nearer sounded the bellows,
" You've got them now ! Put it on, you fellows ! "
Grim and desperate, short and flurried,
Through the Gut we barely worried ;

Near the end they overlapped us,
Made their shot and almost trapped us,
But with a flick of cox's wrist
We swung clear of them, and they missed.

. . . .

You know the moment when, at their height,
The shouts go surging away to the right
And the tumult suddenly dies in your ears
As the long straight homeward reach appears ?
At that moment, while, nearly dead,
I waited the jerk of Jones's head
As if to say " The last spurt now "—
Just as the bobbing enemy bow
Closer and ever closer showed,
Jones deliberately slowed.

For twenty seconds they drew yet nearer . . .
But then I felt the burden lightening,
And every moment, clearer and clearer,
The catch of the stroke behind me tightening.
The heavy-weights ceased to flurry and jerk,
And settled steady again to their work.
Still at the same stroke, grim and slow,
We began to hold the foe.
" Keep it long ! " came a shout from the shore,
And we drained each stroke to its utmost dregs,
While the mingling voices more and more
Gathered and rose in a single roar—
" Legs ! Legs ! Legs ! Legs ! "

We held them off ; we drew away :
And that was really the end of the fray :
Down the Green Bank and past the throng
That clustered on the swaying barges,
Jones kept it steady and kept it long,
And held the enemy's fitful charges,
Till, near the end, when our force was failing
And efforts at time were unavailing,
He quickened our stroke ; we somehow followed,
And safely over the line we wallowed.

Arthur Hugh Sidgwick

DANGERS OF FOOTBALL

Where Covent-Garden's famous temple stands,
That boasts the work of Jove's immortal hands ;
Columns with plain magnificence appear,
And graceful porches lead along the square :
Here oft my course I bend, when lo ! from far
I spy the furies of the foot-ball war :
The 'prentice quits his shop, to join the crew,
Encreasing crowds the flying game pursue.
Thus, as you roll the ball o'er snowy ground,
The gath'ring globe augments with ev'ry round.
But whither shall I run ? The throng draws nigh,
The ball now skims the street, now soars on high ;
The dex'trous glazier strong returns the bound,
And jingling sashes on the pent-house sound.

John Gay

THE RUGGER MATCH

. . . I have seen this day men in the beauty of movement,
A gallant jaw set, the form of a hero that flew,
Cunning, a selfless flinging of self in the fray,
Strength, compassion, control, the obeying of laws,
Victory, and a struggle against defeat.
I know that the Power that gave us the bodies we have
Can only be praised by our use of the things He gave,
That we are not here to turn our backs to the sun,
Or to scorn the delight of our limbs. And for those who have eyes
The beauty of this is the same as the beauty of flowers,
And of eagles and lions and mountains and oceans and stars
And I care not, but rather am glad that the thought will recur
That in Egypt the muscles moved under the shining skins
As here, and in Greece where Olympian champions died,
And in isles long ago, where never a record was kept.

Sir John Squire

CRICKET

Assist, all ye Muses, and join to rehearse
An old English sport, never praised yet in verse :
'Tis Cricket I sing, of illustrious fame,
No nation e'er boasted so noble a game.
Derry down, etc.

Great Pindar has bragg'd of his heroes of old—
Some were swift in the race, some in battles were bold :
The brows of the victor with olive were crown'd :
Hark ! they shout, and Olympia returns the glad sound.

What boasting of Castor and Pollux his brother,
The one famed for riding, for boxing the other ;
Compar'd with our heroes they'll not shine at all—
What were Castor and Pollux to Nyren and Small ?

Here's guarding and catching, and throwing and tossing,
And bowling and striking and running and crossing ;
Each mate must excel in some principal part—
The Pentathlum of Greece could not show so much art.

. . . . . .

Ye bowlers, take heed, to my precepts attend ;
On you the whole fate of the game must depend ;
Spare your vigour at first, now exert all your strength.
But measure each step, and be sure pitch a length.

Ye fieldsmen, look sharp, lest your pains ye beguile ;
Move close like an army, in rank and in file ;
When the ball is return'd, back it sure, for I trow
Whole states have been ruin'd by one overthrow.

Ye strikers, observe when the foe shall draw nigh ;
Mark the bowler, advancing with vigilant eye ;
Your skill all depends upon distance and sight,
Stand firm to your scratch, let your bat be upright.

. . . . . .

Buck, Curry and Hogsflesh, and Barber and Brett,
Whose swiftness in bowling was ne'er equalled yet ;

I had almost forgot, they deserve a large bumper,
Little George, the longstop, and Tom Sueter, the stumper.

Then why should we fear either Sackville or Mann,
Or repine at the loss both of Boynton and Lann ?
With such troops as those we'll be lords of the game,
Spite of Minshull and Miller and Lumpy and Frame.

Then fill up your glass, he's the best that drinks most.
Here's the Hambledon Club ! Who refuses the toast ?
Let's join in the praise of the bat and the wicket,
And sing in full chorus the patrons of cricket.

And when the game's o'er, and our fate shall draw nigh
(For the heroes of cricket, like others, must die),
Our bats we'll resign, neither troubled nor vex'd,
And give up our wickets to those that come next.
Derry down, etc.

Reynell Cotton

BALLADE OF CRICKET

The burden of hard hitting : slog away !
Here shalt thou make a "five" and there a "four",
And then upon thy bat shalt lean, and say,
That thou art in for an uncommon score.
Yea, the loud ring applauding thee shall roar,
And thou to rival Thornton shalt aspire ;
When lo, the Umpire gives thee "leg before"—
"This is the end of every man's desire".

The burden of much bowling, when the stay
Of all thy team is "collared", swift or slower,
When "bailers" break not in their wonted way,
And "yorkers" come not off as here-to-fore ;
When length balls shoot no more—ah never more !
When all deliveries lose their former fire,
When bats seem broader than the broad barn-door—
"This is the end of every man's desire."

The burden of long fielding, when the clay
Clings to thy shoon in sudden shower's downpour,
And running still thou stumblest ; or the ray
Of blazing suns doth bite and burn thee sore,
And blind thee till, forgetful of thy lore,
Thou dost most mournfully misjudge a "skyer",
And lose a match the Fates cannot restore—
" This is the end of every man's desire."

ENVOY

Alas, yet liefer on Youth's hither shore
Would I be some poor Player on scant hire,
Than king among the old who play no more,—
" *This* is the end of every man's desire."

Andrew Lang

AT LORD'S

It is little I repair to the matches of the Southron folk,
Though my own red roses there may blow ;
It is little I repair to the matches of the Southron folk,
Though the red roses crest the caps, I know ;
For the field is full of shades as I near the shadowy coast,
And a ghostly batsman plays to the bowling of a ghost,
And I look through my tears on a soundless-clapping host,
As the run-stealers flicker to and fro,
To and fro :—
Oh my Hornby and my Barlow long ago !

Francis Thompson

CHANT ROYAL OF CRICKET

When earth awakes as from some dreadful night
And doffs her melancholy mourning state,
When May buds burst in blossom and requite
Our weary eyes for Winter's tedious wait,
Then the pale bard takes down his dusty lyre
And strikes the thing with more than usual fire.

Myself, compacted of an earthier clay,
I oil my bats and greasy homage pay
To Cricket, who, with emblems of his court,
Stumps, pads, bails, gloves, begins his summer sway.
Cricket in sooth is Sovran King of Sport.

As yet no shadows blur the magic light,
The glamour that surrounds the opening date.
Illusions yet undashed my soul excite
And of success in luring whispers prate.
I see myself in form : my thoughts aspire
To reach the giddy summit of desire.
Lovers and such may sing a roundelay,
Whate'er that be, to greet returning May ;
For me, not much—the season's all too short ;
I hear the mower hum and scent the fray.
Cricket in sooth is Sovran King of Sport.

A picture stands before my dazzled sight,
Wherein the hero, ruthlessly elate,
Defies all bowlers' concentrated spite.
That hero is myself, I need not state.
'Tis sweet to see their captain's growing ire
And his relief when I at last retire ;
'Tis sweet to run pavilionwards and say,
" Yes, somehow I *was* seeing them today "—
Thus modesty demands that I retort
To murmured compliments upon my play.
Cricket in sooth is Sovran King of Sport.

The truth's resemblance is, I own, but slight
To these proud visions which my soul inflate.
This is the sort of thing : In abject fright
I totter down the steps and through the gate ;
Somehow I reach the pitch and bleat, " Umpire,
Is that one leg ? " What boots it to enquire ?
The impatient bowler takes one grim survey,
Speeds to the crease and whirls—a lightning ray ?
No, a fast yorker. Bang ! the stumps cavort.
Chastened, but not surprised, I go my way.
Cricket in sooth is Sovran King of Sport.

Lord of the Game, for whom these lines I write,
  Fulfil my present hope, watch o'er my fate ;
Defend me from the swerver's puzzling flight ;
  Let me not be run out, at any rate.
As one who's been for years a constant trier,
Reward me with an average slightly higher ;
Let it be double figures. This I pray,
Humblest of boons, before my hair grows grey
  And Time's flight bids me in the last resort
Try golf, or otherwise your cause betray.
  Cricket in sooth is Sovran King of Sport.

King, what though Age's summons I obey,
Resigned to dull rheumatics and decay,
  Still on one text my hearers I'll exhort,
As long as hearers within range will stay :
  " Cricket in sooth is Sovran King of Sport ".

H. S. V. Hodge

WAR

PLEA FOR A NAVY

THE trewe processe of Englysh polycye,
  Of utterwarde [1] to kepe thys regne in rest
Of oure England, that no man may denye,
  Nere say of soth but it is of the best,
  Is thys, that who seith southe, northe, est, and west,
Cheryshe marchandyse, kepe thamyralté,[2]
That we bee maysteres of the narowe see.

Ffor Sigesmondė the grete emperoure,
  Whyche yet regneth, whan he was in this londe
Wyth kynge Herry the Vte, prince of honoure,
  Here mochė glorye as hym thought he fonde ;
  A myghty londė, whyche hadde take on honde
To werre in Ffraunce and make mortalité,
And evere welle kept rounde aboute the see.

And to the kyngė thus he seyde, " My brothere,"
  Whan he perceyved too townes Calys and Dovere,
" Of alle youre townes to chese of one and othere,
  To kepe the see and sonė to come overe
  To werre outwardes and youre regne to recovere,
Kepe these too townes, Sire, and youre mageste,
As youre tweyne eyne to kepe the narowe see."

Ffor if this see be kepte in tyme of werre,
  Who cane here passe withought daungere and woo ?
Who may eschape, who may myschef dyfferre ?
  What marchaundye may for-by be agoo ?
  Ffor nedės hem muste take truse every ffoo,[3]
Fflaundres, and Spayne, and othere, trust to me,
Or ellis hyndered alle for thys narowe see.

[1] *of utterwarde* : outwardly, from foreign attack.
[2] *thamyralté* : the admiralty.
[3] *nedės hem, etc.* : every foe must come to terms.

Therefore I caste me by a lytele wrytinge
  To shewe att eyė thys conclusione,
Ffor concyëns and for myne acquytynge
  Ayenst God and ageyne abusyon
  And cowardyse, and to oure enmyes confusione;
For fourė thynges our noble [1] sheueth to me,
Kyng, shype, and swerde, and pouer of the see.

Where bene oure shippes? Where bene oure swerdes
    become?
  Oure enmyes bid for the shippe sette a shepe.
Allas! oure reule halteth, hit is benome; [2]
  Who dare weel say that lordshyppe shulde take kepe?
  I wolle assaye, thoughe myne herte gynne to wepe,
To do thys werke, yf we wole ever the,[3]
Ffor verry shame, to kepe aboute the see.

Shalle any pryncė, what so be hys name,
  Wheche hathe nobles moche lyche oures,
Be lorde of see, and Fflemmyngs to our blame
  Stoppe us, take us, and so make fade the floures
  Of Englysshe state, and disteyne our honnoures?
Ffor cowardyse, allas! hit shulde so be;
Therefore I gynne to wryte now of the see.

Anonymous (1436)

AGINCOURT

FAIR stood the wind for France
When we our sails advance;
Nor now to prove our chance
    Longer will tarry;
But putting to the main,
At Caux, the mouth of Seine,
With all his martial train
    Landed King Harry;

[1] *noble*: the coin of that name. [2] *benome*: taken away.
[3] *the*: flourish, thrive.

And taking many a fort
Furnished in warlike sort,
Marched towards Agincourt
    In happy hour ;
Skirmishing, day by day,
With those that stopped his way,
Where the French General lay
    With all his power ;

Which, in his height of pride
King Henry to deride,
His ransom to provide
    To the King sending,
Which he neglects the while,
As from a nation vile,
Yet with an angry smile
    Their fall portending.

And turning to his men
Quoth our brave Henry then :
" Though they to one be ten
    Be not amazèd !
Yet have we well begun ;
Battles so bravely won
Have ever to the sun
    By Fame been raisèd !

" And for myself," quoth he,
" This my full rest shall be ;
England ne'er mourn for me,
    Nor more esteem me !
Victor I will remain
Or on this earth lie slain :
Never shall she sustain
    Loss to redeem me.

Poitiers and Cressy tell
When most their pride did swell,
Under our swords they fell ;
    No less our skill is

Than when our Grandsire great,
Claiming the regal seat,
By many a warlike feat
    Lopped the French lilies."

The Duke of York so dread
The eager vaward led ;
With the main, Henry sped
    Among his henchmen :
Excester had the rear,
A braver man not there.
O Lord, how hot they were
    On the false Frenchmen !

They now to fight are gone ;
Armour on armour shone ;
Drum now to drum did groan,
    To hear was wonder ;
That with the cries they make
The very earth did shake.
Trumpet to trumpet spake ;
    Thunder to thunder.

Well it thine age became,
O noble Erpingham,
Which didst the signal aim
    To our hid forces :
When from a meadow by,
Like a storm suddenly
The English archery
    Stuck the French horses.

With Spanish yew so strong,
Arrows a cloth-yard long,
That like to serpents stung,
    Piercing the weather ;
None from his fellow starts,
But playing manly parts
And, like true English hearts,
    Stuck close together.

When down their bows they threw,
And forth their bilbos drew,
And on the French they flew,
    Not one was tardy ;
Arms were from shoulders sent,
Scalps to the teeth were rent,
Down the French peasants went ;
    Our men were hardy.

This while our noble King,
His broadsword brandishing,
Down the French host did ding
    As to o'erwhelm it ;
And many a deep wound lent,
His arms with blood bespent,
And many a cruel dent
    Bruisèd his helmet.

Glo'ster, that Duke so good,
Next of the royal blood,
For famous England stood
    With his brave brother ;
Clarence, in steel so bright,
Though but a maiden knight,
Yet in that furious fight
    Scarce such another.

Warwick in blood did wade ;
Oxford the foe invade,
And cruel slaughter made,
    Still as they ran up,
Suffolk his axe did ply,
Beaumont and Willoughby
Bare them right doughtily,
    Ferrers and Fanhope.

Upon Saint Crispin's Day
Fought was this noble fray,
Which Fame did not delay
    To England to carry :

O when shall Englishmen
With such acts fill a pen,
Or England breed again
Such a King Harry?

Michael Drayton

THE ARMADA

ATTEND, all ye who list to hear our noble England's praise;
I tell of the thrice-famous deeds she wrought in ancient days,
When that great fleet invincible against her bore in vain
The richest spoils of Mexico, the stoutest hearts of Spain.

It was about the lovely close of a warm summer day,
There came a gallant merchant-ship full sail to Plymouth Bay;
Her crew had seen Castile's black fleet, beyond Aurigny's isle,
At earliest twilight, on the waves lie heaving many a mile.
At sunrise she escaped their van by God's especial grace;
And the tall Pinta, till the noon, had held her close in chase.
Forthwith a guard at every gun was placed along the wall;
The beacon blazed upon the roof of Edgecumbe's lofty hall;
Many a light fishing-bark put out to pry along the coast,
And with loose rein and bloody spur rode inland many a post.
With his white hair unbonneted, the stout old sheriff comes;
Behind him march the halberdiers; before him sound the drums;
His yeomen round the market cross make clear an ample space;
For there behoves him to set up the standard of Her Grace.
And haughtily the trumpets peal, and gaily dance the bells,
As slow upon the labouring wind the royal blazon swells.

Look how the Lion of the sea lifts up his ancient crown,
And underneath his deadly paw treads the gay lilies down.
So stalked he when he turned to flight, on that famed
Picard field,
Bohemia's plume, and Genoa's bow, and Caesar's eagle
shield.
So glared he when at Agincourt in wrath he turned to bay,
And crushed and torn beneath his claws the princely
hunters lay.
Ho ! strike the flagstaff deep, Sir Knight : ho ! scatter
flowers, fair maids :
Ho ! gunners, fire a loud salute : ho ! gallants, draw your
blades :
Thou sun, shine on her joyously ; ye breezes, waft her
wide ;
Our glorious SEMPER EADEM, the banner of our pride.
The freshening breeze of eve unfurled that banner's
massy fold ;
The parting gleam of sunshine kissed that haughty scroll
of gold ;
Night sank upon the dusky beach, and on the purple sea,
Such night in England ne'er had been, nor e'er again shall
be.
From Eddystone to Berwick bounds, from Lynn to Milford
Bay,
That time of slumber was as bright and busy as the day ;
For swift to east and swift to west the ghastly war-flame
spread,
High on St. Michael's Mount it shone : it shone on
Beachy Head.
Far on the deep the Spaniard saw, along each southern
shire,
Cape beyond cape, in endless range, those twinkling
points of fire.
The fisher left his skiff to rock on Tamar's glittering waves :
The rugged miners poured to war from Mendip's sunless
caves :
O'er Longleat's towers, o'er Cranbourne's oaks, the fiery
herald flew ;
He roused the shepherds of Stonehenge, the rangers of
Beaulieu.

Right sharp and quick the bells all night rang out from
Bristol town,
And ere the day three hundred horse had met on Clifton
Down ;
The sentinel on Whitehall gate looked forth into the night,
And saw o'erhanging Richmond Hill the streak of blood-
red light.
Then bugle's note and cannon's roar the death-like silence
broke,
And with one start, and with one cry, the royal city woke.
At once on all her stately gates arose the answering fires ;
At once the wild alarum clashed from all her reeling
spires ;
From all the batteries of the Tower pealed loud the voice
of fear ;
And all the thousand masts of Thames sent back a louder
cheer :
And from the farthest wards was heard the rush of hurry-
ing feet,
And the broad streams of pikes and flags rushed down each
roaring street ;
And broader still became the blaze, and louder still the
din,
As fast from every village round the horse came spurring
in :
And eastward straight from wild Blackheath the warlike
errand went,
And roused in many an ancient hall the gallant squires of
Kent.
Southward from Surrey's pleasant hills flew those bright
couriers forth ;
High on bleak Hampstead's swarthy moor they started
for the north ;
And on, and on, without a pause, untired they bounded
still :
All night from tower to tower they sprang ; they sprang
from hill to hill :
Till the proud Peak unfurled the flag o'er Darwin's rocky
dales,
Till like volcanoes flared to heaven the stormy hills of
Wales,

Till twelve fair counties saw the blaze on Malvern's lonely height,
Till streamed in crimson on the wind the Wrekin's crest of light,
Till broad and fierce the star came forth on Ely's stately fane,
And tower and hamlet rose in arms o'er all the boundless plain ;
Till Belvoir's lordly terraces the sign to Lincoln sent,
And Lincoln sped the message on o'er the wide vale of Trent ;
Till Skiddaw saw the fire that burned on Gaunt's embattled pile,
And the red glare on Skiddaw roused the burghers of Carlisle.

Lord Macaulay

THE "REVENGE"

At Flores in the Azores Sir Richard Grenville lay,
And a pinnace, like a flutter'd bird, came flying from far away :
" Spanish ships of war at sea ! We have sighted fifty-three ! "
Then sware Lord Thomas Howard : " 'Fore God, I am no coward ;
But I cannot meet them here, for my ships are out of gear,
And the half my men are sick. I must fly, but follow quick.
We are six ships of the line ; can we fight with fifty-three ? "

Then spake Sir Richard Grenville : " I know you are no coward ;
You fly them for a moment to fight with them again.
But I've ninety men and more that are lying sick ashore.
I should count myself the coward if I left them, my Lord Howard,
To these Inquisition dogs and the devildoms of Spain."

So Lord Howard past away with five ships of war that day,
Till he melted like a cloud in the silent summer heaven ;
But Sir Richard bore in hand all his sick men from the
land
Very carefully and slow,
Men of Bideford in Devon,
And we laid them on the ballast down below ;
For we brought them all aboard,
And they blest him in their pain, that they were not left
to Spain,
To the thumbscrew and the stake, for the glory of the
Lord.

He had only a hundred seamen to work the ship and to
fight,
And he sailed away from Flores till the Spaniard came in
sight,
With his huge sea-castles heaving upon the weather bow.
" Shall we fight or shall we fly ?
Good Sir Richard, tell us now,
For to fight is but to die !
There'll be little of us left by the time this sun be set."
And Sir Richard said again : " We be all good English
men.
Let us bang these dogs of Seville, the children of the devil,
For I never turn'd my back upon Don or devil yet."

Sir Richard spoke and he laugh'd, and we roar'd a hurrah,
and so
The little *Revenge* ran on sheer into the heart of the foe,
With her hundred fighters on deck, and her ninety sick
below ;
For half of their fleet to the right and half to the left were
seen,
And the little *Revenge* ran on thro' the long sea-lane
between.

Thousands of their soldiers look'd down from their decks
and laugh'd,
Thousands of their seamen made mock at the mad little
craft

Running on and on, till delay'd
By their mountain-like *San Philip*, that, of fifteen hundred
 tons,
And up-shadowing high above us with her yawning tiers
 of guns,
Took the breath from our sails, and we stay'd.

And while now the great *San Philip* hung above us like a
 cloud
Whence the thunderbolt will fall
Long and loud,
Four galleons drew away
From the Spanish fleet that day,
And two upon the larboard and two upon the starboard lay,
And the battle-thunder broke from them all.

But anon the great *San Philip*, she bethought herself and
 went
Having that within her womb that had left her ill content ;
And the rest they came aboard us, and they fought us hand
 to hand,
For a dozen times they came with their pikes and mus-
 queteers,
And a dozen times we shook 'em off as a dog that shakes
 his ears
When he leaps from the water to the land.

And the sun went down, and the stars came out far over
 the summer sea,
But never a moment ceased the fight of the one and the
 fifty-three.
Ship after ship, the whole night long, their high-built
 galleons came,
Ship after ship, the whole night long, with her battle-
 thunder and flame ;
Ship after ship, the whole night long, drew back with her
 dead and her shame.
For some were sunk and many were shatter'd, and so could
 fight us no more—
God of battles, was ever a battle like this in the world
 before ?

For he said " Fight on ! fight on ! "
Tho' his vessel was all but a wreck ;
And it chanced that, when half of the short summer night
was gone,
With a grisly wound to be drest he had left the deck,
But a bullet struck him that was dressing it suddenly dead,
And himself he was wounded again in the side and the
head,
And he said " Fight on ! fight on ! "

And the night went down, and the sun smiled out far over
the summer sea,
And the Spanish fleet with broken sides lay round us all in
a ring ;
But they dared not touch us again, for they fear'd that we
still could sting,
So they watch'd what the end would be.
And we had not fought them in vain,
But in perilous plight were we,
Seeing forty of our poor hundred were slain,
And half of the rest of us maim'd for life
In the crash of the cannonades and the desperate strife ;
And the sick men down in the hold were most of them stark
and cold,
And the pikes were all broken or bent, and the powder was
all of it spent ;
And the masts and the rigging were lying over the side ;
But Sir Richard cried in his English pride,
" We have fought such a fight for a day and a night
As may never be fought again !
We have won great glory, my men !
And a day less or more
At sea or ashore,
We die—does it matter when ?
Sink me the ship, Master Gunner—sink her, split her in
twain !
Fall into the hands of God, not into the hands of Spain ! "

And the gunner said " Ay, ay," but the seamen made
reply :
" We have children, we have wives,

And the Lord hath spared our lives.
We will make the Spaniard promise, if we yield, to let us go ;
We shall live to fight again and to strike another blow,"
And the lion there lay dying, and they yielded to the foe.

And the stately Spanish men to their flagship bore him then,
Where they laid him by the mast, old Sir Richard caught at last,
And they praised him to his face with their courtly foreign grace ;
But he rose upon their decks, and he cried :
" I have fought for Queen and Faith like a valiant man and true ;
I have only done my duty as a man is bound to do :
With a joyful spirit I Sir Richard Grenville die ! "
And he fell upon their decks, and he died.

And they stared at the dead that had been so valiant and true,
And had holden the power and glory of Spain so cheap
That he dared her with one little ship and his English few ;
Was he devil or man ? He was devil for aught they knew,
But they sank his body with honour down into the deep,
And they mann'd the *Revenge* with a swarthier alien crew,
And away she sail'd with her loss and long'd for her own ;
When a wind from the lands they had ruin'd awoke from sleep,
And the water began to heave and the weather to moan,
And or ever that evening ended a great gale blew,
And a wave like the wave that is raised by an earthquake grew,
Till it smote on their hulls and their sails and their masts and their flags,
And the whole sea plunged and fell on the shot-shatter'd navy of Spain,
And the little *Revenge* herself went down by the island crags
To be lost evermore in the main.

Lord Tennyson

THE DEATH OF ADMIRAL BLAKE

LADEN with spoil of the South, fulfilled with the glory of achievement,
And freshly crowned with never-dying fame,
Sweeping by shores where the names are the names of the victories of England,
Across the Bay the squadron homeward came.

Proudly they came, but their pride was the pomp of a funeral at midnight,
When dreader yet the lonely morrow looms ;
Few are the words that are spoken, and faces are gaunt beneath the torchlight
That does but darken more the nodding plumes.

Low on the field of his fame, past hope lay the Admiral triumphant,
And fain to rest him after all his pain ;
Yet for the love that he bore to his own land, ever unforgotten,
He prayed to see the Western hills again.

Fainter than stars in a sky long grey with the coming of the daybreak,
Or sounds of night that fade when night is done,
So in the death-dawn faded the splendour and loud renown of warfare
And life of all its longings kept but one.

" Oh ! to be there for an hour when the shade draws in beside the hedgerows,
And falling apples wake the drowsy noon :
Oh ! for the hour when the elms grow sombre and human in the twilight ;
And gardens dream beneath the rising moon.

Only to look once more on the land of the memories of childhood,
Forgetting weary winds and barren foam :

Only to bid farewell to the combe and the orchard and
the moorland,
And sleep at last among the fields of home ! "

So he was silently praying, till now, when his strength
was ebbing faster,
The Lizard lay before them faintly blue ;
Now on the gleaming horizon the white cliffs laughed
along the coast-line,
And now the forelands took the shapes they knew.

There lay the Sound and the Island with green leaves down
beside the water,
The town, the Hoe, the masts, with sunset fired—
Dreams ! ay, dreams of the dead ! for the great heart
faltered on the threshold,
And darkness took the land his soul desired.

Sir Henry Newbolt

GIBRALTAR

Seven weeks of sea, and twice seven days of storm
Upon the huge Atlantic, and once more
We ride into still water and the calm
Of a sweet evening, screened by either shore
Of Spain and Barbary. Our toils are o'er,
Our exile is accomplished. Once again
We look on Europe, mistress as of yore
Of the fair earth and of the hearts of men.
Ay, this is the famed rock which Hercules
And Goth and Moor bequeathed us. At this door
England stands sentry. God ! to hear the shrill
Sweet treble of her fifes upon the breeze,
And at the summons of the rock gun's roar,
To see her red coats marching from the hill !

W. S. Blunt

MARLBOROUGH AT BLENHEIM

But O, my muse, what numbers wilt thou find
To sing the furious troops in battle joined ?
Methinks I hear the drum's tumultuous sound
The victor's shouts and dying groans confound,
The dreadful burst of cannon rend the skies,
And all the thunder of the battle rise.
'Twas then great Marlborough's mighty soul was
proved,
That, in the shock of changing hosts unmoved,
Amidst confusion, horror and despair,
Examined all the dreadful scenes of war ;
In peaceful thought the field of death surveyed,
To fainting squadrons sent the timely aid,
Inspired repulsed battalions to engage,
And taught the doubtful battle where to rage.
So when an angel by divine command
With rising tempests shakes a guilty land,
Such as of late o'er pale Britannia past,
Calm and serene he drives the furious blast ;
And, pleased th' Almighty's orders to perform,
Rides in the whirlwind, and directs the storm.

Joseph Addison

THE "ARETHUSA"

Come, all ye jolly sailors bold,
Whose hearts are cast in honour's mould,
While English glory I unfold,
Huzza to the *Arethusa* !
She is a frigate tight and brave,
As ever stemmed the dashing wave :
Her men are staunch
To their fav'rite launch,
And when the foe shall meet our fire,
Sooner than strike, we'll all expire
On board of the *Arethusa*.

'Twas with the spring fleet she went out
The English Channel to cruise about,
When four French sail, in show so stout,
    Bore down on the *Arethusa.*
The famed *Belle Poule* straight ahead did lie,
The *Arethusa* seemed to fly ;
    Not a sheet, or a tack,
    Or a brace did she slack,
Tho' the Frenchmen laughed and thought it stuff,
But they knew not the handful of men, how tough
    On board of the *Arethusa.*

On deck five hundred men did dance,
The stoutest they could find in France ;
We with two hundred did advance
    On board of the *Arethusa.*
Our captain hailed the Frenchman, " Ho ! "
The Frenchman then cried out, " Hallo ! "
    " Bear down, d'ye see,
    To our Admiral's lee ! "
" No, no," said the Frenchman, " that can't be."
" Then I must lug you along with me,"
    Says the saucy *Arethusa.*

The fight was off the Frenchman's land ;
We forced them back upon their strand ;
For we fought till not a stick could stand
    Of the gallant *Arethusa.*
And now we've driven the foe ashore,
Never to fight with Britons more,
    Let each fill his glass
    To his fav'rite lass !
A health to our captain and officers true,
And all that belong to the jovial crew
    On board of the *Arethusa.*

Prince Hoare

BRITAIN'S BULWARKS

When Britain on her sea-girt shore
  Her ancient Druids erst addressed,
" What aid," she cried, " shall I implore ?—
  What best defence, by numbers pressed ? "

" The hostile nations round thee rise,"
  The mystic oracle replied,
" And view thine isle with envious eyes :
  Their threats defy, their rage deride,
Nor fear invasion from those adverse Gauls,—
Britain's best bulwarks are her wooden walls.

Thine oaks, descending to the main,
  With floating forts shall stem the tide ;
Asserting Britain's liquid reign,
  Where'er her thundering navies ride.
Nor less to peaceful arts inclined
  Where commerce opens all her stores,
In social bonds shall league mankind,
  And join the sea-divided shores :
Spread thy white wings where naval glory calls,—
Britain's best bulwarks are her wooden walls.

Hail, happy isle ! What though thy vales
  No vine-impurpled tribute yield,
Nor fanned with odour-breathing gales,
  Nor crops spontaneous glad the field ?
Yet liberty rewards the toil
  Of industry to labour prone,
Who jocund ploughs the grateful soil,
  And reaps the harvest she has sown :
While other realms tyrannic sway enthralls,—
Britain's best bulwarks are her wooden walls."

Thomas Arne

BATTLE OF THE BALTIC

Of Nelson and the North
Sing the glorious day's renown,
When to battle fierce came forth
All the might of Denmark's crown,
And her arms along the deep proudly shone,—
By each gun the lighted brand
In a bold determined hand ;
And the Prince of all the land
Led them on.

Like leviathans afloat
Lay their bulwarks on the brine,
While the sign of battle flew
On the lofty British line :
It was ten of April morn by the chime :
As they drifted on their path
There was silence deep as death,
And the boldest held his breath
For a time.

But the might of England flushed
To anticipate the scene ;
And her van the fleeter rushed
O'er the deadly space between.
" Hearts of oak ! " our captain cried ; when each gun
From its adamantine lips
Spread a death-shade round the ships,
Like the hurricane eclipse
Of the sun.

Again ! again ! again !
And the havoc did not slack
Till a feeble cheer the Dane
To our cheering sent us back :—
Their shots along the deep slowly boom ;—
Then ceased—and all is wail,
As they strike the shattered sail,
Or in conflagration pale
Light the gloom.

Out spoke the victor then
As he hailed them o'er the wave,
" Ye are brothers ! Ye are men !
And we conquer but to save ;—
So peace instead of death let us bring :
But yield, proud foe, thy fleet
With the crews, at England's feet,
And make submission meet
To our king."

Then Denmark blessed our chief
That he gave her wounds repose ;
And the sounds of joy and grief
From her people wildly rose,
As death withdrew his shades from the day :
While the sun looked smiling bright
O'er a wide and woeful sight,
Where the fires of funeral light
Died away.

Now joy, Old England, raise !
For the tidings of thy might,
By the festal cities' blaze,
While the winecup shines in light ;
And yet, amidst that joy and uproar,
Let us think of them that sleep
Full many a fathom deep
By thy wild and stormy steep,
Elsinore !

Brave hearts ! to Britain's pride
Once so faithful and so true,
On the deck of fame that died
With the gallant good Riou ;—
Soft sigh the winds of heaven o'er their grave !
While the billow mournful rolls
And the mermaid's song condoles,
Singing glory to the souls
Of the brave !

Thomas Campbell

THE FIELD OF WATERLOO

Stop !—for thy tread is on an Empire's dust !
An Earthquake's spoil is sepulchred below !
Is the spot marked with no colossal bust ?
Nor column trophied for triumphal show ?
None ; but the moral's truth tells simpler so,
As the ground was before, thus let it be ;—
How that red rain hath made the harvest grow !
And is this all the world hath gained by thee,
Thou first and last of fields ! king-making Victory ?

And Harold stands upon this place of skulls,
The grave of France, the deadly Waterloo!
How in an hour the power which gave annuls
Its gifts, transferring fame as fleeting too!
In "pride of place" here last the eagle flew,
Then tore with bloody talon the rent plain,
Pierced by the shaft of banded nations through;
Ambition's life and labours all were vain;
He wears the shattered links of the world's broken chain.

Fit retribution! Gaul may champ the bit
And foam in fetters;—but is Earth more free?
Did nations combat to make *One* submit,
Or league to teach all kings true sovereignty?
What! shall reviving Thraldom again be
The patched-up idol of enlightened days?
Shall we, who struck the Lion down, shall we
Pay the Wolf homage? proffering lowly gaze
And servile knees to thrones? No; *prove* before ye praise!

If not, o'er one fallen despot boast no more!
In vain fair cheeks were furrowed with hot tears
For Europe's flowers long rooted up before
The trampler of her vineyards; in vain years
Of death, depopulation, bondage, fears,
Have all been borne, and broken by the accord
Of roused-up millions; all that most endears
Glory, is when the myrtle wreaths a sword
Such as Harmodius drew on Athens' tyrant lord.

There was a sound of revelry by night,
And Belgium's capital had gathered then
Her Beauty and her Chivalry, and bright
The lamps shone o'er fair women and brave men;
A thousand hearts beat happily; and when
Music arose with its voluptuous swell,
Soft eyes looked love to eyes which spake again,
And all went merry as a marriage bell;
But hush! hark! a deep sound strikes like a rising knell!

Did ye not hear it? No; 'twas but the wind,
Or the car rattling o'er the stony street;
On with the dance! let joy be unconfined;
No sleep till morn, when Youth and Pleasure meet
To chase the glowing Hours with flying feet—
But hark!—that heavy sound breaks in once more,
As if the clouds its echo would repeat;
And nearer, clearer, deadlier than before!
Arm! Arm! It is—it is—the cannon's opening roar!

Within a windowed niche of that high hall
Sate Brunswick's fated chieftain; he did hear
That sound the first amidst the festival,
And caught its tone with Death's prophetic ear;
And when they smiled because he deemed it near,
His heart more truly knew that peal too well
Which stretched his father on a bloody bier,
And roused the vengeance blood alone could quell;
He rushed into the field, and, foremost fighting, fell.

Ah! then and there was hurrying to and fro,
And gathering tears, and tremblings of distress,
And cheeks all pale, which but an hour ago
Blushed at the praise of their own loveliness;
And there were sudden partings, such as press
The life from out young hearts, and choking sighs
Which ne'er might be repeated; who could guess
If ever more should meet those mutual eyes,
Since upon night so sweet such awful morn could rise?

And there was mounting in hot haste: the steed,
The mustering squadron, and the clattering car,
Went pouring forward with impetuous speed,
And swiftly forming in the ranks of war;
And the deep thunder peal on peal afar;
And near, the beat of the alarming drum
Roused up the soldier ere the morning star;
While thronged the citizens with terror dumb,
Or whispering with white lips—"The foe! they come! they come!"

And wild and high the " Cameron's gathering " rose !
The war-note of Lochiel, which Albyn's hills
Have heard, and heard, too, have her Saxon foes :—
How in the noon of night that pibroch thrills,
Savage and shrill ! But with the breath which fills
Their mountain-pipe, so fill the mountaineers
With the fierce native daring which instils
The stirring memory of a thousand years,
And Evan's, Donald's fame rings in each clansman's ears !

And Ardennes waves above them her green leaves,
Dewy with nature's tear-drops as they pass,
Grieving, if aught inanimate e'er grieves,
Over the unreturning brave,—alas !
Ere evening to be trodden like the grass
Which now beneath them, but above shall grow
In its next verdure, when this fiery mass
Of living valour, rolling on the foe
And burning with high hope, shall moulder cold and low.

Last noon beheld them full of lusty life,
Last eve in Beauty's circle proudly gay,
The midnight brought the signal-sound of strife,
The morn the marshalling in arms,—the day
Battle's magnificently stern array !
The thunder-clouds close o'er it, which when rent
The earth is covered thick with other clay,
Which her own clay shall cover, heaped and pent,
Rider and horse,—friend, foe,—in one red burial blent !

Lord Byron

ADMIRALS ALL

Effingham, Grenville, Raleigh, Drake,
Here's to the bold and free !
Benbow, Collingwood, Byron, Blake,
Hail to the Kings of the Sea !
Admirals all, for England's sake,
Honour be yours and fame !
And honour, as long as waves shall break,
To Nelson's peerless name !

Admirals all, for England's sake,
Honour be yours and fame!
And honour, as long as waves shall break,
To Nelson's peerless name!

Essex was fretting in Cadiz Bay
With the galleons fair in sight;
Howard at last must give him his way,
And the word was passed to fight.
Never was schoolboy gayer than he,
Since holidays first began:
He tossed his bonnet to wind and sea,
And under the guns he ran.

Drake nor devil nor Spaniard feared,
Their cities he put to the sack;
He singed his Catholic Majesty's beard,
And harried his ships to wrack.
He was playing at Plymouth a rubber of bowls
When the great Armada came;
But he said, "They must wait their turn, good souls,"
And he stooped, and finished the game.

Fifteen sail were the Dutchmen bold,
Duncan he had but two;
But he anchored them fast where the Texel shoaled,
And his colours aloft he flew.
"I've taken the depth to a fathom," he cried,
"And I'll sink with a right good will;
For I know when we're all of us under the tide
My flag will be fluttering still."

Splinters were flying above, below,
When Nelson sailed the Sound:
"Mark you, I wouldn't be elsewhere now,"
Said he, "for a thousand pound!"
The Admiral's signal bade him fly,
But he wickedly wagged his head,
He clapped the glass to his sightless eye
And "I'm damned if I see it," he said.

Admirals all, they said their say,
  (The echoes are ringing still.)
Admirals all, they went their way
  To the haven under the hill.
But they left us a kingdom none can take,
  The realm of the circling sea,
To be ruled by the rightful sons of Blake,
  And the Rodneys yet to be.

Admirals all, for England's sake,
  Honour be yours and fame !
And honour, as long as waves shall break,
  To Nelson's peerless name !

Sir Henry Newbolt

TRAFALGAR DAY

He leads : we hear our Seaman's call
  In the roll of battles won ;
For he is Britain's Admiral
  Till setting of her sun.

When Britain's life was in her ships,
  He kept the sea as his own right ;
And saved us from more fell eclipse
  Than drops on day from blackest night.
Again his battle spat the flame !
  Again his victory-flag men saw !
At sound of Nelson's chieftain-name
  A deeper breath did Freedom draw.

Each trusty captain knew his part :
  They served as men, not marshalled kine :
The pulses they of his great heart,
  With heads to work his main design.
Their Nelson's word, to beat the foe,
  And spare the fall'n, before them shone.
Good was the hour of blow for blow,
  And clear their course while they fought on.

Behold the Envied vanward sweep !—
  A day in mourning weeds adored !
Then Victory was wrought to weep ;
  Then sorrow crowned with laurel soared.
A breezeless flag above a shroud
  All Britain was when wind and wave,
To make her, passing human, proud,
  Brought his last gift from o'er the grave !

Uprose the soul of him a star
  On that brave day of Ocean days :
It rolled the smoke from Trafalgàr
  To darken Austerlitz ablaze.
Are we the men of old, its light
  Will point us under every sky
The path he took ; and must we fight,
  Our Nelson be our battle-cry !

He leads : we hear our Seaman's call
  In the roll of battles won ;
For he is Britain's Admiral
  Till setting of her sun.

George Meredith

WELLINGTON

Who is he that cometh, like an honoured guest,
With banner and with music, with soldier and with priest,
With a nation weeping, and breaking on my rest ?
Mighty Seaman, this is he
Was great by land as thou by sea.
Thine island loves thee well, thou famous man,
The greatest sailor since our world began.
Now, to the roll of muffled drums,
To thee the greatest soldier comes ;
For this is he
Was great by land as thou by sea ;
His foes were thine ; he kept us free ;

O give him welcome, this is he,
Worthy of our gorgeous rites,
And worthy to be laid by thee ;
For this is England's greatest son,
He that gained a hundred fights,
Nor ever lost an English gun ;
This is he that far away
Against the myriads of Assaye
Clashed with his fiery few and won ;
And underneath another sun,
Warring on a later day,
Round affrighted Lisbon drew
The treble works, the vast designs
Of his laboured rampart-lines,
Where he greatly stood at bay,
Whence he issued forth anew,
And ever great and greater grew,
Beating from the wasted vines
Back to France her banded swarms,
Back to France with countless blows,
Till o'er the hills her eagles flew
Beyond the Pyrenean pines,
Followed up in valley and glen
With blare of bugle, clamour of men,
Roll of cannon and clash of arms,
And England pouring on her foes.
Such a war had such a close.
Again their ravening eagle rose
In anger, wheeled on Europe-shadowing wings,
And barking for the thrones of kings ;
Till one that sought but Duty's iron crown
On that loud sabbath shook the spoiler down ;
A day of onsets of despair !
Dashed on every rocky square
Their surging charges foamed themselves away ;
Last, the Prussian trumpet blew ;
Through the long-tormented air
Heaven flashed a sudden jubilant ray,
And down we swept and charged and overthrew.
So great a soldier taught us there,
What long-enduring hearts could do

In that world-earthquake, Waterloo!
Mighty Seaman, tender and true,
And pure as he from taint of craven guile,
O saviour of the silver-coasted isle,
O shaker of the Baltic and the Nile,
If aught of things that here befall
Touch a spirit among things divine,
If love of country move thee there at all,
Be glad, because his bones are laid by thine!
And through the centuries let a people's voice
In full acclaim,
A people's voice,
The proof and echo of all human fame,
A people's voice, when they rejoice
At civic revel and pomp and game,
Attest their great commander's claim
With honour, honour, honour, honour to him,
Eternal honour to his name.

Lord Tennyson

MEN WHO MARCH AWAY

WHAT of the faith and fire within us,
    Men who march away
    Ere the barn-cocks say
    Night is growing grey,
To hazards whence no tears can win us?
  What of the faith and fire within us,
    Men who march away?

. . . .

In our heart of hearts believing
    Victory crowns the just,
    And that braggarts must
    Surely bite the dust,
Press we to the field ungrieving,
  In our heart of hearts believing
    Victory crowns the just.

Thomas Hardy

EPITAPH ON AN ARMY OF MERCENARIES

These, in the day when heaven was falling,
 The hour when earth's foundations fled,
Followed their mercenary calling
 And took their wages and are dead.

Their shoulders held the sky suspended ;
 They stood, and earth's foundations stay ;
What God abandoned, these defended,
 And saved the sum of things for pay.

A. E. Housman

FOR ALL WE HAVE AND ARE

For all we have and are,
For all our children's fate,
Stand up and take the war.
The Hun is at the gate !
Our world has passed away
In wantonness o'erthrown.
There is nothing left today
But steel and fire and stone !
  Though all we knew depart,
  The old Commandments stand :—
  " In courage keep your heart,
  In strength lift up your hand ".

Once more we hear the word
That sickened earth of old :—
" No law except the Sword
Unsheathed and uncontrolled ".
Once more it knits mankind,
Once more the nations go
To meet and break and bind
A crazed and driven foe.

Comfort, content, delight,
The ages' slow-bought gain,
They shrivelled in a night.
Only ourselves remain
To face the naked days
In silent fortitude,
Through perils and dismays
Renewed and re-renewed.
    Though all we made depart,
    The old Commandments stand :—
    " In patience keep your heart,
    In strength lift up your hand ".

No easy hope or lies
Shall bring us to our goal,
But iron sacrifice
Of body, will, and soul.
There is but one task for all—
One life for each to give.
What stands if Freedom fall ?
Who dies if England live ?

Rudyard Kipling

BETWEEN MIDNIGHT AND MORNING

(December 1914)

You that have faith to look with fearless eyes
  Beyond the tragedy of a world at strife,
And trust that out of night and death shall rise
  The dawn of ampler life ;

Rejoice, whatever anguish rend your heart,
  That God has given you, for a priceless dower,
To live in these great times and have your part
  In Freedom's crowning hour.

That you may tell your sons who see the light
  High in the heaven, their heritage to take :—
" I saw the powers of darkness put to flight !
  I saw the morning break ! "

Sir Owen Seaman

THE SOLDIER

If I should die, think only this of me :
  That there's some corner of a foreign field
That is for ever England. There shall be
  In that rich earth a richer dust concealed ;
A dust whom England bore, shaped, made aware,
  Gave, once, her flowers to love, her ways to roam,
A body of England's, breathing English air,
  Washed by the rivers, blest by suns of home.

And think, this heart, all evil shed away,
  A pulse in the eternal mind, no less
    Gives somewhere back the thoughts by England given ;
Her sights and sounds ; dreams happy as her day ;
  And laughter, learnt of friends ; and gentleness,
    In hearts at peace, under an English heaven.

Rupert Brooke

THE VOLUNTEER

Here lies a clerk who half his life had spent
Toiling at ledgers in a city grey,
Thinking that so his days would drift away
With no lance broken in life's tournament :
Yet ever 'twixt the books and his bright eyes
The gleaming eagles of the legions came,
And horsemen, charging under phantom skies,
Went thundering past beneath the oriflamme.

And now those waiting dreams are satisfied ;
From twilight to the halls of dawn he went ;
His lance is broken ; but he lies content
With that high hour, in which he lived and died.
And falling thus, he wants no recompense,
Who found his battle in the last resort ;
Nor needs he any hearse to bear him hence,
Who goes to join the men of Agincourt.

Herbert Asquith

THE DEATH OF THE ZEPPELIN

At last ! At last the wingèd Worm draws near,
The vulture ship that dares not voyage by day,
The man-made Dinosaur that haunts the night.
. . . . .
We marked its course afar,
By dull pulsations of the eager guns,
The grey, lean warders of far-listening London.
. . . . .
The harassed Worm sought covert in a cloud
Which, soon disparted, gave him for a prey
To the implacable airman hovering near,
Who pierced his bowels with a fiery bolt.
The Monster writhed in self-engendered flames,
Which brake forth in the likeness of a rose,
A torch of hell brandished at heaven's gate,
A piercing wonder to the million eyes
Of waking London. . . . At last he dropped,
A sombre coal of fading crimson fire,
Into his burial-place, a field defiled.
And then, but not till then, arose the cry,
Prolonged, unpitying, a cordite cheer
Of the old valiant city, stark as Time,
Which wills not mercy for the merciless.

Anonymous

WAR-WORKER

(1916)

Far from their homes they lie, the men who fell
Fighting in Flanders clay, in Tigris sand ;
He who lies here died for the cause as well,
Whom neither bayonet killed nor bursting shell,
But his own heart that loved its native land.

Arundell Esdaile

TRAFALGAR SQUARE

September 1917

Fool that I was: my heart was sore,
Yea sick for the myriad wounded men,
The maim'd in the war: I had grief for each one:
And I came in the gay September sun
To the open smile of Trafalgar Square;
Where many a lad with a limb fordone
Loll'd by the lion-guarded column
That holdeth Nelson statued thereon
Upright in the air.

The Parliament towers and the Abbey towers,
The white Horseguards and grey Whitehall,
He looketh on all,
Past Somerset House and the river's bend
To the pillar'd dome of St. Paul,
That slumbers confessing God's solemn blessing
On England's glory, to keep it ours—
While children true to her prowess renew
And throng from the ends of the earth to defend
Freedom and honour—till Earth shall end.

The gentle unjealous Shakespeare, I trow,
In his country tomb of peaceful fame,
Must feel exiled from life and glow
If he think of this man with his warrior claim,
Who looketh o'er London as if 'twere his own,
As he standeth in stone, aloft and alone,
Sailing the sky with one arm and one eye.

Robert Bridges

TO A BULL-DOG

(W. H. S., Capt. [Acting Major] R.F.A.; killed April 12, 1917.)

We shan't see Willy any more, Mamie,
He won't be coming any more:
He came back once and again and again,
But he won't get leave any more.

We looked from the window and there was his cab,
  And we ran downstairs like a streak,
And he said " Hullo, you bad dog," and you crouched
    to the floor,
  Paralysed to hear him speak,

And then let fly at his face and his chest
  Till I had to hold you down,
While he took off his cap and his gloves and his coat,
  And his bag and his thonged Sam Browne.

We went upstairs to the studio,
  The three of us, just as of old,
And you lay down and I sat and talked to him
  As round the room he strolled.

Here in the room where, years ago
  Before the old life stopped,
He worked all day with his slippers and his pipe,
  He would pick up the threads he'd dropped.

Fondling all the drawings he had left behind,
  Glad to find them all still the same,
And opening the cupboards to look at his belongings
  . . . Every time he came.

But now I know what a dog doesn't know,
  Though you'll thrust your head on my knee,
And try to draw me from the absent-mindedness
  That you find so dull in me.

And all your life you will never know
  What I wouldn't tell you even if I could,
That the last time we waved him away
  Willy went for good.

But sometimes, as you lie on the hearthrug
  Sleeping in the warmth of the stove,
Even through your muddled old canine brain
  Shapes from the past may rove.

You'll scarcely remember, even in a dream,
  How we brought home a silly little pup,
With a big square head and little crooked legs
  That could scarcely bear him up,

But your tail will tap at the memory
  Of a man whose friend you were,
Who was always kind though he called you a naughty dog
  When he found you on his chair ;

Who'd make you face a reproving finger
  And solemnly lecture you,
Till your head hung downwards and you looked very sheepish :
  And you'll dream of your triumphs too,

Of summer evening chases in the garden
  When you dodged us all about with a bone :
We were three boys, and you were the cleverest,
  But now we're two alone.

When summer comes again,
  And the long sunsets fade,
We shall have to go on playing the feeble game for two
  That since the war we've played.

And though you run expectant as you always do
  To the uniforms we meet,
You'll never find Willy among all the soldiers
  In even the longest street,

Nor in any crowd ; yet, strange and bitter thought,
  Even now were the old words said,
If I tried the old trick and said " Where's Willy ? "
  You would quiver and lift your head.

And your brown eyes would look to ask if I were serious,
  And wait for the word to spring.
Sleep undisturbed : I shan't say that again,
  You innocent old thing.

I must sit, not speaking, on the sofa,
  While you lie asleep on the floor ;
For he's suffered a thing that dogs couldn't dream of,
  And he won't be coming here any more.

Sir John Squire

IN FLANDERS FIELDS

In Flanders fields the poppies blow
Between the crosses, row on row,
    That mark our place ; and in the sky
    The larks, still bravely singing, fly
Scarce heard amid the guns below.

We are the Dead. Short days ago
We lived, felt dawn, saw sunset glow,
  Loved and were loved, and now we lie
    In Flanders fields.

Take up our quarrel with the foe :
To you from failing hands we throw
    The torch ; be yours to hold it high.
    If ye break faith with us who die,
We shall not sleep, though poppies grow
    In Flanders fields.

John MacCrae

NIGHT BOMBERS

Eastward they climb, black shapes against the grey
Of falling dusk, gone with the nodding day
From English fields. Not theirs the sudden glow
Of triumph that their fighter-brothers know ;
Only to fly through cloud, through storm, through night,
Unerring, and to keep their purpose bright,
Nor turn until, their dreadful duty done,
Westward they climb to race the awakened sun.

Anonymous

WHEN THE PLANE DIVED

When the plane dived and the machine-gun spattered
The deck, in his numb clutch the tugging wheel
Bucked madly as he strove to keep the keel
Zig-zagging through the steep and choppy sea—
To keep zig-zagging, that was all that mattered . . .
To keep the ship zig-zagging endlessly,
Dodging that diving devil. Now again
The bullets spattered like a squall of rain
About him ; and again with desperate grip
He tugged, to port the helm . . . to keep the ship
Zig-zagging . . . zagging through eternity ;
To keep the ship. . . . A sudden scalding pain
Shot through his shoulder and the whole sky shattered
About him in red fire ; and yet his grip
Tightened upon the wheel. . . . To keep the ship
Zig . . . zig . . . zig-zagging, that was all that mattered.

Wilfrid Gibson

MINE-SWEEPERS

Not ours the fighter's glow,
  The glory and the praise ;
Unnoticed to and fro
  We pass our dangerous ways.

We sift the drifting sea
  And blindly grope beneath ;
Obscure and toilsome we,
  The fishermen of death.

But when the great ships go
  To battle through the gloom,
Our hearts beat high to know
  We cleared their path of doom.

E. Hilton Young

SOLDIER

(1940)

So, friend of all men, and the wide world's lover,
  You are learning, between willing and unwilling,
  The trade of the fighting-man, the old trade of killing,
Whose best is this, to stand and die and suffer.

The Prince of Peace and God of Battles, making
  Of peace new morning and of battle ending,
  Give you, in life, not death, your part in mending
His broken world you had no part in breaking.

Arundell Esdaile

THE HEAP

Still in the crystal light
Of Winter's cold sunrise
A heap of rubble lies.
As in hag-ridden sleep
With unbelieving eyes
He stares at the still heap—
That heap that but last night
Was home—that heap that lies
Still in the crystal light
Of Winter's cold sunrise.

Wilfrid Gibson

THE BIAS

If there be some wild beauty worth
My love in every land on earth,
How claim impartial Nature yields
No riches but in English fields?—
  And yet forgive me if I hold it treason
  Not to love those fields past reason.

If some dark, festering homeland town
Call anger on its makers down,
How claim none but a foreign State
Has store of evil worth my hate?—
  And yet forgive me if I turn my anger,
  Fresh and whole, against the stranger.

Though love, when peace resumes, may roam
To tryst with beauty far from home,
And anger then find chiefest mark
In England, where some town lies dark—
  Yet still forgive me if my heart discover
  Proof that I am England's lover.

G. Rostrevor Hamilton

THE OTHER LITTLE BOATS

A PAUSE came in the fighting and England held her breath,
For the battle was not ended and the ending might be death.
Then out they came, the little boats, from all the Channel shores:
Free men were these who hauled the ropes and sweated at the oars.
From Itchenor and Shoreham, from Deal and Winchelsea,
They put out into the Channel to keep their country free.

Not of Dunkirk this story, but of boatmen long ago,
When our Queen was Gloriana and King Philip was the foe,
And galleons rode the narrow seas, and Effingham and Drake
Were out of shot and powder, with all England still at stake.

They got the shot and powder, they charged the guns again,
The guns that guarded England from the galleons of Spain,

And the men that helped them do it, helped them still to
hold the sea,
Men from Itchenor and Shoreham, men from Deal and
Winchelsea,
Looked out happily from Heaven and cheered to see the
work
Of their grandsons' grandsons' grandsons on the beaches of
Dunkirk.

Edward Shanks

ON A GRAVE IN MESOPOTAMIA

Soldiers of England,
Her sons and her servants,
Following homeward
The dreams that outspeed you,
Here lies a soldier,
His labours ended,
Even of England
Dreamless for ever.

Anonymous

REFLECTION

DEAR COUNTRY

. . . Deare countrey ! O ! how dearely deare
Ought thy rembraunce and perpetuall band
Be to thy foster Childe, that from thy hand
Did commun breath and nouriture receave.
How brutish is it not to understand
How much to her we owe, that all us gave ;
That gave unto us all what ever good we have.

Edmund Spenser

THE LIE

Go, soul, the body's guest,
  Upon a thankless arrant ;
Fear not to touch the best ;
  The truth shall be thy warrant.
    Go, since I needs must die,
    And give the world the lie.

Say to the court, it glows
  And shines like rotten wood ;
Say to the church, it shows
  What's good, and doth no good ;
    If church and court reply,
    Then give them both the lie.

Tell potentates, they live
  Acting by others' action,
Not loved unless they give,
  Not strong but by their faction :
    If potentates reply,
    Give potentates the lie.

Tell men of high condition
  That manage the estate,
Their purpose is ambition,
  Their practice only hate :
    And if they once reply,
    Then give them all the lie.

Tell them that brave it most,
  They beg for more by spending,
Who, in their greatest cost,
  Like nothing but commending :
    And if they make reply,
    Then give them all the lie.

Tell zeal it wants devotion ;
  Tell love it is but lust ;
Tell time it meets but motion ;
  Tell flesh it is but dust :
    And wish them not reply,
    For thou must give the lie.

Tell age it daily wasteth ;
  Tell honour how it alters ;
Tell beauty how she blasteth ;
  Tell favour how it falters :
    And if they shall reply,
    Give every one the lie.

Tell wit how much it wrangles
  In tickle points of niceness ;
Tell wisdom she entangles
  Herself in over-wiseness :
    And when they do reply,
    Straight give them both the lie.

Tell physic of her boldness ;
  Tell skill it is prevention ;
Tell charity of coldness ;
  Tell law it is contention :
    And as they do reply
    So give them still the lie.

Tell fortune of her blindness ;
  Tell nature of decay ;
Tell friendship of unkindness ;
  Tell justice of delay :
    And if they will reply,
    Then give them all the lie.

Tell arts they have no soundness,
  But vary by esteeming ;
Tell schools they want profoundness,
  And stand so much on seeming :
    If arts and schools reply,
    Give arts and schools the lie.

Tell faith it's fled the city ;
  Tell how the country erreth ;
Tell, manhood shakes off pity ;
  Tell, virtue least preferreth :
    And if they do reply,
    Spare not to give the lie.

So when thou hast, as I
  Commanded thee, done blabbing,
Because to give the lie
  Deserves no less than stabbing,
    Stab at thee he that will,
    No stab thy soul can kill.

Sir Walter Raleigh

A FAREWELL TO ARMS

To Queen Elizabeth

His golden locks Time hath to silver turned ;
O Time too swift, O swiftness never ceasing !
His youth 'gainst time and age hath ever spurned,
  But spurn'd in vain ; youth waneth by increasing :
Beauty, strength, youth, are flowers but fading seen ;
Duty, faith, love, are roots, and ever green.

His helmet now shall make a hive for bees ;
  And, lovers' sonnets turn'd to holy psalms,
A man-at-arms must now serve on his knees,
  And feed on prayers, which are age his alms :[1]
But though from court to cottage he depart,
His Saint is sure of his unspotted heart.

And when he saddest sits in homely cell,
  He'll teach his swains this carol for a song :
" Blest be the hearts that wish my sovereign well,
  Curst be the souls that think her any wrong ! "
Goddess, allow this agèd man his right
To be your beadsman now that was your knight.

George Peele

SACRED RELIGION

  Sacred Religion ! Mother of form, and fear !
How gorgeously sometimes dost thou sit deck'd !
What pompous vestures do we make thee wear !
What stately piles we prodigal erect !
How sweet perfum'd thou art, how shining clear !
How solemnly observ'd, with what respect !
  Another time all plain, all quite threadbare,
Thou must have all within and nought without ;
Sit poorly, without light, disrob'd ; no care
Of outward grace t' amuse the poor devout ;
Pow'rless, unfollow'd ; scarcely men can spare
The necessary rites to set thee out.
  Either truth, goodness, virtue are not still
The self-same which they are and always one,
But alter to the project of our will ;
Or we our actions make them wait upon,
Putting them in the liv'ry of our skill,
And cast them off again when we have done.
  You, mighty lords, that with respected grace
Do at the stern of fair example stand,
And all the body of this populace
Guide with the turning of your hand,
Keep a right course ; bear up from all disgrace

[1] *age his alms* : the alms of his old age.

Observe the point of glory to our land.
  Hold up disgracèd knowledge from the ground ;
Keep virtue in request ; give worth her due ;
Let not neglect with barb'rous means confound
So fair a good, to bring in night anew ;
Be not, O be not accessory found
Unto her death that must give life to you !
  Where will you have your virtuous name safe laid ?
In gorgeous tombs, in sacred cells secure ?
Do you not see those prostrate heaps betray'd
Your fathers' bones and could not keep them sure ?
And will you trust deceitful stones fair laid
And think they will be to your honour truer ?
  No, no ! unsparing Time will proudly send
A warrant unto wrath, that with one frown
Will all these mock'ries of vain glory rend
And make them, as before, ungrac'd, unknown ;
Poor idle honours, that can ill defend
Your memories that cannot keep their own.
  And whereto serves that wondrous Trophy now
That on the goodly plain near Wilton stands,
That huge dumb heap [1] that cannot tell us how
Nor what nor whence it is, nor with whose hands,
Nor for whose glory it was set to show
How much our pride mocks that of other lands.

Samuel Daniel

THIS ENGLAND

This royal throne of kings, this sceptred isle,
This earth of majesty, this seat of Mars,
This other Eden, demi-paradise,
This fortress built by Nature for herself
Against infection and the hand of war,
This happy breed of men, this little world,
This precious stone set in the silver sea,
Which serves it in the office of a wall,
Or as a moat defensive to a house ;
Against the envy of less happier lands,
This blessed plot, this earth, this realm, this England.

William Shakespeare

[1] *That huge dumb heap* : Stonehenge.

GROWING IN GRACE

To Sir Henry Goodyere

Who makes the last a pattern for next year,
  Turns no new leaf, but still the same things reads ;
Seen things he sees again, heard things doth hear,
  And makes his life but like a pair of beads.

A palace, when 'tis that which it should be,
  Leaves growing, and stands such, or else decays ;
But he which dwells there is not so, for he
  Strives to urge upward, and his fortune raise.

So had your body her morning, hath her noon,
  And shall not better ; her next change is night ;
But her fair, larger guest, to whom sun and moon
  Are sparks, and short-lived, claims another right.

The noble soul by age grows lustier ;
  Her appetite and her digestion mend.
We must not starve nor hope to pamper her
  With women's milk, and pap, unto the end.

Provide you manlier diet. You have seen
  All libraries, which are schools, camps and courts ;
But ask your garners if you have not been
  In harvest too indulgent to your sports.

Would you redeem it ? Then yourself transplant
  Awhile from hence. Perchance outlandish ground
Bears no more wit than ours ; but yet more scant
  Are those diversions there, which here abound.

To be a stranger hath that benefit.
  We can beginnings, but not habits choke.
Go—whither ? hence. You get, if you forget ;
  New faults, till they prescribe to us, are smoke.

Our soul, whose country's heaven, and God her Father,
  Into this world, corruption's sink, is sent ;
Yet so much in her travel she doth gather,
  That she returns home wiser than she went.

It pays you well, if it teach you to spare,
  And make you ashamed to make your hawk's praise
    yours,
Which when herself she lessens in the air,
  You then first say that high enough she towers.

However, keep the lively taste you hold
  Of God ; love Him as now, but fear Him more ;
And in your afternoons think what you told
  And promised Him at morning prayer before.

Let falsehood like a discord anger you ;
  Else be not froward. But why do I touch
Things of which none is in your practice new ?
  And tables or fruit-trenchers teach as much.

But thus I make you keep your promise, Sir ;
  Riding I had you, though you still stay'd there ;
And in these thoughts, although you never stir,
  You came with me to Mitcham, and are here.

John Donne

IN WESTMINSTER ABBEY

Mortality, behold and fear !
What a change of flesh is here !
Think how many royal bones
Sleep within this heap of stones !
Here they lie had realms and lands,
Who now want strength to stir their hands.
Where from their pulpits sealed with dust
They preach, " In greatness is no trust ".

Here is an acre sown indeed
With the richest, royall'st seed
That the earth did e'er suck in,
Since the first man died for sin.
Here the bones of birth have cried,
" Though gods they were, as men they died."
Here are sands, ignoble things,
Dropt from the ruined sides of kings ;
Here's a world of pomp and state,
Buried in dust, once dead by fate.

Francis Beaumont

AN OCEAN HOME

Others may use the ocean as their road,
Only the English make it their abode,
Whose ready sails with ev'ry wind can fly,
And make a cov'nant with th' inconstant sky ;
Our oaks secure, as if they there took root,
We tread on billows with a steady foot.

Edmund Waller

IN THE CLOISTER

But let my due feet never fail
To walk the studious cloister's pale,
And love the high embowed roof,
With antique pillars massy proof,
And storied windows richly dight,
Casting a dim religious light.
There let the pealing organ blow
To the full-voic'd quire below,
In service high, and anthems clear,
As may with sweetness, through mine ear,
Dissolve me into ecstasies,
And bring all Heav'n before mine eyes.

John Milton

BRAVE TOMB

THE moon shone clear on the becalmèd flood,
Where, while her beams like glittering silver play,
Upon the deck our careful General stood,
And deeply mus'd on the succeeding day.

That happy sun, said he, will rise again,
Who twice victorious did our Navy see :
And I alone must view him rise in vain,
Without one ray of all his star for me.

Yet like an English Gen'ral will I die,
And all the ocean make my spacious grave :
Women and cowards on the land may lie,
The sea's a tomb that's proper for the Brave.

John Dryden

VAIN GLORY

THE boast of heraldry, the pomp of power,
  And all that beauty, all that wealth e'er gave,
Awaits alike th' inevitable hour.
  The paths of glory lead but to the grave.

Nor you, ye Proud, impute to these the fault,
  If Mem'ry o'er their tomb no trophies raise,
Where thro' the long-drawn aisle and fretted vault
  The pealing anthem swells the note of praise.

Can storied urn or animated bust
  Back to its mansion call the fleeting breath ?
Can Honour's voice provoke the silent dust,
  Or Flatt'ry soothe the dull cold ear of Death ?

Perhaps in this neglected spot is laid
  Some heart once pregnant with celestial fire ;
Hands, that the rod of empire might have swayed,
  Or waked to ecstasy the living lyre.

His little, nameless, unremembered acts
Of kindness and of love. Nor less, I trust,
To them I may have owed another gift,
Of aspect more sublime ; that blessed mood,
In which the burthen of the mystery,
In which the heavy and the weary weight
Of all this unintelligible world
Is lightened :—that serene and blessed mood,
In which the affections gently lead us on,—
Until, the breath of this corporeal frame
And even the motion of our human blood
Almost suspended, we are laid asleep
In body, and become a living soul :
While with an eye made quiet by the power
Of harmony, and the deep power of joy,
We see into the life of things.

William Wordsworth

THE COUNTRYMAN IN EXILE

I TRAVELLED among unknown men,
  In lands beyond the sea ;
Nor, England ! did I know till then
  What love I bore to thee.

'Tis past, that melancholy dream !
  Nor will I quit thy shore
A second time ; for still I seem
  To love thee more and more.

Among thy mountains did I feel
  The joy of my desire ;
And she I cherished turned her wheel
  Beside an English fire.

Thy mornings shewed, thy nights concealed,
  The bowers where Lucy played ;
And thine too is the last green field
  That Lucy's eyes surveyed.

William Wordsworth

THE HERITAGE OF FREEDOM

It is not to be thought of that the Flood
  Of British freedom, which, to the open sea
  Of the world's praise, from dark antiquity
Hath flowed, " with pomp of waters unwithstood ",
Roused though it be full often to a mood
  Which spurns the check of salutary bands,
  That this most famous Stream in bogs and sands
Should perish ; and to evil and to good
Be lost for ever. In our halls is hung
  Armoury of the invincible Knights of old :
We must be free or die, who speak the tongue
  That Shakespeare spake ; the faith and morals hold
Which Milton held.—In everything we are sprung
  Of Earth's first blood, have titles manifold.

William Wordsworth

DEAR BRITAIN, MOTHER ISLE

. . . O my Mother Isle !
Needs must thou prove a name most dear and holy
To me, a son, a brother, and a friend,
A husband, and a father ! who revere
All bonds of natural love, and find them all
Within the limits of thy rocky shores.
O native Britain ! O my Mother Isle !
How shouldst thou prove aught else but dear and holy
To me, who from thy lakes and mountain-hills,
Thy clouds, thy quiet dales, thy rocks and seas,
Have drunk in all my intellectual life,
All sweet sensations, all ennobling thoughts,
All adoration of the God in nature,
All lovely and all honourable things,
Whatever makes this mortal spirit feel
The joy and greatness of its future being ?
There lives nor form nor feeling in my soul
Unborrowed from my country ! O divine
And beauteous island ! thou hast been my sole

And most magnificent temple, in the which
I walk with awe, and sing my stately songs,
Loving the God that made me !—May my fears,
My filial fears, be vain ! and may the vaunts
And menace of the vengeful enemy
Pass like the gust, that roared and died away
In the distant tree ; which, heard and only heard
In this low dell, bowed not the delicate grass.

Samuel Taylor Coleridge

ENGLAND

Peace, Freedom, Happiness, have loved to wait
  On the fair islands, fenced by circling seas ;
  And ever of such favoured spots as these
Have the wise dreamers dreamed, who would create
That perfect model of a happy state
  Which the world never saw ! Oceana,
  Utopia such, and Plato's isle that lay
Westward of Gades and the Great Sea's gate.
Dreams are they all, which yet have helped to make
  That underneath fair polities we dwell,
    Though marred in part by envy, faction, hate ;
Dreams which are dear, dear England, for thy sake,
  Who art indeed that sea-girt citadel
    And nearest image of that perfect state.

Archbishop Trench

LETTY'S GLOBE

When Letty had scarce passed her third glad year
  And her young artless words began to flow,
One day we gave the child a coloured sphere
  Of the wide earth, that she might mark and know
By tint and outline all its sea and land.
  She patted all the world ; old empires peeped
Between her baby fingers : her soft hand
  Was welcome at all frontiers. How she leaped
  And laughed and prattled in her world-wide bliss ;

But when we turned her sweet, unlearned eye
On our own isle, she raised a joyous cry—
" Oh ! yes, I see it, Letty's home is there ! "
   And while she hid all England with a kiss,
Bright over Europe fell her golden hair.

Charles Tennyson-Turner

SOBER-SUITED FREEDOM

You ask me, why, tho' ill at ease,
   Within this region I subsist,
   Whose spirits falter in the mist,
And languish for the purple seas.

It is the land that freemen till,
   That sober-suited Freedom chose,
   The land where, girt with friends or foes
A man may speak the thing he will ;

A land of settled government,
   A land of just and old renown,
   Where Freedom slowly broadens down
From precedent to precedent ;

Where faction seldom gathers head,
   But by degrees to fulness wrought,
   The strength of some diffusive thought
Hath time and space to work and spread.

Should banded unions persecute
   Opinion, and induce a time
   When single thought is civil crime,
And individual freedom mute ;

Tho' Power should make from land to land
   The name of Britain trebly great—
   Tho' every channel of the State
Should fill and choke with golden sand—

Yet waft me from the harbour-mouth,
  Wild wind ! I seek a warmer sky,
  And I will see before I die
The palms and temples of the South.

Lord Tennyson

HOME-THOUGHTS, FROM ABROAD

O, to be in England
Now that April's there !
And whoever wakes in England
Sees, some morning, unaware,
That the lowest boughs and the brushwood sheaf
Round the elm-tree bole are in tiny leaf,
While the chaffinch sings on the orchard bough
In England—now !

And after April, when May follows,
And the whitethroat builds, and all the swallows !
Hark, where my blossomed pear-tree in the hedge
Leans to the field and scatters on the clover
Blossoms and dewdrops—at the bent spray's edge—
That's the wise thrush ; he sings each song twice over,
Lest you should think he never could recapture
The first fine careless rapture !
And though the fields look rough with hoary dew,
All will be gay when noontide wakes anew
The buttercups, the little children's dower
—Far brighter than this gaudy melon flower !

Robert Browning

HOME-THOUGHTS, FROM THE SEA

Nobly, nobly Cape Saint Vincent to the North-West died
  away ;
Sunset ran, one glorious blood-red, reeking into Cadiz Bay ;
Bluish 'mid the burning water, full in face Trafalgar lay ;
In the dimmest North-East distance, dawn'd Gibraltar
  grand and grey ;

" Here and here did England help me : how can I help England ? "—say,
Whoso turns as I, this evening, turn to God to praise and pray,
While Jove's planet rises yonder, silent over Africa.

Robert Browning

THE FAIR BRASS

An effigy of brass,
Trodden by careless feet
Of worshippers that pass,
Beautiful and complete,

Lieth in the sombre aisle
Of this old church unwreckt,
And still from modern style
Shielded by kind neglect.

It shows a warrior arm'd :
Across his iron breast
His hands by death are charm'd
To leave his sword at rest,

Wherewith he led his men
O'ersea, and smote to hell
The astonisht Saracen,
Nor doubted he did well.

Would we could teach our sons
His trust in face of doom,
Or give our bravest ones
A comparable tomb :

Such as to look on shrives
The heart of half its care ;
So in each line survives
The spirit that made it fair ;

So fair the characters,
With which the dusty scroll,
That tells his title, stirs
A requiem for his soul.

Yet dearer far to me,
And brave as he are they,
Who fight by land and sea
For England at this day ;

Whose vile memorials,
In mournful marbles gilt,
Deface the beauteous walls
By growing glory built :

Heirs of our antique shrines,
Sires of our future fame,
Whose starry honour shines
In many a noble name

Across the deathful days,
Link'd in the brotherhood
That loves our country's praise,
And lives for heavenly good.

Robert Bridges

PRO REGE NOSTRO

What have I done for you,
England, my England ?
What is there I would not do,
England, my own ?
With your glorious eyes austere,
As the Lord were walking near,
Whispering terrible things and dear
As the Song on your bugles blown,
England—
Round the world on your bugles blown !

Where shall the watchful Sun,
  England, my England,
Match the master-work you've done,
  England, my own ?
When shall he rejoice agen
Such a breed of mighty men
As come forward, one to ten,
  To the Song on your bugles blown,
      England—
  Down the years on your bugles blown ?

Ever the faith endures,
  England, my England :—
Take and break us : we are yours,
  England, my own !
Life is good, and joy runs high
Between English earth and sky :
Death is death ; but we shall die
  To the Song on your bugles blown,
      England—
  To the stars on your bugles blown !

They call you proud and hard,
  England, my England :
You with worlds to watch and ward,
  England, my own !
You whose mailed hand keeps the keys
Of such teeming destinies,
You could not know nor dread nor ease,
  Were the Song on your bugles blown,
      England—
  Round the Pit on your bugles blown !

Mother of Ships whose might,
  England, my England,
Is the fierce old Sea's delight,
  England, my own,
Chosen daughter of the Lord,
Spouse-in-chief of the ancient Sword,

There's the menace of the Word
In the Song on your bugles blown,
England—
Out of Heaven on your bugles blown !

W. E. Henley

OLD SHEPHERD'S PRAYER

Up to the bed by the window, where I be lyin',
Comes bells and bleat of the flock wi' they two children's clack.
Over, from under the eaves there's the starlings flyin',
And down in yard, fit to burst his chain, yapping out at Sue, I do hear young Mac.

Turning around like a falled-over sack
I can see team ploughin' in Withybush field and meal carts startin' up road to Church Town ;
Saturday arternoon, the men goin' back
And the women from market, trapin' home over the down.

Heavenly Master, I wud like to wake to they same green places
Where I be know'd for breakin' dogs and follerin' sheep.
And if I may not walk in th' old ways and look on th' old faces
I wud sooner sleep.

Charlotte Mew

IN THE TRAIN

I am in a long train gliding through England,
Gliding past green fields and gentle grey willows,
Past huge dark elms and meadows full of buttercups,
And old farms dreaming among mossy apple trees.

Now we are in a dingy town of small ugly houses
And tin advertisements of cocoa and Sunlight Soap,

Now we are in a dreary station built of coffee-coloured
wood,
Where barmaids in black stand in empty Refreshment
Rooms,
And shabby old women sit on benches with suitcases.

Now we are by sidings where coal-trucks lurk discon-
solate,
Bright skies overarch us with shining cloud palaces,
Sunshine flashes on canals and then the rain comes,
Silver rain from grey skies lashing our window panes.
Then it is bright again and white smoke is blowing
Gaily over a pale blue sky among the telegraph wires.

Northward we rush under bridges, up gradients,
Through black, smoky tunnels, over iron viaducts,
Past platelayers and signal-boxes, factories and ware-
houses ;
Afternoon is fading among the tall brick chimney-stacks
In the murky Midlands where meadows grow more
colourless.

Northward, O train, you rush, resolute, invincible,
Northward to the night where your banner of flying
smoke
Will glow in the darkness with burning spark and ruddy
flame.
Be the train, my life, see the shining meadows,
Glance at the quiet farms, the gardens and shady lanes,

But do not linger by them, look at the dingy misery
Of all those silly towns, see it, hate it and remember it,
But never accept it. You must only accept your own
road :
The strong unchanging steel rails of necessity,
The ardent power that drives you towards night and the
unknown terminus.

Vivian de Sola Pinto

VALE

Farewell, this is the first, the worst Farewell,
  Good-bye to the long dream ;
I hear the tolling of my boyhood's knell,
  And I must cross the stream.

Good-bye, South Meadow, Athens, Cuckoo Weir,
  Good-bye, tall Brocas trees ;
To me you are more sacred and more fair
  Than the Hesperides.

Good-bye, dear Library, dear musty shelves,
  Worn books and marble bust,
Where over tables scholars skipped like elves,
  And raised a cloud of dust.

But there I saw—as through a misty veil
  A chalice of white fire—
The light of Shelley's song, and heard the tale
  Of his divine desire.

'Twas there I read how, led by fatal chance,
  A mortal loved the Moon ;
And thus I learnt the language of romance,
  And heard the magic tune.

The little book was like a silver key
  To many-coloured lands,
Where wondrous harps upon a ghostly sea
  Answer a mermaid's hands.

Tomorrow I shall be beyond the spell,
  The fields behind ; the road
Before me ; banished from the wishing well,
  And on my back a load.

Yet none can steal the tasted happiness,
  And if I meet dark hours,
Dear Mother, I will turn in my distress
  Back to thy chiming towers.

Though pangs begotten of sweet memory
Make worse the present woe,
I'll turn to thee and say : " At Eton I
Was happy long ago.

What can I give thee, Mother, in return
For all thy gifts to me ?
What if no laurel shall adorn my urn,
Nor deed of high degree ?

Others with honour, glory and green bays
Shall brighten thy bright fame ;
I with no more than love, can swell thy praise
With one forgotten name."

Maurice Baring

VAGABOND

Dunno a heap about the what an' why,
Can't say's I ever knowed.
Heaven to me's a fair blue stretch of sky,
Earth's jest a dusty road.

Dunno the names o' things, nor what they are,
Can't say's I ever will.
Dunno about God—He's jest the noddin' star
Atop the windy hill.

Dunno about Life—it's jest a tramp alone
From wakin'-time to doss.
Dunno about Death—it's jest a quiet stone
All over-grey wi' moss.

An' why I live, an' why the old world spins,
Are things I never knowed ;
My mark's the gypsy fires, the lonely inns,
An' jest the dusty road.

John Masefield

TESTAMENT

When I am dead, let not my limbs be given
To rot amongst the dead I never knew,
But cast my ashes wide under wide heaven,
Or to my garden let me still be true,

And, like the ashes I was wont to save
Preciously from the hearth beneath my fire,
Lighten the soil with mine. Not, not the grave !
I loved the soil I fought, and this is my desire.

V. Sackville-West

THE MAP

How tiny England is this map will show,
  And how she is the butt of many seas
  That shaped her landscape to its subtleties,
How few her rivers are, her hills how low.
This map will tell you, faintly, of her towns
  (Pin-point for London, Thames a thread of hair),
But will not tell of dewponds on the Downs,
  Or how the leaves of Warwick green the air.
This map will tell you nothing of the way
  The coltish April skips across her skies,
  Nor how, in autumn nights, the curlew cries,
Or thrush or blackbird harmonise in May.
  For these such things consult that wiser chart
  Engraved upon the exiled English heart.

James Walker

FANCY'S KNELL

When lads were home from labour
  At Abdon under Clee,
A man would call his neighbour
  And both would send for me.

And where the light in lances
  Across the mead was laid,
There to the dances
  I fetched my flute and played.

Ours were idle pleasures,
  Yet oh, content we were,
The young to wind the measures,
  The old to heed the air ;
And I to lift with playing
  From tree and tower and steep
The light delaying,
  And flute the sun to sleep.

The youth toward his fancy
  Would turn his brow of tan,
And Tom would pair with Nancy
  And Dick step off with Fan ;
The girl would lift her glances
  To his, and both be mute :
Well went the dances
  At evening to the flute.

Wenlock Edge was umbered,
  And bright was Abdon Burf,
And warm between them slumbered
  The smooth green miles of turf ;
Until from grass and clover
  The upshot beam would fade,
And England over
  Advanced the lofty shade.

The lofty shade advances,
  I fetch my flute and play :
Come, lads, and learn the dances
  And praise the tune to-day.
To-morrow, more's the pity,
  Away we both must hie,
To air the ditty,
  And to earth I.

A. E. Housman

HUMOUR

THE FRIAR

A FRERE ther was, a wantown and a merye,
A limitour,[1] a ful solempne man.
In alle the ordres foure is noon that can
So muche of daliaunce and fair langage.
He hadde maad ful many a mariage
Of yonge wommen, at his owne cost.
Un-to his ordre he was a noble post.
Ful wel biloved and famulier was he
With frankeleyns over-al in his contree,
And eek with worthy wommen of the toun :
For he had power of confessioun,
As seyde him-self, more than a curat,
For of his ordre he was licentiat.
Ful swetely herde he confessioun,
And pleasunt was his absolucioun ;
He was an esy man to yeve penaunce
Ther as he wiste to han a good pitaunce ;
For unto a povre ordre for to yive
Is signe that a man is wel y-shrive.
For if he yaf,[2] he dorste make avaunt,[3]
He wiste that a man was repentaunt.
For many a man so hard is of his herte,
He may nat wepe al-thogh him sore smerte.
Therfore, in stede of weping and preyeres,
Men moot yeve silver to the povre freres.
His tipet[4] was ay farsed[5] ful of knyves
And pinnes, for to yeven faire wyves.
And certeinly he hadde a mery note ;
Wel coude he singe and pleyen on a rote.
Of yeddinges[6] he bar utterly the prys.
His nekke whyt was as the flour-de-lys ;

[1] *limitour* : friar licensed to beg locally.
[2] *yaf* : gave. [3] *avaunt* : boast. [4] *tipet* : hood.
[5] *farsed* : stuffed. [6] *yeddinges* : songs.

Ther-to he strong was as a champioun.
He knew the tavernes wel in every toun,
And everich hostiler and tappestere
Bet than a lazar[1] or a beggestere ;
For un-to swich a worthy man as he
Acorded nat, as by his facultee,
To have with seke lazars aqueyntaunce,
It is nat honest, it may nat avaunce
For to delen with no swich poraille,[2]
But al with riche and sellers of vitaille.
And over-al, ther as profit sholde aryse,
Curteys he was, and lowly of servyse.
Ther nas no man no-wher so vertuous.
He was the beste beggere in his hous ;
And yaf a certeyn ferme[3] for the graunt ;
Noon of his bretheren cam ther in his haunt ;
For thogh a widwe hadde noght a sho,[4]
So plesaunt was his " *In principio* ",
Yet wolde he have a ferthing, er he wente.
His purchas was wel bettre than his rente.[5]
And rage he coude, as it were right a whelpe.
In love-dayes ther coude he muchel helpe.
For there he was nat lyk a cloisterer,
With a thredbar cope, as is a povre scoler,
But he was lyk a maister or a pope.
Of double worsted was his semi-cope,
That rounded as a belle out of the presse.
Somwhat he lipsed, for his wantownesse,
To make his English swete up-on his tonge ;
And in his harping, whan that he had songe,
His eyen twinkled in his heed aright,
As doon the sterres in the frosty night.

Geoffrey Chaucer

TAVERN SCENE

THEN goeth Glutton in and great oaths after him.
Cis the shoe-seller sat on the bench,
Wat the warrener and his wife also,

[1] *lazar* : leper. [2] *poraille* : poor people. [3] *ferme* : rent.
[4] *sho* : shoe. [5] *rente* : income.

Tim the tinker and twain of his prentices,
Hick the hackney-man, and Hugh the needler,
Clarice of Cock-lane, and the clerk of the church,
Davy the ditcher, and a dozen others ;
Sir Piers of Pridie and Pernel of Flanders,
A fiddler, a ratter, a Cheapside sweeper,
A roper,[1] a rider, and Rose the dish-seller,
Godfrey of Garlichithe and Griffin the Welshman,
And a heap of upholsterers, in the morning early
Gave Glutton with glad cheer good ale to hansel.[2]
Then Clement the cobbler cast off his cloak,
And at the new fair [3] he wagered it for sale ;
Hick the hackney-man threw down his hood,
And bade Bat the butcher be on his side.
Then chapmen [4] were chosen the chaffer to appraise ;
He that had the hood should have amends for the cloke.
The two rose up readily and whispered together,
Appraising these pennyworths apart by themselves.
They could not in their conscience accord together,
Till Robin the roper arose for the truth,
And named himself umpire to end the dispute,
Then Hick the hostler had the cloak,
In covenant that Clement should fill the cup,
And have Hick's hood and hold himself quit ;
Whoso first repented should rise up after
And greet Sir Glutton with a gallon of ale.
There was laughing and lowering and " let go the cup ! "
They sat so till evensong, and sang now and then,
Till Glutton had gulped down a gallon and a gill.

. . . . . .

He could neither step nor stand until he had his staff ;
Then gan he to go like a gleeman's dog,
Sometimes aside and sometimes arear,
As one that layeth lines, birds to ensnare.
When he drew nigh the door, then dim were his eyes ;
He stumbled on the threshold and fell on the floor.
Clement the cobbler caught him by the middle,

[1] *roper* : rope-maker.
[2] *to hansel* : as an earnest of good will.
[3] *at the new fair* : the name of a popular form of barter.
[4] *chapmen* : traders.

And to lift him aloft, laid him on his knees ;
But Glutton was a great churl and grievous to lift,
And coughed up a caudle [1] in Clement's lap. . . .
. . . . . .

With all woe in the world his wife and his daughter
Bore him home to his bed and put him therein.
And after this surfeit he had a fit of sloth,
And slept Saturday and Sunday till the sun went down.
Then he awoke from his slumber, and wiped both his eyes,
And the first word he said was, " Where is the bowl ? "
Then his wife did upbraid him for his wicked ways
And also Repentance rebuked him thus :
" Both in words and in works thou hast evilly wrought ;
Shrive thee therefore with shame and shew it with thy mouth."
" I, Glutton," said the man, " confess me guilty ;
I have trespassed with tongue, I cannot tell how oft,
Have sworn ' By God's soul ' and ' So help me the Saints ',
Where never was need, nine hundred times.
I have surfeited at supper and sometimes at noon,
Till I, Glutton, threw it up, ere I had gone a mile,
And spilt what should spared be and spent on the hungry.
Too daintily on fast days I have drunken and eaten,
Sitting so long that I slept and ate at once.
To hear tales in taverns and to drink more I dined
And feasted ere noon on the fasting days."
" This showing shrift shall be merit to thee."
Then Glutton gan groan and great dole [2] he made
For the wicked life he had lived the while,
And vowed to fast : " For hunger or thirst
Shall no fish on Friday defy [3] in my maw,
Till Abstinence, my Aunt, hath given me leave ;
And yet have I hated her all my life-time."

William Langland

THE COURT OF FAME

I STODE up, halfe sodenly afrayd ;
Suppleyng to Fame, I besought her grace,

[1] *caudle* : drink. [2] *dole* : lamentation. [3] *defy* : be digested.

And that it wolde please her, full tenderly I prayd,
Owt of her bokis *Apollo* to rase.[1]
" Nay, sir," she sayd, " what so in this place
Of our noble courte is ones spoken owte,
It must nedes after rin all the worlde aboute."

God wote, theis wordes made me full sad ;
And when that I sawe it wolde no better be,
But that my peticyon wolde not be had,
What shulde I do but take it in gre ?[2]
For, by Juppiter and his high mageste,
I did what I cowde to scrape out the scrollis,
Apollo to rase out of her ragman rollis.[3]

Now hereof it erkith me lenger to wryte ;
To Occupacyon I wyll agayne resorte,
Which redde on still, as it cam to her syght,
Rendrynge my devisis I made in disporte,
Of the Mayden of Kent callid Comforte,
Of Lovers testamentis and of there wanton wyllis,
And how Jollas lovyd goodly Phillis ;

Diodorus Siculus of my translacyon
Out of fresshe Latine into owre Englysshe playne,
Rcountyng commoditis of many a straunge nacyon ;
Who redyth it ones wolde rede it agayne ;
Sex volumis engrosid together it doth containe :
But when of the laurell she made rehersall,
All orators and poetis, with other grete and smale,

A thowsande thowsande, I trow, to my dome,[4]
Triumpha, triumpha ! they cryid all aboute ;
Of trumpetis and clariouns the noyse went to Rome ;
The starry hevyn, me thought, shoke with the showte ;
The grownde gronid and tremblid, the noyse was so
stowte :
The Quene of Fame commaundid shett fast the boke ;
And therwith sodenly out of my dreme I woke.

[1] *rase* : erase. [2] *in gre* : in good part.
[3] *ragman rollis* : catalogue. [4] *to my dome* : in my judgement.

My mynde of the grete din was somdele amasid,
I wypid myne eyne for to make them clere ;
Then to the hevyn sperycall upwarde I gasid,
Where I saw Janus, with his double chere ;[1]
Makynge his almanak for the new yere ;
He turnyd his tirikkis,[2] his volvell[3] ran fast :
Good luk this new yere ! the olde yere is past.

John Skelton

HONEST TRADESMEN

When shoomakers make shoes,
That are wel sowed, with never a stitch amisse,
And use no crafte, in uttring of the same :
When taylours steale no stuffe from gentlemen,
When tanners are with corriers[4] wel agreede,
And both so dresse their hydes that we go dry :
When cutlers leave to sel old rustie blades,
And hide no crackes with soder[5] nor deceit :
When tinkers make no more holes than they founde,
When thatchers thinke their wages worth their worke,
When colliers put no dust into their sacks,
When maltemen make us drink no fermentie,
When Davie Diker diggs, and dallies not,
When smithes shoo horses as they would be shod,
When millers toll not with a golden thumbe,
When bakers make not barme[6] beare price of wheat,
When brewers put no bagage[7] in their beere,
When butchers blowe not over al their fleshe,
When horsecorsers beguile no friends with jades,
When weavers weight is found in huswives web.
(But why dwel I so long among these lowts ?)
When mercers make more bones to swere and lye,
When vintners mix no water with their wine,
When printers passe none errours in their books,
When hatters use to bye none olde cast robes,
When goldsmithes get no gains by sodred crownes,

[1] *chere* : face. [2] *tirikkis* : swivels.
[3] *volvell* : a mechanical almanac.
[4] *corriers* : one who curries leather after it has been tanned.
[5] *soder* : solder. [6] *barme* : yeast. [7] *bagage* : rubbish.

When upholsters sel fethers without dust,
When pewterers infect no tin with leade,
When drapers draw no gaines by giving day,[1]
When perchmentiers[2] put in no ferret silke,[3]
When surgeons heale al wounds without delay.
When al these things are ordred as they ought,
And see themselves within my glasse of steele,
Even then (my priests) may you make holyday
And pray no more but ordinarie prayers.

George Gascoigne

A BORE

He, like to a high-stretched lute-string, squeakt, " O sir,
'Tis sweet to talk of kings." " At Westminster,"
Said I, " the man that keeps the Abbey tombs,
And for his price doth with whoever comes
Of all our Harries and our Edwards talk,
From king to king, and all their kin can walk :
Your ears shall hear nought but kings ; your eyes meet
Kings only ; the way to it is Kingstreet."
He smack'd and cried, " He's base, mechanic, coarse,
So are all your Englishmen in their discourse.
Are not your Frenchmen neat ? " " Mine ? as you see,
I have but one, sir, look—he follows me."
" Certes they're neatly clothed. I of this mind am,
Your only wearing is your grogaram." [4]
" Not so, sir, I have more." Under this pitch
He would not fly ; I chaffed him. But as itch
Scratch'd into smart, and as blunt iron ground
Into an edge, hurts worse ; so I, fool, found
Crossing hurt me. To fit my sullenness,
He to another key his style doth dress,
And asks, " What news ? " I tell him of new plays.
He takes my hand, and as a still which stays
A semibreve, 'twixt each drop, he niggardly,
As loth to enrich me, so tells many a lie.

[1] *giving day* : giving credit.
[2] *perchmentiers* : makers of parchment.
[3] *ferret silke* : a narrow tape made of silk.
[4] *grogaram* : garment of coarse texture.

More than ten Holinsheds, or Halls, or Stows,
Of trivial household trash he knows ; he knows
When the Queen frown'd, or smiled, and he knows what
A subtle statesman may gather of that ;
He knows who loves whom ; and who by poison
Hastes to an office's reversion ;
He knows who hath sold his land, and now doth beg
A licence, old iron, boots, shoes, and egg-
Shells to transport ; shortly boys shall not play
At span-counter, or blow-point, but shall pay
Toll to some courtier ; and wiser than all us,
He knows what lady is not painted. Thus
He with home meats cloys me.

John Donne

ON THE UNIVERSITY CARRIER

Here lieth one who did most truly prove,
That he could never die while he could move ;
So hung his destiny, never to rot
While he might still jog on, and keep his trot ;
Made of sphere-metal, never to decay
Until his revolution was at stay.
Time numbers motion, yet (without a crime
'Gainst old truth) motion numbered out his time ;
And like an engine moved with wheel and weight,
His principles being ceased, he ended straight.
Rest that gives all men life, gave him his death,
And too much breathing put him out of breath ;
Nor were it contradiction to affirm
Too long vacation hastned on his term.
Merely to drive the time away he sickn'd,
Fainted, and died, nor would with ale be quickn'd ;
" Nay," quoth he, on his swooning bed outstretcht,
" If I mayn't carry, sure I'll ne'er be fetcht ;
" But vow, though the cross doctors all stood hearers,
" For one carrier put down to make six bearers."
Ease was his chief disease, and to judge right,
He died for heaviness that his cart went light ;
His leisure told him that his time was come,

And so God save the Regent, Church, and King !
Which means that I like all and everything.

Our standing army, and disbanded seamen,
  Poor's rate, Reform, my own, the nation's debt,
Our little riots just to show we are free men,
  Our trifling bankruptcies in the Gazette,
Our cloudy climate, and our chilly women,
  All these I can forgive, and those forget,
And greatly venerate our recent glories,
And wish they were not owing to the Tories.

Lord Byron

NO !

No sun—no moon !
No morn—no noon—
No dawn—no dusk—no proper time of day—
No sky—no earthly view—
No distance looking blue—
No road—no street—no " t'other side the way "—
No end to any Row—
No indications where the crescents go—
No top to any steeple—
No recognitions of familiar people—
No courtesies for showing 'em—
No knowing 'em !—
No travelling at all—no locomotion,
No inkling of the way—no notion—
" No go "—by land or ocean—
No mail—no post—
No news from any foreign coast—
No Park—no Ring—no afternoon gentility—
No company—no nobility,—
No warmth, no cheerfulness, no healthful ease,
No comfortable feel in any member—
No shade, no shine, no butterflies, no bees,
No fruits, no flowers, no leaves, no birds—
November !

Thomas Hood

MR. LEAR

" How pleasant to know Mr. Lear !
  Who has written such volumes of stuff !
Some think him ill-tempered and queer,
  But a few think him pleasant enough.

His mind is concrete and fastidious,
  His nose is remarkably big ;
His visage is more or less hideous,
  His beard it resembles a wig.

He has ears, and two eyes, and ten fingers,
  Leastways if you reckon two thumbs ;
Long ago he was one of the singers,
  But now he is one of the dumbs.

He sits in a beautiful parlour,
  With hundreds of books on the wall ;
He drinks a great deal of Marsala,
  But never gets tipsy at all.

He has many friends, laymen and clerical,
  Old Foss is the name of his cat :
His body is perfectly spherical,
  He weareth a runcible hat.

When he walks in a waterproof white,
  The children run after him so !
Calling out, " He's come out in his night-
  gown, that crazy old Englishman, oh ! "

He weeps by the side of the ocean,
  He weeps on the top of the hill ;
He purchases pancakes and lotion,
  And chocolate shrimps from the mill.

He reads but he cannot speak Spanish,
  He cannot abide ginger-beer :
Ere the days of his pilgrimage vanish,
  How pleasant to know Mr. Lear ! "

Edward Lear

THE BLESSED BELL

But hark ! a sound is stealing on my ear—
  A soft and silvery sound—I know it well.
Its tinkling tells me that a time is near
  Precious to me—it is the Dinner Bell.
O blessed Bell ! Thou bringest beef and beer,
  Thou bringest good things more than tongue may tell :
Seared is, of course, my heart—but unsubdued
Is, and shall be, my appetite for food.

I go. Untaught and feeble is my pen :
  But on one statement I may safely venture :
That few of our most highly gifted men
  Have more appreciation of the trencher.
I go. One pound of British beef, and then
  What Mr. Swiveller called a " modest quencher " ;
That home-returning I may " soothly say ",
" Fate cannot touch me : I have dined today."

C. S. Calverley

ETIQUETTE

The *Ballyshannon* foundered off the coast of Cariboo,
And down in fathoms many went the captain and the crew ;
Down went the owners—greedy men whom hope of gain allured :
Oh, dry the starting tear, for they were heavily insured.

Besides the captain and the mate, the owners and the crew,
The passengers were also drowned excepting only two :
Young Peter Gray, who tasted teas for Baker, Croop, and Co.,
And Somers, who from Eastern shores imported indigo.

These passengers, by reason of their clinging to a mast,
Upon a desert island were eventually cast.
They hunted for their meals, as Alexander Selkirk used,
But they couldn't chat together—they had not been introduced.

For Peter Gray, and Somers too, though certainly in
trade,
Were properly particular about the friends they made ;
And somehow thus they settled it without a word of
mouth—
That Gray should take the northern half, while Somers
took the south.

On Peter's portion oysters grew—a delicacy rare,
But oysters were a delicacy Peter couldn't bear.
On Somers' side was turtle, on the shingle lying thick,
Which Somers couldn't eat, because it always made him
sick.

Gray gnashed his teeth with envy as he saw a mighty store
Of turtle unmolested on his fellow-creature's shore.
The oysters at his feet aside impatiently he shoved,
For turtle and his mother were the only things he loved.

And Somers sighed in sorrow as he settled in the south,
For the thought of Peter's oysters brought the water to his
mouth.
He longed to lay him down upon the shelly bed, and stuff :
He had often eaten oysters, but had never had enough.

How they wished an introduction to each other they had
had
When on board the *Ballyshannon* ! And it drove them
nearly mad
To think how very friendly with each other they might get,
If it wasn't for the arbitrary rule of etiquette !

One day, when out a-hunting for the *mus ridiculus*,
Gray overheard his fellow-man soliloquising thus :
" I wonder how the playmates of my youth are getting on,
M'Connell, S. B. Walters, Paddy Byles, and Robin-
son ? "

These simple words made Peter as delighted as could be,
Old chummies at the Charterhouse were Robinson and he !

He walked straight up to SOMERS, then he turned extremely red,
Hesitated, hummed and hawed a bit, then cleared his throat, and said :

" I beg your pardon—pray forgive me if I seem too bold,
But you have breathed a name I knew familiarly of old.
You spoke aloud of ROBINSON—I happened to be by.
You know him ? " " Yes, extremely well." " Allow me, so do I."

It was enough : they felt they could more pleasantly get on,
For (ah, the magic of the fact !) they each knew ROBINSON !
And MR. SOMERS' turtle was at PETER's service quite,
And MR. SOMERS punished PETER's oyster-beds all night.

They soon became like brothers from community of wrongs :
They wrote each other little odes and sang each other songs ;
They told each other anecdotes disparaging their wives ;
On several occasions, too, they saved each other's lives.

They felt quite melancholy when they parted for the night,
And got up in the morning soon as ever it was light ;
Each other's pleasant company they reckoned so upon,
And all because it happened that they both knew ROBINSON !

They lived for many years on that inhospitable shore,
And day by day they learned to love each other more and more.
At last, to their astonishment, on getting up one day,
They saw a frigate anchored in the offing of the bay.

To PETER an idea occurred. " Suppose we cross the main ?
So good an opportunity may not be found again."
And SOMERS thought a minute, then ejaculated, " Done !
I wonder how my business in the City's getting on ? "

" But stay," said MR. PETER : " when in England, as you know,
I earned a living tasting teas for BAKER, CROOP, AND CO.,

I may be superseded—my employers think me dead ! ”
“ Then come with me,” said Somers, “ and taste indigo
instead.”

But all their plans were scattered in a moment when they
found
The vessel was a convict ship from Portland, outward
bound ;
When a boat came off to fetch them, though they felt it
very kind,
To go on board they firmly but respectfully declined.

As both the happy settlers roared with laughter at the
joke,
They recognised a gentlemanly fellow pulling stroke :
’Twas Robinson—a convict, in an unbecoming frock !
Condemned to seven years for misappropriating stock ! ! !

They laughed no more, for Somers thought he had been
rather rash
In knowing one whose friend had misappropriated cash ;
And Peter thought a foolish tack he must have gone upon
In making the acquaintance of a friend of Robinson.

At first they didn’t quarrel very openly, I’ve heard ;
They nodded when they met, and now and then exchanged
a word :
The word grew rare, and rarer still the nodding of the
head,
And when they meet each other now, they cut each other
dead.

To allocate the island they agreed by word of mouth,
And Peter takes the north again, and Somers takes the
south ;
And Peter has the oysters, which he hates, in layers
thick,
And Somers has the turtle—turtle always makes him sick.

Sir W. S. Gilbert

A POLITICAL ALLEGORY

ONCE there was a famous nation
  With a long and glorious past :
Very splendid was its station,
  And its territory vast ;
It had won the approbation,
The applause and admiration,
Of the states who'd had occasion,
In a time of tribulation,
And of disorganisation,
Not to mention degradation,
And profound humiliation,
  To observe it standing fast
Without any trepidation,
Or a sign of vacillation,
  Firm and faithful to the last.

Came a time of dire distraction,
  Full of terror and despair,
When a delicate transaction
  Called for unexampled care ;
But the people were directed,
Both the well and ill-affected,
To a wholly unexpected
And surprising course of action,
  Based on motives new and rare
(Being governed by a faction,
  As they generally were).

In a little time the nation
  Had a chance of saying whether
It and its administration
  Seemed inclined to pull together :
And it spoke its mind with vigour :—
  " Such disgraceful conduct must
Everlastingly disfigure
  Future annals, and disgust
Evermore the candid student :
You have been unwise, imprudent,
  Pusillanimous, unjust,

And neglectful of the glory
  Appertaining to our name
Till this melancholy story
  Put a period to our fame."

So this faction, disappointed,
  Lost the national good graces,
And their rivals were anointed,
  And were set in the high places.

Pretty soon arose conditions
  Most embarrassing and hard,
And the party politicians
  Had to be upon their guard.
Illegitimate ambitions,
Democratic rhetoricians,
Persons prone to base submissions,
Men of warlike dispositions,
Wild and wicked statisticians,
Metaphysical magicians,
People apt to sign petitions,
Men inclined to make conditions,
  And a host of wary foes,
Compassed round the ruling faction :
But a certain line of action
  They incontinently chose :
And with great determination,
And extreme discrimination,
Not untouched by exaltation,
After proper preparation,
And profound examination,
Wrought it out with acclamation,
And each other's approbation,
Till the national taxation
  Not unnaturally rose.

To the nation now occurred an
  Opportunity of saying
What they thought about the burden
  Which the government was laying

On their shoulders : and they said it
  In uncompromising terms :—
" Your behaviour would discredit
  Tigers, crocodiles, and worms :
You have ruined and disgraced us,
And successfully effaced us
From the proud commanding station
Where the zeal and penetration
Of our ancestors had placed us.
Go ! we are a ruined nation ;
  But before our dissolution
We pronounce your condemnation—
  Sappers of our constitution,
Slayers of our reputation ! "

But the nation—mark the moral,
  For its value is untold—
During each successive quarrel
  Grew and prospered as of old.

J. K. Stephen

THE ENGLISHMAN

St. George he was for England,
  And before he killed the dragon
He drank a pint of English ale
  Out of an English flagon.
For though he fast right readily
  In hair-shirt or in mail,
It isn't safe to give him cakes
  Unless you give him ale.

St. George he was for England,
  And right gallantly set free
The lady left for dragon's meat
  And tied up to a tree ;
But since he stood for England
  And knew what England means,
Unless you give him bacon
  You mustn't give him beans.

St. George he is for England,
  And shall wear the shield he wore
When we go out in armour
  With the battle-cross before.
But though he's jolly company
  And very pleased to dine,
It isn't safe to give him nuts
  Unless you give him wine.

G. K. Chesterton

HOW THEY DO IT

(Sir Henry Newbolt)

It was eight bells in the forenoon and hammocks running sleek
  (*It's a fair sea flowing from the West*),
When the little Commodore came a-sailing up the Creek
  (*Heave Ho ! I think you'll know the rest*).
Thunder in the halyards and horses leaping high,
Blake and Drake and Nelson are listenin' where they lie,
Four and twenty blackbirds a-bakin' in a pie,
  And the *Pegasus* came waltzing from the West.

Now the little Commodore sat steady on his keel
  (*It's a fair sea flowing from the West*),
A heart as stout as concrete reinforced with steel
  (*Heave Ho ! I think you'll know the rest*).
Swinging are the scuppers, hark, the rudder snores,
Plugging at the Frenchmen, downing 'em by scores,
Porto Rico, Vera Cruz, and also the Azores,
  And the *Pegasus* came waltzing from the West.

So three cheers more for the little Commodore
  (*It's a fair sea flowing from the West*),
I tell you so again as I've told you so before
  (*Heigh Ho ! I think you know the rest*).
Aged is the Motherland, old but she is young
  (Easy with the tackle there—don't release the bung),
And I sang a song like all the songs that I have ever sung
  When the *Pegasus* came sailing from the West.

Sir John Squire

THE EMIGRANT'S RETURN

From India to an English April

" Courage ! " they cried, and pointed to the shore ;
" Yon rift among the headlands that appears
Is Plymouth, and in sixty minutes more
Thereby we anchor and the ending nears."
But I was drinking toddy in the bar
And wishing I were back in Bow Bazaar,
For the thermometer was lower far
Than I had seen thermometer for years.

And presently I ventured on the deck
And saw a bleak land buffeted by hail,
Whereon it seemed no isolated speck
Of light or life or colour could prevail ;
But black trees bent before an icy breeze,
Lead-coloured cliffs confronted sable seas,
And all things said, " You will most surely freeze
On landing here and perish without fail."

" Ah, frore and bitter island, why so hard,
So loveless to thy late-returning son ?
Where is thy English April which the bard "—
Thus I reflected—" has enthused upon ?
Where is the laughing goddess of the Spring,
The bleating lamb, the lark upon the wing,
The daffodil—and many another thing
Wherewith the poet peoples Avalon ? "

So, loud-protesting, I was led ashore,
And found me in a little cobbled street
Where the rude Boreas vexed me more and more
And the rain smote me and the subtle sleet ;
Yet sudden there was something in the air
That said, " I may be desolate and bare,
But I am England ; do not yet despair,
For you will find me rather hard to beat."

And so Odysseus won to his hotel
And real hot water running from the tap
And rosy maids responding to the bell
And fires of coal and many things to lap
The body in content ; and no more noise
Of peons and coolies, watermen and boys,
But kindly countrymen whose simple joys
Lay, it would seem, in waiting on a chap.

Then a great peace descended on my soul,
And, as the shades of eve began to fall,
" Than Blighty," I remarked, " upon the whole
There are worse spots on the terrestrial ball.
To Hind the tropic ease, the sun's embrace,
Light, colour, and the seasons' gentle pace ;
Blighty is Arctic—yet a sounder place,
A comfortabler country, after all."

Hilton Brown

OLD MRS. HAGUE

Old Mrs. Hague,
The Gardener's wife,
Was not to be enclosed in any formulas.
She seems to stand upon a little mound
Of pansies,
    Primroses,
        And primulas.
Outlined against the pale blue eye of northern spring,
Heavily planted in this printed muslin beauty
Of clumps and spots and dots and tiger-stripes,
She swelled with ideas and ideals of duty,
Emphatic,
    Rheumatic.

Mrs. Thatch,
The wife, she was sorry to say,
Of Lord X's gardener
—If such one could call him—

Was silly, town-bred, what Mrs. Hague would call
—Well, she really did not like to say it,
Did not know what to call it ;
Shall we say a Ne'er-do-Well ?
And all the time the primroses, the wind-flowers
Opened their eyes and pressed their nodding heads
Against her, and the moss seemed ready to
Run up those rugged limbs,
The lichen ready
To crystallise its feathery formations
Along these solid branches.

If not upon this flower-sprinkled mound,
Then Mrs. Hague stood
Pressed in the narrow framework of her door,
And fills it to our minds for evermore.
Out of the slender gaps
Between the figure and its frame,
Was wafted the crusty, country odour
Of new bread,
Which was but one blossom of the hedges
That Mrs. Hague had planted.

For Mrs. Hague was childless,
And so had wisely broken up her life
With fences of her own construction,
Above which she would peer
With bovine grace,
Kind nose, kind eyes
Wide open in wide face.
For

Monday was Washing Day,
Tuesday was Baking Day,
Wednesday h'Alfred 'as 'is dinner h'early,
Thursday was Baking Day again,
Friday was a busy day, a very busy day,
And Saturday prepared the way for Sunday,
Black satin bosoms and a brooch,
A bonnet and a Bible.

Nor were these all :
There were other more imposing barriers
Of Strawberry Jam in June
And Blackberry Jelly in October :
For each fruit contributed a hedge
To the garden of Mrs. Hague's days.

These fences made life safe for Mrs. Hague :
Each barrier of washing, mending, baking
Was a barricade
Thrown up against being lonely or afraid.
This infinitive perspective
—The week, the month, the year—
Showed in the narrow gaps
Between her and the door,
As she stood there in the doorway,
Narrow as a coffin.

Oh, who can describe the grace of Mrs. Hague,
A Mrs. Noah limned by Botticelli,
'Mid flowering trees, green winds and pensive flowers ;
A Rousseau portrait, inflated by Picasso ;
Or seen in summer,
As through a tapestry
Of pool, exotic flower and conifer ?

As Daphne was transformed into a tree,
So some old elm had turned to Mrs. Hague,
Thick bole, wide arms and rustic dignity.

Sir Osbert Sitwell

THE ENGLISHMAN

A Very Patriotic Song

When Earth in Eden did awake
  And Man was made and mated,
The earliest men, by some mistake,
  Were foreigners all created ;

And in this fix the world began,
Till Heaven conceived a nobler plan
And there was born an Englishman—

With a fa, la, la, fa, la, la, la, la, la, la,
With a fa, la, la, la, la, la, la!

Still half the sphere in darkness sat,
But Britons went and found it ;
The heathen swore the Earth was flat—
We flung the flag all round it ;
And if the sea, with stealthy care,
Threw up an island anywhere,
An Englishman was always there—

With a fa, la, la, fa, la, la, la, la, la, la,
With a fa, la, la, la, la, la, la!

Then round the globe we looked, and lo!
The foreigners did not shave, Sir,
Nor did we shrink from saying so
In accents bold and brave, Sir ;
We pointed out from day to day
What we should do if we were they—
We made them love us in this way—

With a fa, la, la, fa, la, la, la, la, la, la,
With a fa, la, la, la, la, la, la!

And I am tempted, I confess,
To self-congratulation
When I reflect that I possess
The virtues of my nation,
And daily let my neighbours see
How different their lives might be
If they would but be ruled by me—

With a fa, la, la, fa, la, la, la, la, la, la,
With a fa, la, la, la, la, la, la!

The simple mind and manly air,
  Not Brains so much as Breeding,
With *joie de vivre* and *savoir faire*,
  Are constantly succeeding ;
Not men of words, we live to do,
Nor speak till we are spoken to,
Then answer " Cock-a-doodle-doo ! "—

With a fa, la, la, fa, la, la, la, la, la, la,
With a fa, la, la, la, la, la, la !

Alas, for all our kindly pain,
  The world is sick and sore, Sir,
And Frenchmen mulishly remain
  As foreign as before, Sir,
Thus ends the tale as it began ;
Conceive the difference, if you can,
Had Adam been an Englishman—

With a fa, la, la, fa, la, la, la, la, la, la,
With a fa, la, la, la, la, la, la !

A. P. Herbert

TO MRS. GAMP IN ELYSIUM

(Suggested by Lord Baldwin's declaration that, after paying due honour in another world to " good Sir Walter " and " Jane ", he would like to " go into a corner " and hold converse with Mrs. Gamp.)

We know there is, in some far nook of space,
A wondrous high-walled place
Where Rosinante feeds with Sancho's ass
On clover-speckled grass ;

Dominie Sampson dwells within these gates,
And Crusoe and Miss Bates,
And Monsieur Jourdain and Yseult the Fair,
And lo ! thou too art there.

Thou too art there ; thy pattens clink upon
Bright paths of azure stone,
And thy umbrella hangs upon the wall
With Gram and Durandal.

Now leaning o'er a " parapidge " of gold
Thy profile we behold.
(We had not thought of this, yet who dares doubt
That it has come about ?)

Surely thou hast thy russet tea-pot still,
And " cowcumbers " at will ;
The spicy groves will yield thee store enough
Of choice and fragrant snuff.

With Mrs. Harris and her voiceful nine
Thou mayest sit and dine,
While she, if ever things should " go contrairy ",
May still breathe, " Send for Sairey ! "

And surely the perfection of thy bliss
Beyond the stars is this :
That Mrs. Harris is no figment now,
But quite as real as thou.

Dorothy Margaret Stuart

TO A LONDON TYPIST, 1940

TYPIST of the shingled hair,
  Cigarette in coloured lips,
Frail of form, degenerate air
  To your painted finger-tips :
Symbol of a falling race,
  Trembling hands and slipping feet,
Yielding up its pride of place,
  Once imperial, now effete.

When the German Leader flung
  Aerial terror on your town,
Why was not your nerve unstrung
  Nor your courage broken down ?
Why, impervious to the Hun,
  Did you tramp to work each day,
When the railways did not run,
  When the rubble blocked your way ?

Only those can tell that know
  This unreasonable land
Better than a foreign foe,
  Who will never understand.
Anyway you've proved, my dear,
  When the hour for proof was ripe,
What the English think of fear
  By remaining true to type.

Guy Boas

ART

Poets

DEATH OF CHAUCER

Alas ! my worthi master honorable,
  This landès very treasure and richesse !
Death by thy death hath harm irreparable
  Unto us done : hir vengeable duress
  Despoilèd hath this land of the sweetness
    Of rhetoric ; for unto Tullius
    Was never man so like amongès us.

Also, who was heir in philosophy
  To Aristotle, in our tongue, but thou ?
The steppès of Virgile in poesy
  Thou folwedest eke, men wot well enow.
  That combre-world,[1] that thee, my master, slow[2]—
    Would I slain werė !—Death was too hastyf
    To run on thee, and revė[3] thee thy life.

. . . . .

She might have tarried her vengeance awhile
  Till that some man had equal to thee be ;
Nay, let be that ! She knew well that this isle
  May never man forth bringè like to thee ;
  And her officè nedès do mot[4] she ;
    God bad her so, I trust as for the best ;
    O master, master, God thy soulè rest !

Thomas Hoccleve

EDMUND SPENSER

Witness our Colin ; whom though all the Graces,
And all the Muses nursed ; whose well taught song
Parnassus self, and Glorian embraces,

1 *combre-world* : earth-encumberer.
2 *slow* : slew.
3 *reve* : take (from).
4 *mot* : must.

And all the learn'd and all the shepherds throng ;
  Yet all his hopes were crossed, all suits denied ;
  Discouraged, scorned, his writing vilified :
Poorly (poor man) he lived ; poorly (poor man) he died.

And had not that great Heart (whose honoured head
Ah ! lies full low) pitied thy woeful flight ;
There hadst thou lain unwept, unburièd,
Unblessed, nor graced with any common rite :
  Yet shalt thou live, when thy great foe shall sink
  Beneath his mountain tomb, whose fame shall stink ;
And time his blacker name shall blur with blackest ink.

O let th' iambic Muse revenge that wrong
Which can not slumber in thy sheets of lead :
Let thy abusèd honour cry as long
As there be quills to write, or eyes to read :
  On his rank name let thine own votes be turned,
  Oh may that man that hath the Muses scorned,
Alive nor dead, be ever of a Muse adorned !

Phineas Fletcher

CHRISTOPHER MARLOWE

CROWNED, girdled, garbed and shod with light and fire,
  Son first-born of the morning, sovereign star !
  Soul nearest ours of all, that wert most far,
Most far off in the abysm of time, thy lyre
Hung highest above the dawn-enkindled quire
  Where all ye sang together, all that are,
  And all the starry songs behind thy car
Rang sequence, all our souls acclaim thee sire.

" If all the pens that ever poets held
  Had fed the feelings of their masters' thoughts "
  And as with rush of hurtling chariots
The flight of all their spirits were impelled
  Toward one great end, thy glory—nay, not then,
  Not yet might'st thou be praised enough of men.

Algernon Charles Swinburne

I LIKE TO THINK OF SHAKESPEARE

I LIKE to think of Shakespeare, not as when
In our old London of the spacious time
He took all amorous hearts with honeyed rhyme ;
Or flung his jest at Burbage and at Ben ;
Or speared the flying follies with his pen ;
Or, in deep hour, made Juliet's love sublime ;
Or from Lear's kindness and Iago's crime
Caught tragic hint of heaven's dark way with men.
These were great memories, but he laid them down.
And when, with brow composed and friendly tread,
He sought the little streets of Stratford town,
That knew his dreams and soon must hold him dead,
I like to think how Shakespeare pruned his rose,
And ate his pippin in his orchard close.

Sir E. K. Chambers

AN ODE FOR BEN JONSON

AH, Ben !
Say how or when
Shall we thy guests
Meet at those lyric feasts,
Made at the Sun,
The Dog, the triple Tun ?
Where we such clusters had,
As made us nobly wild, not mad ;
And yet each verse of thine
Out-did the meat, out-did the frolic wine.

My Ben !
Or come again :
Or send to us,
Thy wit's great over-plus ;
But teach us yet
Wisely to husband it ;

Lest we that talent spend :
And having once brought to an end
That precious stock ; the store
Of such a wit the world should have no more.

Robert Herrick

MILTON

An Ode

Soul of England, dost thou sleep,
Lulled or dulled, thy mighty youth forgotten ?
Of the world's wine hast thou drunk too deep ?
Hast thou sown more than thy hands can reap ?
Turn again thine ear
To that song severe
In thine hour of storm and war begotten !

Here in towered London's throng,
In her streets, with Time's new murmur seething,
Milton pacing mused his haughty song.
Here he sleeps out feud and fret and wrong.
Nay, that spirit august
Tramples death's low dust,
Still for us is kindled, burning, breathing.

He, on whose earth-darkened sight
Rose horizons of the empyrean
And the ordered spheres' unhasting flight ;
He, who saw where, round the heart of Light,
Seraphs ardent-eyed
Flamed in circle wide,
Quiring music of their solemn paean,

When through space a trouble ran
(Like a flush on serene skies arisen)
That from this dim spot of earth began—
Rumour of the world's new marvel, Man,
From whose heart's beat sped
Hope, hazard, and dread
Past earth's borders to hell's fiery prison :

He, who saw the Anarch's hate
Tower, winged for woe ; the serpent charming
Eve in her imperilled bower ; the Gate
Barred, and those two forms that, desolate
Mid the radiant spheres,
Wept first human tears ;
Earlier war in heaven, and angels arming :

He, who, like his Samson, bowed
Toiling, hardly-tasked and night-enfolded,
Steered his proud course to one purpose vowed,
As an eagle beats through hailing cloud
Strong-winged and alone,
Seeking skies unknown :
He whose verse, majestically moulded,

Moves like armed and bannered host
Streaming irresistible, or abounding
River in a land's remoteness lost,
Poured from solitary peaks of frost,
And far histories brings
Of old realms and kings,
With high fates of fallen Man resounding :

This is England's voice that rang
Over Europe ; this the soul unshaken
That from darkness a great splendour sang,
Beauty mightier for the cost and pang ;
Of our blood and name
Risen, our spirits to claim,
To enlarge, to summon, to awaken !

Laurence Binyon

POPE AND DRYDEN

TIME was, ere yet in these degenerate days
Ignoble themes obtain'd mistaken praise,
When sense and wit with poesy allied,
No fabled graces, flourish'd side by side ;

From the same fount their inspiration drew,
And, rear'd by taste, bloom'd fairer as they grew.
Then, in this happy isle, a Pope's pure strain
Sought the rapt soul to charm, nor sought in vain ;
A polish'd nation's praise aspired to claim,
And raised the people's, as the poet's fame.
Like him great Dryden pour'd the tide of song,
In streams less smooth, indeed, yet doubly strong.

Lord Byron

COWPER AT OLNEY

In this green valley where the Ouse
Is looped in many a silver pool,
Seeking God's mercy and his muse
Went Cowper sorrowful.

Like the pale gleam of wintry sun
His genius lit the obscure place,
Where, battling with despair, lived one
Of melancholy's race.

By quiet waters, by green fields
In winter sweet as summer hay,
By hedgerows where the chaffinch builds
He went his brooding way.

And not a berry or a leaf,
Or stirring bough or fragrant wind,
But, in its moment, soothed the grief
Of his tormented mind.

And since, like the belovèd sheep
Of David's shepherd, he was led
By streams and pastures quiet as sleep—
Was he not comforted ?

Sylvia Lynd

TO WILLIAM WORDSWORTH

Composed on the night after his Recitation of a Poem
on the Growth of an Individual Mind

Friend of the wise ! and Teacher of the Good !
Into my heart have I received that Lay
More than historic, that prophetic Lay
Wherein (high theme by thee first sung aright)
Of the foundations and the building up
Of a Human Spirit thou hast dared to tell
What may be told, to the understanding mind
Revealable ; and what within the mind
By vital breathings secret as the soul
Of vernal growth, oft quickens in the heart
Thoughts all too deep for words !
Theme hard as high !
Of smiles spontaneous, and mysterious fears
(The first-born they of Reason and twin-birth) ;
Of tides obedient to external force,
And currents self-determined, as might seem,
Or by some inner Power ; of moments awful,
Now in thy inner life, and now abroad,
When power streamed from thee, and thy soul received
The light reflected, as a light bestowed ;
Of fancies fair, and milder hours of youth,
Hyblaean murmurs of poetic thought
Industrious in its joy, in vales and glens
Native or outland, lakes and famous hills !
Or on the lonely high-road, when the stars
Were rising ; or by secret mountain-streams,
The guides and the companions of thy way !

Of more than Fancy, of the Social Sense
Distending wide, and man beloved as man,
Where France in all her towns lay vibrating
Like some becalmèd bark beneath the burst
Of Heaven's immediate thunder, when no cloud
Is visible, or shadow on the main.
For thou wert there, thine own brows garlanded,
Amid the tremor of a realm aglow,

Amid a mighty nation jubilant,
When from the general heart of human kind
Hope sprang forth like a full-born Deity !
——Of that dear Hope afflicted and struck down,
So summoned homeward, thenceforth calm and sure
From the dread watch-tower of man's absolute self,
With light unwaning on her eyes, to look
Far on—herself a glory to behold,
The Angel of the vision ! Then (last strain)
Of Duty, chosen Laws controlling choice,
Action and joy !—An orphic song indeed,
A song divine of high and passionate thoughts
To their own music chaunted !

Samuel Taylor Coleridge

DEATH OF BYRON

When Byron's eyes were shut in death,
We bow'd our head and held our breath
He taught us little ; but our soul
Had *felt* him like the thunder's roll.
With shivering heart the strife we saw
Of passion with eternal law ;
And yet with reverential awe
We watch'd the fount of fiery life
Which served for that Titanic strife.

Matthew Arnold

AH, DID YOU ONCE SEE SHELLEY PLAIN

Ah, did you once see Shelley plain,
  And did he stop and speak to you,
And did you speak to him again ?
  How strange it seems and new !

But you were living before that,
  And also you are living after ;
And the memory I started at—
  My starting moves your laughter.

I crossed a moor, with a name of its own
And a certain use in the world no doubt,
Yet a hand's-breadth of it shines alone
'Mid the blank miles round about :

For there I picked up on the heather
And there I put inside my breast
A moulted feather, an eagle-feather !
Well, I forget the rest.

Robert Browning

KEATS'S IMMORTALITY

PEACE, peace ! he is not dead, he doth not sleep—
He hath awakened from the dream of life—
'Tis we, who lost in stormy visions, keep
With phantoms an unprofitable strife,
And in mad trance, strike with our spirit's knife
Invulnerable nothings.—*We* decay
Like corpses in a charnel ; fear and grief
Convulse us and consume us day by day,
And cold hopes swarm like worms within our living clay.

He has outsoared the shadow of our night ;
Envy and calumny and hate and pain,
And that unrest which men miscall delight,
Can touch him not and torture not again ;
From the contagion of the world's slow stain
He is secure, and now can never mourn
A heart grown cold, a head grown grey in vain,
Nor, when the spirit's self has ceased to burn,
With sparkless ashes load an unlamented urn.

He lives, he wakes—'tis Death is dead, not he ;
Mourn not for Adonais.—Thou young Dawn,
Turn all thy dew to splendour, for from thee
The spirit thou lamentest is not gone ;
Ye caverns and ye forests, cease to moan !
Cease, ye faint flowers and fountains, and thou Air,
Which like a mourning veil thy scarf hadst thrown
O'er the abandoned Earth, now leave it bare
Even to the joyous stars which smile on its despair !

He is made one with Nature: there is heard
His voice in all her music, from the moan
Of thunder, to the song of night's sweet bird;
He is a presence to be felt and known
In darkness and in light, from herb and stone,
Spreading itself where'er that Power may move
Which has withdrawn his being to its own;
Which wields the world with never-wearied love,
Sustains it from beneath, and kindles it above.

He is a portion of the loveliness
Which once he made more lovely: he doth bear
His part, while the one Spirit's plastic stress
Sweeps through the dull dense world, compelling there
All new successions to the forms they wear;
Torturing th' unwilling dross that checks its flight
To its own likeness, as each mass may bear;
And bursting in its beauty and its might
From trees and beasts and men into the Heaven's light.

The splendours of the firmament of time
May be eclipsed, but are extinguished not;
Like stars to their appointed height they climb,
And death is a low mist which cannot blot
The brightness it may veil. When lofty thought
Lifts a young heart above its mortal lair,
And love and life contend in it, for what
Shall be its earthly doom, the dead live there
And move like winds of light on dark and stormy air.

. . . . . .

The One remains, the many change and pass;
Heaven's light for ever shines, Earth's shadows fly;
Life, like a dome of many-coloured glass,
Stains the white radiance of eternity,
Until Death tramples it to fragments.—Die,
If thou wouldst be with that which thou dost seek!
Follow where all is fled!—Rome's azure sky,
Flowers, ruins, statues, music, words, are weak
The glory they transfuse with fitting truth to speak.

Percy Bysshe Shelley

DEATH OF TENNYSON

Low, like another's, lies the laurelled head :
The life that seemed a perfect song is o'er :
Carry the last great bard to his last bed.
Land that he loved, thy noblest voice is mute.
Land that he loved, that loved him ! nevermore
Meadow of thine, smooth lawn or wild sea-shore,
Gardens of odorous bloom and tremulous fruit,
Or woodlands old, like Druid couches spread,
The master's feet shall tread.
Death's little rift hath rent the faultless lute :
The singer of undying songs is dead.

Lo, in this season pensive-hued and grave,
While fades and falls the doomed, reluctant leaf
From withered Earth's fantastic coronal,
With wandering sighs of forest and of wave
Mingles the murmur of a people's grief
For him whose leaf shall fade not, neither fall.
He hath fared forth, beyond these suns and showers.
For us, the autumn glow, the autumn flame,
And soon the winter silence shall be ours :
Him the eternal spring of fadeless fame
Crowns with no mortal flowers.

What needs his laurel our ephemeral tears,
To save from visitation of decay ?
Not in this temporal light alone, that bay
Blooms, nor to perishable mundane ears
Sings he with lips of transitory clay.

Reft though he be from us,
Virgil salutes him, and Theocritus ;
Catullus, mightiest-brained Lucretius, each
Greets him, their brother, on the Stygian beach ;
Proudly a gaunt right-hand doth Dante reach ;
Milton and Wordsworth bid him welcome home ;
Keats, on his lips the eternal rose of youth,
Doth in the name of Beauty that is Truth

A kinsman's love beseech ;
Coleridge, his locks aspersed with fairy foam,
Calm Spenser, Chaucer suave,
His equal friendship crave :
And godlike spirits hail him guest, in speech
Of Athens, Florence, Weimar, Stratford, Rome.

. . . .

The seasons change, the winds they shift and veer ;
The grace of yesteryear
Is dead ; the birds depart, the groves decay :
Empires dissolve and peoples disappear :
Song passes not away.
Captains and conquerors leave a little dust,
And kings a dubious legend of their reign ;
The swords of Caesars, they are less than rust :
The poet doth remain.
Dead is Augustus, Maro is alive ;
And thou, the Mantuan of this age and soil,
With Virgil shalt survive,
Enriching Time with no less honeyed spoil,
The yielded sweet of every Muse's hive ;
Heeding no more the sound of idle praise
In that great calm our tumults cannot reach,—
Master who crown'st our immelodious days
With flower of perfect speech.

Sir William Watson

EARLY SPRING AND THOMAS HARDY

Always these loitering, melancholy dusks
Of early spring will now belong to you.
They hold the essence of the spirit we loved
As yours : the musing greyness of despair
Shot with dim, brooding sweetnesses of hope ;
The portent in the promise, the far view
Looking beyond bud, leafage, to the end.
In this pre-blossoming stillness of the spring
Life stares, as in a mirror, at its own face ;
Here is a time you loved, a chosen theme,
Your soul's familiar place.

To these hushed, faintly lighted evenings
(If anywhere this side the moon)
The native in you, from death's foreign sojourn,
Must return.

V. H. Friedlaender

IN MEMORY OF WILFRED OWEN

I HAD half-forgotten among the soft blue waters
And the gay-fruited arbutus of the hill
Where never the nightingales are silent,
And the sunny hours are warm with honey and dew ;

I had half-forgotten as the stars slid westward
Year after year in grave majestic order,
In the strivings and in the triumphs of manhood,
The world's voice, and the touch of beloved hands.

But I have never quite forgotten, never forgotten
All you who lie there so lonely, and never stir
When the hired buglers call unheeded to you,
Whom the sun shall never warm nor the frost chill.

Do you remember . . . but why should you remember ?
Have you not given all you had, to forget ?
Oh, blessed, blessed be Death ! They can no more vex
you,
You for whom memory and forgetfulness are one.

Richard Aldington

LASCELLES ABERCROMBIE

LIFE, manifest in beauty and ugliness,
You apprehended ever with intense
Zest for the sensuous visible evidence
Of the creative energy in stress
Evolving form—perceiving none the less

In every image the spiritual effluence
  Illuming with divine intelligence
The show of things that, else, were nothingness.
In the beginning was the Word—the Word
  Evoking cosmos from chaotic night :
" Let there be light ! " across the void was heard
  The living voice of God ; and there was light ;
And still God speaks through poets, uttering
Ever new universes when they sing.

Wilfrid Gibson

Painting, Architecture, Sculpture

CHRIST CHURCH CATHEDRAL WINDOWS, OXFORD

Shadows do everywhere for substance pass,
You'd think the sands were in an hour-glass.
You that do live with surgeons, have you seen
A spring of blood forc'd from a swelling vein ?
So from a touch of Moses' rod doth jump
A cataract, the rock is made a pump :
At sight of whose o'erflowings many get
Themselves away for fear of being wet.
Have you beheld a sprightful lady stand
To have her frame drawn by a painter's hand ?
Such lively look and presence, such a dress
King Pharaoh's daughter's image doth express ;
Look well upon her gown and you will swear
The needle, not the pencil, hath been there :
At sight of her some gallants do dispute
Whether i' th' Church 'tis lawful to salute.
Next Jacob kneeling, where his kids-skin's such
As it may well cosen old Isaac's touch :
A shepherd, seeing how thorns went round about
Abraham's ram, would needs have helped it out.
Behold the Dove descending to inspire
The Apostles' heads with cloven tongues of fire,

And in a superficies there you'll see
The gross dimensions of profundity :
'Tis hard to judge which is best built and higher
The arch-roof in the window or the choir.

Anonymous (17th century)

SIR JOHN VANBRUGH

UNDER this stone, reader, survey
Dead Sir John Vanbrugh's house of clay :
Lie heavy on him, Earth ! for he
Laid many heavy loads on thee.

Abel Evans

SIR JOSHUA REYNOLDS

HERE Reynolds is laid, and to tell you my mind,
He has not left a better or wiser behind :
His pencil was striking, resistless and grand ;
His manners were gentle, complying, and bland ;
Still born to improve us in every part,
His pencil our faces, his manners our heart :
To coxcombs averse, yet most civilly steering,
When they judg'd without skill, he was still hard of hearing ;
When they talk'd of their Raphaels, Correggios and stuff,
He shifted his trumpet, and only took snuff.

Oliver Goldsmith

SIR JOSHUA REYNOLDS'S PAINTED WINDOW AT NEW COLLEGE, OXFORD

AH, stay thy treacherous hand, forbear to trace
Those faultless forms of elegance and grace !
Ah, cease to spread the bright transparent mass,
With Titian's pencil, o'er the speaking glass !

Nor steal, by strokes of art with truth combin'd,
The fond illusions of my wayward mind !
For long, enamour'd of a barbarous age,
A faithless truant to the classic page,
Long have I loved to catch the simple chime
Of minstrel-harps, and spell the fabling rime ;
To view the festive rites, the knightly play,
That deck'd heroic Albion's elder day ;
To mark the mouldering halls of Barons bold,
And the rough castle, cast in giant mould ;
With Gothic manners Gothic arts explore,
And muse on the magnificence of yore.

. . . . . .

Such was a pensive bard's mistaken strain—
But, oh, of ravish'd pleasures why complain ?
No more the matchless skill I call unkind
That strives to disenchant my cheated mind.
For when again I view thy chaste Design,
The just proportion, and the genuine line ;
Those native pourtraitures of Attic art,
That from the lucid surface seem to start ;
Those tints, that steal no glories from the day,
Nor ask the sun to lend his streaming ray ;
The doubtful radiance of contending dyes,
That faintly mingle, yet distinctly rise ;
Twixt light and shade the transitory strife ;
The feature blooming with immortal life ;
The stole in casual foldings taught to flow,
Not with ambitious ornaments to glow ;
The tread majestic and the beaming eye,
That lifted speaks its commerce with the sky ;
Heaven's golden emanation, gleaming mild
O'er the mean cradle of the Virgin's child :
Sudden, the sombrous imagery is fled,
Which late my visionary rapture fed :
Thy powerful hand has broke the Gothic chain,
And brought my bosom back to truth again ;
To truth, by no peculiar taste confin'd,
Whose universal pattern strikes mankind ;
To truth, whose bold and unresisted aim
Checks frail caprice, and fashion's fickle claim ;

To truth, whose charms deception's magic quell,
And bind coy Fancy in a stronger spell.

. . . . . .

Reynolds, 'tis thine, from the broad window's height,
To add new lustre to religious light :
Not of its pomp to strip this ancient shrine,
But bid that pomp with purer radiance shine :
With arts unknown before, to reconcile
The willing Graces to the Gothic pile.

Thomas Warton

THE THREE PARTS OF PAINTING

I ASKED my dear friend Orator Prig :
" What's the first part of oratory ? " He said : " A great wig."
" And what is the second ? " Then, dancing a jig
And bowing profoundly, he said : " A great wig."
" And what is the third ? " Then he snored like a pig,
And puffing his cheeks out, replied, " A great wig."
So if a great painter with questions you push,
" What's the first part of painting ? " he'll say : " A paint-brush."
" And what is the second ? " with most modest blush,
He'll smile like a cherub and say : " A paint-brush."
" And what is the third ? " he'll bow like a rush,
With a leer in his eye, he'll reply : " A paint-brush."
Perhaps this is all a painter can want :
But look yonder—that house is the house of Rembrandt !

" O dear Mother Outline ! of wisdom most sage,
What's the first part of painting ? " She said : " Patronage."
" And what is the second, to please and engage ? "
She frowned like a fury, and said : " Patronage."
" And what is the third ? " She put off old age,
And smil'd like a siren, and said : " Patronage."

William Blake

NEWTON'S STATUE

The Evangelist St. John my patron was :
Three Gothic courts are his, and in the first
Was my abiding-place, a nook obscure ;
Right underneath, the College kitchens made
A humming sound, less tuneable than bees,
But hardly less industrious ; with shrill notes
Of sharp command and scolding intermixed.
Near me hung Trinity's loquacious clock,
Who never let the quarters, night or day,
Slip by him unproclaimed, and told the hours
Twice over with a male and female voice.
Her pealing organ was my neighbour too ;
And from my pillow, looking forth by light
Of moon or favouring stars, I could behold
The antechapel where the statue stood
Of Newton with his prism and silent face,
The marble index of a mind for ever
Voyaging through strange seas of Thought, alone.

William Wordsworth

KING'S COLLEGE CHAPEL

Tax not the royal Saint with vain expense
With ill-matched aims the architect who planned—
Albeit labouring for a scanty band
Of white-robed Scholars only—this immense
And glorious Work of fine intelligence !
Give all thou canst ; high Heaven rejects the lore
Of nicely-calculated less or more ;
So deemed the man who fashioned for the sense
These lofty pillars, spread that branching roof
Self-poised, and scooped into ten thousand cells,
Where light and shade repose, where music dwells
Lingering—and wandering on as loth to die ;
Like thoughts whose very sweetness yieldeth proof
That they were born for immortality.

William Wordsworth

PEELE CASTLE IN A STORM

I WAS thy neighbour once, thou rugged Pile !
Four summer weeks I dwelt in sight of thee ;
I saw thee every day ; and all the while
Thy form was sleeping on a glassy sea.

So pure the sky, so quiet was the air !
So like, so very like, was day to day !
Whene'er I looked, thy image still was there ;
It trembled, but it never passed away.

How perfect was the calm ! it seemed no sleep ;
No mood, which season takes away, or brings ;
I could have fancied that the mighty deep
Was even the gentlest of all gentle things.

Ah ! then, if mine had been the Painter's hand,
To express what then I saw ; and add the gleam,
The light that never was, on sea or land,
The consecration, and the Poet's dream ;

I would have planted thee, thou hoary Pile,
Amid a world how different from this,
Beside a sea that could not cease to smile ;
On tranquil land, beneath a sky of bliss.

. . . . .

So once it would have been,—'tis so no more ;
I have submitted to a new control ;
A power is gone, which nothing can restore ;
A deep distress hath humanised my Soul.

Not for a moment could I now behold
A smiling sea, and be what I have been ;
The feeling of my loss will ne'er be old ;
This, which I know, I speak with mind serene.

Then, Beaumont, Friend ! who would have been the
Friend,
If he had lived, of Him whom I deplore,

This work of thine I blame not, but commend ;
This sea in anger, and that dismal shore.

O 'tis a passionate Work yet wise and well,
Well chosen is the spirit that is here ;
That Hulk which labours in the deadly swell,
This rueful sky, this pageantry of fear !

And this huge Castle, standing here sublime,
I love to see the look with which it braves,
Cased in the unfeeling armour of old time,
The lightning, the fierce wind, and trampling waves.

William Wordsworth

LINDISFARNE ABBEY

In Saxon strength that Abbey frown'd,
With massive arches broad and round,
That rose alternate, row and row,
On ponderous columns, short and low,
  Built ere the art was known,
By pointed aisle, and shafted stalk,
The arcades of an alley'd walk
  To emulate in stone.
On the deep walls the heathen Dane
Had pour'd his impious rage in vain.

. . . . .

Not but that portions of the pile,
Rebuilded in a later style,
Show'd where the spoiler's hand had been ;
Not but the wasting sea-breeze keen
Had worn the pillar's carving quaint,
And moulder'd in his niche the saint,
And rounded with consuming power
The pointed angles of each tower ;
Yet still entire the Abbey stood,
Like veteran, worn, but unsubdu'd.

Sir Walter Scott

TO THE ARTISTS CALLED P.R.B.

(1851)

I THANK you, brethren in sincerity,—
  One who, within the temperate climes of Art,
  From the charmed circle humbly stands apart,
Scornfully also, with a listless eye
Watching old marionettes' vitality ;
  For you have shown, with youth's brave confidence,
  The honesty of true speech and the sense
Uniting life with " nature ", earth with sky.

In faithful hearts Art strikes its roots far down,
  And bears both flower and fruit with seeded core ;
  When Truth dies out, the fruit appears no more,
But the flower hides a worm within its crown.
  God speed you onward ! once again our way
  Shall be made odorous with fresh flowers of May.

William Bell Scott

TURNER

TURNER had strength to bear that tempering
That shatters weaker hearts and breaks their hope.
He still pursued his journey step by step—
First modestly attired in quiet grey,
As well became sincere humility ;
Then with a plume of colour he adorned
His simple raiment and so walked awhile ;
Until at last, like his belovèd Sun,
He set in forms of strangest phantasy,
Coloured with gold and scarlet, and the lands
Of his conception grew as dim and vague
As shadows. So his mighty brain declined.

. . . . . .

Turner bequeathed his riches unto Art,
And to extend his fame—a noble wish ;
And from the grave he challenged Claude Lorraine,
And still they try their prowess side by side,

Living on canvas in strange rivalry.
But you who would be judges in this cause
Must go to Nature, the great law-giver,
And having studied her eternal code,
Give your decision without any fear
Of prejudice or withered connoisseurs.

Philip Gilbert Hamerton

IN ST. PAUL'S A WHILE AGO

Summer and winter close commune
On this July afternoon
As I enter chilly Paul's,
With its chasmal classic walls,
—Drifts of gray illumination
From the lofty fenestration
Slant them down in bristling spines that spread
Fan-like upon the vast dust-moted shade.
Moveless here, no whit allied
To the daemonian din outside,
Statues stand, cadaverous, wan,
Round the loiterers looking on
Under the yawning dome and nave,
Pondering whatnot, giddy or grave.
Here a verger moves a chair,
Or a red rope fixes there :—
A brimming Hebe, rapt in her adorning,
Brushes an Artemisia craped in mourning ;
Beatrice Benedick piques, coquetting ;
All unknowing or forgetting
That strange Jew, Damascus-bound,
Whose name, thereafter travelling round
To this precinct of the world,
Spread here like a flag unfurled :
Anon inspiring architectural sages
To frame this pile, writ his throughout the ages :
Whence also the encircling mart
Assumed his name, of him no part,

And to his vision-seeing mind
Charmless, blank in every kind ;
And whose displays, even had they called his eye,
No gold or silver had been his to buy ;
Whose haunters, had they seen him stand
On his own steps here, lift his hand
In stress of eager, stammering speech,
And his meaning chanced to reach,
Would have proclaimed him as they passed
An epilept enthusiast.

Thomas Hardy

BY THE STATUE OF KING CHARLES AT CHARING CROSS

Sombre and rich, the skies ;
Great glooms, and starry plains.
Gently the night wind sighs ;
Else a vast silence reigns.

The splendid silence clings
Around me ; and around
The saddest of all kings
Crowned, and again discrowned.

Comely and calm, he rides
Hard by his own Whitehall :
Only the night wind glides :
No crowds, nor rebels, brawl.

Gone, too, his Court ; and yet,
The stars his courtiers are :
Stars in their stations set ;
And every wandering star.

Alone he rides, alone,
The fair and fatal king :
Dark night is all his own,
That strange and solemn thing.

Which are more full of fate :
The stars ; or those sad eyes ?
Which are more still and great :
Those brows ; or the dark skies ?

Although his whole heart yearn
In passionate tragedy :
Never was face so stern
With sweet austerity.

Vanquished in life, his death
By beauty made amends :
The passing of his breath
Won his defeated ends.

Brief life, and hapless ? Nay :
Through death, life grew sublime.
Speak after sentence ? Yea :
And to the end of time.

Armoured he rides, his head
Bare to the stars of doom :
He triumphs now, the dead,
Beholding London's gloom.

Our wearier spirit faints,
Vexed in the world's employ :
His soul was of the saints ;
And art to him was joy.

King, tried in fires of woe !
Men hunger for thy grace :
And through the night I go,
Loving thy mournful face.

Yet, when the city sleeps ;
When all the cries are still :
The stars and heavenly deeps
Work out a perfect will.

Lionel Johnson

HE CARVED IN STONE

He carved in stone. Out of his quiet life
He watched as any faithful seaman charged
With tidings of the myriad-faring sea,
And thoughts and premonitions through his mind
Sailing as ships from strange and storied lands
His hungry spirit held, till all they were
Found living witness in the chiselled stone.
Slowly out of the dark confusion, spread
By life's innumerable venturings
Over his brain, he would triumph into the light
Of one clear mood, unblemished of the blind
Legions of errant thought that cried about
His rapt seclusion : as a pearl unsoiled,
Nay, rather washed to lonelier chastity,
In gritty mud. And then would come a bird,
A flower, or the wind moving upon a flower,
A beast at pasture, or a clustered fruit,
A peasant face as were the saints of old,
The leer of custom, or the bow of the moon
Swung in miraculous poise—some stray from the world
Of things created by the eternal mind
In joy articulate. And his perfect mood
Would dwell about the token of God's mood
Until in bird or flower or moving wind
Or flock or shepherd or the troops of heaven
It sprang in one fierce moment of desire
To visible form.
Then would his chisel work among the stone,
Persuading it of petal or of limb
Or starry curve, till risen anew there sang
Shape out of chaos, and again the vision
Of one mind single from the world was pressed
Upon the daily custom of the sky
Or field or the body of man.

John Drinkwater

VIROCONIUM

VIROCON—Virocon—
Still the ancient name rings on
And brings, in the untrampled wheat,
The tumult of a thousand feet.

Where trumpets rang and men marched by,
None passes but the dragon-fly.
Athwart the grassy town, forlorn,
The lone dor-beetle blows his horn.

The poppy standards droop and fall
Above one rent and mournful wall ;
In every sunset-flame it burns,
Yet towers unscathed when day returns.

And still the breaking seas of grain
Flow havenless across the plain :
The years wash on, their spindrift leaps
Where the old city, dreaming, sleeps.

Grief lingers here, like mists that lie
Across the dawns of ripe July ;
On capital and corridor
The pathos of the conqueror.

The pillars stand, with alien grace,
In churches of a younger race ;
The chiselled column, black and rough,
Becomes a roadside cattle-trough :

The skulls of men who, right or wrong,
Still wore the splendour of the strong,
Are shepherds' lanterns now, and shield
Their candles in the lambing field.

But when, through evening's open door,
Two lovers tread the broken floor,
And the wild-apple petals fall
Round passion's scarlet festival ;

When cuckoos call from the green gloom,
Where dark, shelving forests loom ;
When foxes bark beside the gate,
And the grey badger seeks his mate—

There haunts within them secretly
One that lives while empires die,
A shrineless god whose songs abide
Forever in the countryside.

Mary Webb

Music

A SONG TO THE LUTE IN MUSIC

WHERE griping griefs the heart would wound,
  And doleful dumps the mind oppress,
There music with her silver sound
  With speed is wont to send redress :
Of troubled minds, in every sore,
Sweet music hath a salve in store.

In joy it makes our mirth abound,
  In woe it cheers our heavy sprites ;
Bestraughted heads relief hath found
  By music's pleasant sweet delights ;
Our senses all—what shall I say more ?—
Are subject unto music's lore.

The gods by music have their praise ;
  The life, the soul therein doth joy ;
For, as the Roman poet says,
  In seas, whom pirates would destroy,
A dolphin saved from death most sharp
Arion playing on his harp.

O heavenly gift that rules the mind,
  Even as the stern doth rule the ship !
O music, whom the gods assign'd
  To comfort man whom cares would nip !

Since thou both man and beast do'st move,
What beast is he will thee disprove?

Richard Edwardes

TO A FRIEND IN PRAISE OF MUSIC AND POETRY

If music and sweet poetry agree,
As they must needs, the sister and the brother,
Then must the love be great 'twixt thee and me,
Because thou lov'st the one and I the other.
Dowland to thee is dear whose heavenly touch
Upon the lute doth ravish human sense,
Spenser to me, whose deep conceit [1] is such
As passing all conceit needs no defence.
Thou lov'st to hear the sweet melodious sound
That Phoebus' lute, the queen of music, makes,
And I in deep delight am chiefly drowned,
Whenas himself to singing he betakes.
One god is god of both, as poets feign,
One knight loves both, and both to thee remain.

Richard Barnfield

WHEN TO HER LUTE CORINNA SINGS

When to her lute Corinna sings,
Her voice revives the leaden strings,
And doth in highest notes appear
As any challenged echo clear;
But when she doth of mourning speak,
E'en with her sighs the strings do break.

And as her lute doth live or die,
Led by her passion, so must I:
For when of pleasure she doth sing,
My thoughts enjoy a sudden spring;
But if she doth of sorrow speak,
E'en from my heart the strings do break.

Thomas Campion

[1] *conceit*: conception, thought.

ENGLISH MUSICAL INSTRUMENTS

Of sundry sorts that were, as the musician likes,
On which the practis'd hand with perfect fingering strikes,
Whereby their height of skill might liveliest be exprest.
The trembling lute some touch, some strain the viol best
In sets which there were seen, the music wondrous choice.
Some likewise there affect the gamba [1] with the voice,
To show that England could variety afford.
Some that delight to touch the sterner wiry chord
The cittern, the pandore,[2] and the theorbo [3] strike ;
The gittern [4] and the kit [5] the wand'ring fiddles like.
So were there some again, in this their learned strife,
Loud instruments that loved ; the cornet and the fife,
The hautboy,[6] sackbut [7] deep, recorder and the flute,
Even from the shrillest shawm [8] onto the cornamute.[9]
Some blow the bagpipe up that plays the country round,
The tabor and the pipe some take delight to sound.

Michael Drayton

MUSIC FOR THE MORRIS DANCE

Ho ! who comes here along with bagpiping and drumming ?
O 'tis the morris dance I see, the morris dance a-coming.
  Come ladies out, come quickly !
And see about how trim they dance and trickly.
Hey ! there again ! how the bells shake it !
Hey ho ! now for our town ! and take it !
Soft awhile, piper, not away so fast ! They melt them.
Be hanged, knave ! see'st thou not the dancers swelt them ? [10]
  Stand out awhile ! you come too far ! I say, in !
  There give the hobby-horse more room to play in !

Anonymous (16th century)

1 *gamba* : viol held between the legs.
2 *pandore* : a type of cittern.
3 *theorbo* : large lute.
4 *gittern* : guitar.
5 *kit* : small stringed instrument.
6 *hautboy* : oboe.
7 *sackbut* : trombone.
8 *shawm* : upper oboe.
9 *cornamute* : form of bagpipe.
10 *swelt them* : become faint with heat.

LUTESTRINGS CAT-EATEN

Are these the strings that poets feign
Have clear'd the air, and calm'd the main ?
Charm'd wolves, and from the mountain crests
Made forests dance with all their beasts ?
Could these neglected shreds you see
Inspire a lute of ivory
And make it speak ? Oh ! think then what
Hath been committed by my cat,
Who in the silence of this night
Hath gnawn these cords, and marr'd them quite ;
Leaving such relics as may be
For frets,[1] not for my lute, but me.
Puss, I will curse thee ; may'st thou dwell
With some dry hermit in a cell
Where rat ne'er peep'd, where mouse ne'er fed,
And flies go supperless to bed ;
Or with some close-par'd brother,[2] where
Thou'lt fast each Sabbath in the year ;
Or else, profane, be hang'd on Monday,
For butchering a mouse on Sunday.

. . . . .

Thus, Puss, thou seest what might betide thee ;
But I forbear to hurt or chide thee ;
For maybe Puss was melancholy ;
And so to make her blithe and jolly,
Finding these strings, she'ld have a fit
Of mirth ; nay, Puss, if that were it,
Thus I revenge me, that as thou
Hast played on them, I've played on you ;
And as thy touch was nothing fine,
So I've but scratch'd these notes of mine.

Thomas Master

[1] *frets.* A play on the two meanings of " fret ", as an interlaced pattern and an irritation.

[2] *close-par'd brother* : closely shorn Puritan.

TO MR. H. LAWES, ON HIS AIRS

Harry, whose tuneful and well measur'd song
First taught our English music how to span
Words with just note and accent, not to scan
With Midas ears, committing short and long ;
Thy worth and skill exempts thee from the throng,
With praise enough, for envy to look wan ;
To after age thou shalt be writ the man,
That with smooth air couldst humour best our tongue.
Thou honour'st Verse, and Verse must send her wing
To honour thee, the priest of Phoebus' choir
That tun'st their happiest lines in hymn, or story.
Dante shall give Fame leave to set thee higher
Than his Casella, whom he wooed to sing
Met in the milder shades of Purgatory.

John Milton

ON THE DEATH OF MR. PURCELL

Mark how the lark and linnet sing,
With rival notes
They strain their warbling throats
To welcome in the spring.
But in the close of night,
When Philomel begins her heav'nly lay,
They cease their mutual spite,
Drink in her music with delight,
And list'ning and silent, and silent and list'ning,
and list'ning and silent, obey.

So ceas'd the rival crew, when Purcell came,
They sung no more, or only sung his fame,
Struck dumb, they all admir'd
The godlike man,
Alas, too soon retir'd,
As he too late began.

We beg not hell our Orpheus to restore ;
Had he been there,
Their sovereign's fear
Had sent him back before.
The pow'r of harmony too well they knew ;
He long ere this had tun'd their jarring sphere
And left no hell below.

The heav'nly choir, who heard his notes from high,
Let down the scale of music from the sky :
They handed him along,
And all the way he taught, and all the way they
sung.
Ye brethren of the lyre and tuneful voice,
Lament his lot : but at your own rejoice.
Now live secure, and linger out your days,
The gods are pleas'd alone with Purcell's lays,
Nor know to mend their choice.

John Dryden

CHRISTMAS MUSIC

At break of day, O how the bells did ring !
To Thee, my King,
The bells did ring ;
To Thee the angels sing :
Thy goodness did produce this other spring,
For this it is they make the bells to ring :
The sounding bells do through the air
Proclaim Thy welcome far and near ;
While I alone with Thee inherit
All these joys, beyond my merit.
Who would not always sing
To such a King ?

. . . . .

Hark how remoter Parishes do sound !
Far off they ring
For Thee, my King,
Ev'n round about the Town :

The churches scatter'd over all the ground
Serve for Thy praise, who art with glory crown'd.
This city is an engine great
That makes my pleasure more complete ;
The sword, the mace, the magistrate,
To honour Thee, attend in state ;
The whole assembly sings ;
The minster rings.

Thomas Traherne

POLITE MUSIC

In days of old, when Englishmen were men,
Their music, like themselves, was grave and plain ;
The manly trumpet, and the simple reed,
Alike with citizen and swain agreed ;
Whose songs, in lofty sense, but humble verse,
Their loves and wars alternately rehearse ;
Sung by themselves, their homely cheer to crown,
In tunes from sire to son deliver'd down.
But now, since Britons are become polite,
Since few can read, and fewer still can write ;
Since South-Sea schemes have so enrich'd the land,
That footmen 'gainst their lords for boroughs stand ;
Since masquerades and op'ras made their entry,
And Heydegger reign'd guardian of our gentry ;
A hundred various instruments combine,
And foreign songsters in the concert join :
The Gallic horn, whose winding tube in vain
Pretends to emulate the trumpet's strain ;
The shrill-toned fiddle and the warbling flute,
The grave bassoon, deep base, and tinkling lute,
All league, melodious nonsense to dispense,
And give us sound, and show, instead of sense ;
In unknown tongues mysterious dullness chant,
Make love in tune, or thro' the gamut rant.

James Miller

THE EOLIAN HARP

My pensive Sara ! thy soft cheek reclined
Thus on mine arm, most soothing sweet it is
To sit beside our cot, our cot o'ergrown
With white-flowered Jasmin, and the broad-leaved
    Myrtle,
(Meet emblems they of Innocence and Love !),
And watch the clouds, that late were rich with light,
Slow saddening round, and mark the star of eve
Serenely brilliant (such should wisdom be)
Shine opposite ! How exquisite the scents
Snatched from yon bean-field ! and the world so
    hushed !
The stilly murmur of the distant sea
Tells us of silence. And that simplest lute,
Placed length-ways in the clasping casement, hark !
How by the desultory breeze caressed,
Like some coy maid half yielding to her lover,
It pours such sweet upbraiding, as must needs
Tempt to repeat the wrong ! And now, its strings
Boldlier swept, the long sequacious notes
Over delicious surges sink and rise,
Such a soft floating witchery of sound
As twilight Elfins make, when they at eve
Voyage on gentle gales from Fairy-Land,
Where melodies round honey-dropping flowers,
Footless and wild, like birds of Paradise,
Nor pause, nor perch, hovering on untamed wing !
O ! the one life within us and abroad,
Which meets all motion and becomes its soul,
A light in sound, a sound-like power in light,
Rhythm in all thought, and joyance everywhere—
Methinks, it should have been impossible
Not to love all things in a world so filled ;
Where the breeze warbles, and the mute still air
Is Music slumbering on her instrument.

Samuel Taylor Coleridge

THE ORGANIST IN HEAVEN

When Wesley died, the Angelic Orders,
  To see him at the state,
Pressed so incontinent that the warders
  Forgot to shut the gate.
So I, that hitherto had followed
  As one with grief o'ercast,
Where for the doors a space was hollowed,
  Crept in, and heard what passed.
And God said :—" Seeing thou hast given
  Thy life to my great sounds,
Choose thou through all the cirque of Heaven
  What most of bliss redounds."
Then Wesley said : " I hear the thunder
  Low growling from Thy seat—
Grant me that I may bind it under
  The trampling of my feet."
And Wesley said : " See, lightning quivers
  Upon the presence walls—
Lord, give me of it four great rivers,
  To be my manuals."
And then I saw the thunder chidden
  As slave to his desire ;
And then I saw the space bestridden
  With four great bands of fire ;
And stage by stage, stop stop subtending,
  Each lever strong and true,
One shape inextricable blending,
  The awful organ grew.
Then certain angels clad the Master
  In very marvellous wise,
Till clouds of rose and alabaster
  Concealed him from mine eyes.
And likest to a dove soft brooding,
  The innocent figure ran ;
So breathed the breath of his preluding,
  And then the fugue began—
Began, but, to his office turning,
  The porter swung his key ;

Wherefore, although my heart was yearning,
 I had to go ; but he
Played on ; and, as I downward clomb,
 I heard the mighty bars
Of thunder-gusts, that shook heaven's dome,
 And moved the balanced stars.

T. E. Brown

HENRY PURCELL

Have fair fallen, O fair, fair have fallen, so dear
To me, so arch-especial a spirit as heaves in Henry Purcell,
An age is now since passed, since parted ; with the reversal
Of the outward sentence low lays him, listed to a heresy, here.

Not mood in him nor meaning, proud fire or sacred fear,
Or love or pity or all that sweet notes not his might nursle :
It is the forgèd feature finds me : it is the rehearsal
Of own, of abrupt self there so thrusts on, so throngs the ear.

Let him, oh ! with his air of angels then lift me, lay me ! only I'll
Have an eye to the sakes of him, quaint moonmarks, to his pelted plumage under
Wings : so some great storm fowl, whenever he has walked his while

The thunder-purple sea beach plumèd purple-of-thunder,
If a wuthering of his palmy snow-pinions scatter a colossal smile
Off him, but meaning motion fans fresh our wits with wonder.

Gerard Manley Hopkins

CONCERT PARTY

(Egyptian Base Camp)

THEY are gathering round. . . .
Out of the twilight ; over the grey-blue sand,
Shoals of low-jargoning men drift inward to the sound,—
The jangle and throb of a piano . . . tum-ti-tum. . . .
Drawn by a lamp they come
Out of the glimmering lines of their tents, over the shuffling
sand.

O sing us the songs, the songs of our own land,
You warbling ladies in white.
Dimness conceals the hunger in our faces,
This wall of faces risen out of the night,
These eyes that keep their memories of the places
So long beyond their sight.

Jaded and gay, the ladies sing ; and the chap in brown
Tilts his grey hat ; jaunty and lean and pale,
He rattles the keys . . . some actor-bloke from town. . . .
" *God send you home* " ; and then " *A long long trail* " ;
" *I hear you calling me* " ; and " *Dixieland* ". . . .
Sing slowly . . . now the chorus . . . one by one.
We hear them, drink them ; till the concert's done.
Silent, I watch the shadowy mass of soldiers stand,
Silent, they drift away, over the glimmering sand.

Siegfried Sassoon

THE LITTLE DANCERS

LONELY, save for a few faint stars, the sky
Dreams ; and lonely, below, the little street
Into its gloom retires, secluded and shy.
Scarcely the dumb roar enters this soft retreat ;
And all is dark, save where come flooding rays
From a tavern window : there, to the brisk measure
Of an organ that down in an alley merrily plays,
Two children, all alone and no one by,

Holding their tattered frocks, through an airy maze
Of motion, lightly threaded with nimble feet,
Dance sedately : face to face they gaze,
Their eyes shining, grave with a perfect pleasure.

Laurence Binyon

BETSINDA DANCES

On a carpet red and blue
Sits Betsinda not quite two,
Tracing with baby-starfish hand
The patterns that a Persian planned.
Suddenly she sees me go
Towards the box whence dances flow,
Where embalmed together lie
Symphony and lullaby.
Out of her round and silken head
Fly patterns blue and patterns red ;
She hoists her tiny self upright
And, shining-eyed, awaits delight.
  Now at full speed the record spins ;
The wizard needle-point begins
(Perceptive as a blind man's finger)
To thread the secret paths where linger
The ghosts of poignant violins.
Out of a limbo black as jet
It conjures horn and clarinet ;
And spectral harp and phantom flute
And shades of oboes long since mute
It rouses, like the trump of doom,
To glory from their waxen tomb.
  Then, as the tide of sound advances,
With grave delight Betsinda dances :
One arm flies up, the other down,
To lift her Lilliputian gown,
And round she turns on clumsy, sweet,
Unrhythmical, enraptured feet ;
And round and round again she goes
On hopeful, small, precarious toes.
  Dance, Betsinda, dance, while I

Weave from this a memory ;
Thinking, if I chance to hear
That record in some future year,
The needle-point shall conjure yet
Horn and harp and clarinet :
But O ! it shall not conjure you—
Betsinda, dancing, not quite two.

Jan Struther

CHARACTER

BOADICEA

When the British warrior queen,
  Bleeding from the Roman rods,
Sought, with an indignant mien,
  Counsel of her country's gods,

Sage beneath a spreading oak
  Sat the Druid, hoary chief;
Every burning word he spoke
  Full of rage, and full of grief.

"Princess! if our agèd eyes
  Weep upon thy matchless wrongs,
'Tis because resentment ties
  All the terrors of our tongues.

Rome shall perish—write that word
  In the blood that she has spilt;
Perish, hopeless and abhorred,
  Deep in ruin as in guilt.

Rome, for empire far renowned,
  Tramples on a thousand states;
Soon her pride shall kiss the ground—
  Hark! the Gaul is at her gates!

Other Romans shall arise,
  Heedless of a soldier's name;
Sounds, not arms, shall win the prize—
  Harmony the path to fame.

Then the progeny that springs
  From the forests of our land,
Armed with thunder, clad with wings,
  Shall a wider world command.

Regions Caesar never knew
  Thy posterity shall sway,
Where his eagles never flew,
  None invincible as they."

Such the bard's prophetic words,
  Pregnant with celestial fire,
Bending, as he swept the chords
  Of his sweet but awful lyre.

She, with all a monarch's pride,
  Felt them in her bosom glow ;
Rushed to battle, fought, and died ;
  Dying, hurled them at the foe.

" Ruffians, pitiless as proud,
  Heaven awards the vengeance due ;
Empire is on us bestowed,
  Shame and ruin wait for you."

William Cowper

THE ROMAN CENTURION'S SONG

Roman Occupation of Britain, A.D. 300

LEGATE, I had the news last night—my cohort ordered home
By ship to Portus Itius and thence by road to Rome.
I've marched the companies aboard, the arms are stowed below ;
Now let another take my sword. Command me not to go !

I've served in Britain forty years, from Vectis to the Wall.
I have none other home than this, nor any life at all.
Last night I did not understand, but, now the hour draws near
That calls me to my native land, I feel that land is here.

Here where men say my name was made, here where my work was done,

Here where my dearest dead are laid—my wife—my wife
and son ;
Here where time, custom, grief and toil, age, memory,
service, love,
Have rooted me in British soil. Ah, how can I remove ?

For me this land, that sea, these airs, those folk and fields
suffice ;
What purple Southern pomp can match our changeful
Northern skies,
Black with December snows unshed or pearled with August
haze—
The clanging arch of steel-grey March, or June's long-
lighted days ?

You'll follow widening Rhodanus till vine and olive lean
Aslant before the sunny breeze that sweeps Nemausus clean
To Arelate's triple gate ; but let me linger on,
Here where our stiff-necked British oaks confront Euro-
clydon !

You'll take the old Aurelian Road through shore-descending
pines
Where, blue as any peacock's neck, the Tyrrhene Ocean
shines.
You'll go where laurel crowns are won, but—will you e'er
forget
The scent of hawthorn in the sun, or bracken in the wet ?

Let me work here for Britain's sake—at any task you will—
A marsh to drain, a road to make, or native troops to drill.
Some Western camp (I know the Pict) or granite Border
keep,
'Mid seas of heather derelict, where our old messmates sleep.

Legate, I come to you in tears—My cohort ordered home !
I've served in Britain forty years. What should I do in
Rome ?
Here is my heart, my soul, my mind—the only life I know.
I cannot leave it all behind. Command me not to go !

Rudyard Kipling

KING CANUTE

KING CANUTE was weary-hearted ; he had reigned for years a score,
Battling, struggling, pushing, fighting, killing much and robbing more ;
And he thought upon his actions, walking by the wild sea-shore.

'Twixt the Chancellor and Bishop walked the King with steps sedate,
Chamberlains and grooms came after, silversticks and goldsticks great,
Chaplains, aides-de-camp, and pages—all the officers of state.

Sliding after like a shadow, pausing when he chose to pause,
If a frown his face contracted, straight the courtiers dropped their jaws ;
If to laugh the King was minded, out they burst in loud hee-haws.

But that day a something vexed him, that was clear to old and young :
Thrice his Grace had yawned at table, when his favourite gleemen sung,
Once the Queen would have consoled him, but he bade her hold her tongue.

" Something ails my gracious master," cried the Keeper of the Seal ;
" Sure, my Lord, it is the lampreys served to dinner, or the veal ? "
" Psha ! " exclaimed the angry monarch ; " Keeper, 'tis not that I feel.

'Tis the *heart* and not the dinner, fool, that doth my rest impair ;
Can a king be great as I am, prithee, and yet know no care ?

Oh, I'm sick, and tired, and weary." Some one cried,
"The King's arm-chair!"

Then towards the lacqueys turning, quick my Lord the Keeper nodded,
Straight the King's great chair was brought him by two footmen able-bodied;
Languidly he sank into it: it was comfortably wadded.

"Leading on my fierce companions," cried he, "over storm and brine,
I have fought and I have conquered! Where was glory like to mine?"
Loudly all the courtiers echoed, "Where is glory like to thine?"

"What avail me all my kingdoms? Weary am I now and old;
Those fair sons I have begotten long to see me dead and cold;
Would I were, and quiet buried underneath the silent mould!

Oh, remorse, the writhing serpent! at my bosom tears and bites!
Horrid, horrid things I look on, though I put out all the lights;
Ghosts of ghastly recollections troop about my bed at nights.

Cities burning, convents blazing, red with sacrilegious fires;
Mothers weeping, virgins screaming vainly for their slaughtered sires"—
"Such a tender conscience," cries the Bishop, "every one admires.

But for such unpleasant bygones cease, my gracious Lord, to search;
They're forgotten and forgiven by our Holy Mother Church;
Never, never does she leave her benefactors in the lurch.

Look ! the land is crowned with minsters, which your
Grace's bounty raised ;
Abbeys filled with holy men, where you and Heaven are
daily praised ;
You, my Lord, to think of dying ? On my conscience I'm
amazed ! "

" Nay, I feel," replied King Canute, " that my end is
drawing near."
" Don't say so," exclaimed the courtiers (striving each to
squeeze a tear),
" Sure your Grace is strong and lusty, and may live this
fifty year."

" Live these fifty years ! " the Bishop roared, with actions
made to suit ;
" Are you mad, my good Lord Keeper, thus to speak of
King Canute ?
Men have lived a thousand years, and sure His Majesty
will do't.

Adam, Enoch, Lamech, Cainan, Mahaleel, Methuselah,
Lived nine hundred years apiece, and mayn't the King as
well as they ? "
" Fervently," exclaimed the Keeper, " fervently I trust he
may."

" *He* to die ? " resumed the Bishop. " He a mortal like to
us ?
Death was not for him intended, though *communis omnibus* :
Keeper, you are irreligious for to talk and cavil thus.

With his wondrous skill in healing ne'er a doctor can
compete ;
Loathsome lepers, if he touch them, start up clean upon
their feet ;
Surely he could raise the dead up, did his Highness think
it meet.

Did not once the Jewish captain stay the sun upon the
hill ?

And, the while he slew the foemen, bid the silver moon
stand still ?
So, no doubt, could gracious Canute, if it were his sacred
will."

" Might I stay the sun above us, good Sir Bishop ? "
Canute cried ;
" Could I bid the silver moon to pause upon her heavenly
ride ?
If the moon obeys my orders, sure I can command the
tide.

Will the advancing waves obey me, Bishop, if I make the
sign ? "
Said the Bishop, bowing lowly, " Land and sea, my Lord,
are thine."
Canute turned towards the ocean—" Back ! " he said,
" thou foaming brine.

From the sacred shore I stand on I command thee to
retreat ;
Venture not, thou stormy rebel, to approach thy master's
seat ;
Ocean, be thou still ! I bid thee come not nearer to my
feet ! "

But the sullen ocean answered with a louder, deeper roar,
And the rapid waves drew nearer, falling sounding on the
shore ;
Back the Keeper and the Bishop, back the King and
courtiers bore.

And he sternly bade them never more to kneel to human
clay,
But alone to praise and worship That which earth and
seas obey ;
And his golden crown of empire never wore he from that
day.
King Canute is dead and gone : Parasites exist alway.

William Makepeace Thackeray

ROBIN HOOD AND GUY OF GISBORNE

WHEN shaws [1] beene sheene, and shradds [2] full fayre,
  And leaves both large and longe,
Itt is merrye walking in the fayre forrèst
  To hear the small birdes songe.

The woodweele [3] sang, and wold not cease,
  Sitting upon the spraye,
So lowde, he wakened Robin Hood,
  In the greenwood where he lay.

" Now by my faye," sayd jolly Robin,
  " A sweaven [4] I had this night ;
I dreamt me of two wighty yemen,
  That fast with me can fight.

Methought they did mee beate and binde,
  And tooke my bow mee froe ;
If I be Robin alive in this lande,
  I'le be wroken on them towe."

" Sweavens are swift, master," quoth John,
  " As the wind that blowes ore a hill ;
For if itt be never so loude this night,
  Tomorrow itt may be still."

" Buske [5] yee, bowne yee, my merry men all,
  And John shall goe with mee,
For I'le goe seeke yond wight yeomen,
  In greenwood where they bee."

They cast on them their gownes of grene,
  And tooke theyr bowes each one ;
And they away to the greene forrèst
  A shooting forth are gone ;

Until they came to the merry greenwood,
  Where they had gladdest bee,

[1] *shaws* : groves. [2] *shradds* : copses.
[3] *woodweele* : golden ouzel or thrush. [4] *sweaven* : dream.
[5] *Buske* : get ready, dress.

There were they ware of a wight yeoman,
His body leaned to a tree.

A sword and a dagger he wore by his side,
Of manye a man the bane ;
And he was clad in his capull hyde [1]
Topp and tayll and mayne.

" Stand you still, master," quoth Little John,
" Under this tree so grene,
And I will go to yond wight yeoman
To know what he doth meane."

" Ah ! John, by me thou settest noe store,
And that I farley [2] finde :
How offt send I my men beffore,
And tarry my selfe behinde ?

It is no cunning a knave to ken,
An a man but heare him speake ;
An itt were not for bursting of my bowe,
John, I thy head wold breake."

As often wordes they breeden bale,
So they parted Robin and John ;
And John is gone to Barnesdale :
The gates [3] he knoweth each one.

[Little John is taken by the Sheriff of Nottingham and bound to a tree.]

. . . . .

Let us leave talking of Little John,
And thinke of Robin Hood,
How he is gone to the wight yeoman,
Where under the leaves he stood.

" Good morrowe, good fellowe," sayd Robin so fayre,
" Good morrowe, good fellowe," quoth he ;
" Methinkes by this bowe thou beares in thy hande
A good archere thou sholdst bee."

. . . . .

[1] *capull hyde* : horse hide. [2] *farley* : strange.
[3] *gates* : ways.

" I seeke an outlawe," the stranger sayd,
" Men call him Robin Hood ;
Rather I'ld meet with that proud outlawe
Than fortye pound soe good."

" Now come with me, thou wighty yeoman,
And Robin thou soone shalt see :
But first let us some pastime find
Under the greenwood tree."

. . . . . .

They cutt them downe two summer shroggs,[1]
That grew both under a breere,
And sett them threescore rood in twaine
To shoot the prickes y-fere.[2]

. . . . . .

The first time Robin shot at the pricke,
He mist but an inch it froe :
The yeoman he was an archer good,
But he cold never shoote soe.

The seconde shoote had the wightye yeman,
He shote within the garlánde :
But Robin he shott far better than hee,
For he clave the good pricke wande.

" A blessing upon thy heart," he sayd ;
" Good fellowe, thy shooting is goode ;
For an thy hart be as good as thy hand,
Thou wert better than Robin Hoode.

Now tell me thy name, good fellowe," sayd he,
Under the leaves of lyne.[3]
" Nay, by my faith," quoth bolde Robin,
" Till thou have told me thine."

" I dwell by dale and downe," quoth hee,
" And Robin to take I'me sworne ;
And when I am called by my right name
I am Guye of good Gisborne."

shroggs : underwood. [2] *prickes y-fere* : at the mark together.
[3] *lyne* : the linden tree.

"My dwelling is in this wood," sayes Robin,
  "By thee I set right nought;
I am Robin Hood of Barnesdale,
  Whom thou so long hast sought."

He that had neither beene kithe nor kin,
  Might have seene a full fayre sight,
To see how together these yeomen went
  With blades both browne and bright.

To see how these yeomen together they fought
  Two howrres of a summers day:
Yett neither Robin Hood nor sir Guy
  Them fettled [1] to flye away.

Robin was reachles [2] on a roote,
  And stumbled at that tyde;
And Guy was quicke and nimble with-all,
  And hitt him ore the left side.

"Ah, deere lady," sayd Robin Hood,
  "That art both mother and may," [3]
I think it was never mans destinye
  To dye before his day."

Robin though on our ladye deere,
  And soone leapt up againe,
And strait he came with a backward stroke,
  And he sir Guy hath slayne.

He took sir Guys head by the hayre,
  And sticked itt on his bowes end:
"Thou hast beene a traytor all thy liffe,
  Which thing must have an ende."

Robin did off his gowne of greene,
  And on sir Guy did it throwe,
And hee put on that capull hyde,
  That cladd him topp to toe.

. . . . .

[1] *fettle*: get ready. [2] *reachles*: reckless, careless.
[3] *may*: maid.

Robin Hood sett Guyes horne to his mouth,
  And a loud blast in it did blow.
That beheard the Sheriffe of Nottingham,
  As he leaned under a lowe.[1]
. . . . .

" Come hyther, come hyther, thou good sir Guy,
  Aske what thou wilt of mee."
" O I will none of thy gold," sayd Robin,
  " Nor will I none of thy fee :

But now I have slaine the master," he sayes,
  " Let me go strike the knave ;
This is all the rewarde I aske ;
  Nor noe other will I have."
. . . . .

Fast Robin hee hyed him to Little John,
  He thought to loose him belive ;[2]
The sheriffe and all his companye
  Fast after him did drive.

" Stand abacke, stand abacke," sayd Robin Hood ;
  " Why draw you mee soe neere ?
Itt was never the use in our countrye
  One's shrift another shold heere."

But Robin pulled forth an Irysh kniffe,
  And losed John hand and foote,
And gave him sir Guyes bow into his hand,
  And bade it be his boote.

Then John he took Guyes bow in his hand,
  His boltes and arrowes eche one :
When the sheriffe saw Little John bend his bow,
  He fettled him to be gone.
. . . . .

But he cold neither runne soe fast,
  Nor away soe fast cold runne,
But Little John with an arrow so broad
  Did cleave his herte in twinne.

Anonymous (14th century)

[1] *lowe* : knoll.   [2] *belive* : speedily.

THE PATIENT GRISELD

Amonges thise povre folk ther dwelte a man
Which that was holden povrest of hem alle ;
But hye God som tyme senden can
His grace into a litel oxes stalle :
Janicula men of that throp him calle.
A doghter hadde he, fair ynogh to sighte,
And Grisildis this yonge mayden highte.[1]

But for to speke of vertuous beautee,
Than was she oon the faireste under sonne ;
For povreliche y-fostred up was she,
No likerous lust was thurgh her herte y-ronne ;
Wel ofter of the welle than of the tonne[2]
She drank, and for she wolde vertu plese,
She knew wel labour, but non ydel ese.

But thogh this mayde tendre were of age,
Yet in the brest of hir virginitee
Ther was enclosèd rype and sad corage ;
And in greet reverence and charitee
Hir olde povre fader fostred she ;
A fewe sheep spinning on feeld she kepte,
She wolde noght been ydel til she slepte.

And whan she hoomward cam, she wolde bringe
Wortes or othere herbes tymes ofte,
The whiche she shredde and seeth for hir livinge,
And made hir bed ful harde and no-thing softe ;
And ay she kepte hir fadres lyf on-lofte
With everich obeisáunce and diligence
That child may doon to fadres reverence.

Geoffrey Chaucer

THE PARSON

A good man was ther of religioun,
And was a povre Persoun of a toun ;
But rich he was of holy thoght and werk.
He was also a lerned man, a clerk,

[1] *highte*, called. [2] *tonne* : tun, barrel.

That Cristes gospel trewely wolde preche ;
His parisshens devoutly wolde he teche.
Benigne he was and wonder diligent,
And in adversitee ful pacient ;
And swich he was y-preved ofte sythes.
Ful looth were him to cursen for his tythes,
But rather wolde he yeven, out of doubte,
Unto his povre parisshens aboute
Of his offring and eek of his substaunce.
He coude in litel thing han suffisaunce.
Wyd was his párisshe, and hoúses fer asonder,
But he ne lafte nat, for reyn ne thonder,
In siknes nor in meschief, to visyte
The ferrest in his parisshe, much and lyte,
Upon his feet, and in his hand a staf.
This noble ensample to his sheep he yaf,
That first he wroghte, and afterward he taughte ;
Out of the gospel he tho wordes caughte ;
And this figure he added eek ther-to,
That if gold ruste, what shal iren do ?
For if a preest be foul, on whom we truste,
No wonder is a lewèd man [1] to ruste ;
And shame it is, if a preest take keep,
A shiten [2] shepherde and a clene sheep.
Wel oghte a preest ensample for to yive,
By his clennesse, how that his sheep shold live.
He sette nat his benefice to hyre
And leet his sheep encombred in the myre,
And ran to London unto Seÿnt Poules,
To seken him a chaunterie for soules,
Or with a bretherhed to ben withoolde ;
But dwelte at hoom and kepte wel his folde,
So that the wolf ne made it nat miscarie ;
He was a shepherde and no mercenarie.
And though he holy were and vertuous,
He was to sinful man not despitous,
Ne of his speche daungerous [3] ne digne,[4]
But in his teching discreet and benigne.

[1] *lewed man* : layman, unlearned.
[2] *shiten* : befouled.
[3] *daungerous* : forbidding.
[4] *digne* : proud.

To drawen folk to heven by fairnesse,
By good ensample, was his bisinesse :
But it were any persone obstinat,
What-so he were, of heigh or lowe estat,
Him wolde he snibben sharply for the nones.
A bettre preest I trow that nowher noon is.
He wayted áfter no pómpe and reverence,
Ne maked him a spyced [1] conscience,
But Cristes lore and his apostles twelve,
He taughte, and first he folwed it him-selve.

Geoffrey Chaucer

GOD SAVE KING HARRY !

Glade in god, call hom youre herte,
In joye and blisse youre merthe encres,
And kepe goddis lawe in querte ; [2]
This holy tyme, let sorwe ases ; [3]
Among oure self, god sende us pes !
Therto eche man be boun : [4]
To letten [5] fooles of here res, [6]
Stonde with the kyng, mayntene the croun.

. . . . .

A kyngdom must be governed by right,
To chastyse false [7] that ar aspyed.
Falsed and trouthe to-gydre wole fight,
Til oon that other hath distroyd ;
Til trouthe be fro treson tryed,
Shal nevere be pes in regyoun.
In all kyngdomes that man hath gyed, [8]
To the place of vertues god geveth the crowne.

. . . . .

That lord loveth lityl hym selve,
That geveth his blisse for sorwe and woo ;
For the love of ten or twelve
Make alle folk his foo,

[1] *spyced* : over-scrupulous.
[2] *querte* : health.
[3] *ases* : cease.
[4] *boun* : ready.
[5] *letten* : stop.
[6] *here res* : their assault.
[7] *false* : false persons.
[8] *gyed* : governed.

And lese the love of God also,
For fawte of perfeccyone.
Though he had no vauntage but of tho,
He myghte were a symple crowne.
. . . . .

The fadir the wanton child wole kenne [1]
Chastyse with yerde,[2] and bete hit sore.
So after, the fadyr the yerde wole brenne,
When child is wys, and taketh to lore.
We han ben goddis yerde yore,
Chastysed kyngdom, castell, and towne.
Twyggis of oure yerde we have forlore.[3]
God save the kyng, and kepe the crowne !

Englische men dede maystryyes make ; [4]
Thurgh all the world, here word it sprong.
Cristen and hethen they mad to quake,
Tok and slowen kynges strong.
God let nevere werre be us among,
To lese that blo [5] of gret renowne,
Ne nevere oure right be turned to wrong ;
God save the kyng, and kepe the crowne !

Among oure self, yif fight be raysed,
Than stroye we oure awen nest.
That hath victor, wol be evel payed,
So many good men ben lest.
Yhit is beter bowe than brest.[6]
Eche man is bounden to resoun.
Ye, that ben wysest, take the best ;
Conseile the kyng, mayntene the crowne !

A comons myght sone be shent,[7]
With-outen kyng or governour,
And a kynge withoute rent [8]
Myght lightly trussen [9] his tresour,
For comons mayntene lordis honour,
Holy chirche, and religyoun,

[1] *kenne* : teach. [2] *yerde* : rod. [3] *forlore* : lost.
[4] *maystryyes make* : make masteries, perform wonderful feats.
[5] *blo* : repute. [6] *brest* : burst. [7] *shent* : ruined.
[8] *rent* : revenue. [9] *lightly trussen* : make a light bundle of.

For comouns is the fayrest flour
That evere god sette on erthely crown.

God, lete this kyngdom nevere be lorn [1]
Among oure self, in no distance !
Other kyngdomes laughe us not to skorn,
And say, for synne god sends vengeance.
God, geve us space of repentance,
Good lyf, and devocioun ;
And, God, kepe in thy governance
Our comely kyng, and save the crowne !

Anonymous (1413)

A QUEEN'S FAITH

(Speech by Queen Elizabeth from *Will Shakespeare*)

I AM not drunken with religious dream
Like the poor blissful fools of kingdom come :
I know the flesh is sweetest, when all's said
And summer's hey-day and the love of men :
I know well what I lose. I'm head of the Church
And stoop my neck on Sunday—to what Christ ?
The God of little children ? I have none.
The God of love ? What love has come to me ?
The God upon His ass ? I am not meek,
Nor is he meek, the stallion that I ride,
The great white horse of England. I'll not bow
To the gentle Jesus of the women, I—
But to the man who hung 'twixt earth and heaven
Six mortal hours, and knew the end (as strength
And custom was) three days away, yet ruled
His soul and body so, that when the sponge
Blessed his cracked lips with promise of relief
And quick oblivion, he would not drink :
He turned his head away and would not drink :
Spat out the anodyne and would not drink.
This was a god for kings and queens of pride,
And him I follow.

Clemence Dane

[1] *lorn* : lost.

DRAKE'S CHAIR

Sitting and Drinking in the Chair made out of the Relics of Sir Francis Drake's Ship

CHEER up, my mates ! the wind does fairly blow.
  Clap on more sail and never spare !
  Farewell all lands, for now we are
  In the wide sea of drink, and merrily we go.
Bless me ! 'tis hot ! Another bowl of wine
  And we shall cut the burning line.
Hey, boys ! She scuds away ! And by my head I know
  We round the world are sailing now.
What dull men are those who tarry at home,
When abroad they might wantonly roam
  And gain such experience, and spy too
  Such countries and wonders as I do !
But prithee, good Pilot ! take heed what you do,
  And fail not to touch at Peru.
  With gold there the vessel we'll store,
  And never and never be poor ;
  No, never be poor any more !

What do I mean ? What thoughts do me misguide ?
As well upon a staff may witches ride
  Their fancied journeys in the air
As I sail round the ocean in this Chair.
'Tis true ; but yet this Chair which here you see,
For all its quiet now and gravity,
  Has wander'd and has travell'd more
Than ever beast or fish or bird or ever tree before ;
In every air, and every sea 't has been.
'T has compass'd all the earth and all the heav'ns 't has seen ;
Let not the Pope's itself with this compare !
This is the only Universal Chair !

The pious wand'rer's fleet, sav'd from the flame,
(Which still the relics did of Troy pursue
  And took them for its due),

A squadron of immortal nymphs became.
Still with their arms they row about the seas,
And still make new and greater voyages.
Nor has the first poetic ship of Greece,
(Though now a star she so triumphant show
And guide her sailing successors below
Bright as her ancient freight the shining Fleece ;)
Yet to this day a quiet harbour found ;
The tide of heav'n still carries her around.
Only Drake's sacred vessel, which before
  Had done and had seen more
  Than those have done or seen,
Ev'n since they Goddesses and this a star has been,
As a reward for all her labour past
  Is made the seat of rest at last.
  Let the case now quite alter'd be ;
And as thou went'st abroad the world to see,
  Let the world now come to see thee !

The world will do't. For Curiosity
Does no less than Devotion pilgrims make.
And I myself, who now love quiet too
As much almost as any chair can do,
  Would yet a journey take,
An old wheel of that chariot to see
  Which Phaeton so rashly brake ;
Yet what could that say more than these remains of
    Drake ?
Great relic ! Thou too in this port of ease
Hast still one way of making voyages.
The breath of Fame, like an auspicious gale,
  (The great Trade Wind which ne'er does fail)
Shall drive thee round the world, and thou shalt run
  As long around it as the sun.
The straits of Time too narrow are for thee ;
Launch forth into an undiscover'd sea,
And steer the endless course of vast Eternity !
Take for thy sail this verse, and for thy Pilot me !

Abraham Cowley

TO THE LORD GENERAL

CROMWELL, our chief of men, who through a cloud
Not of war only, but detractions rude,
Guided by faith and matchless fortitude,
To peace and truth thy glorious way hast ploughed,
And on the neck of crownèd Fortune proud
Hast reared God's trophies, and his work pursued,
While Darwen stream, with blood of Scots imbrued,
And Dunbar field, resounds thy praises loud,
And Worcester's laureate wreath : yet much remains
To conquer still ; peace hath her victories
No less renowned than war : new foes arise,
Threatening to bind our souls with secular chains.
Help us to save free conscience from the paw
Of hireling wolves whose gospel is their maw.

John Milton

THE SONG OF THE WESTERN MEN

A GOOD sword and a trusty hand !
A merry heart and true !
King James's men shall understand
What Cornish lads can do.

And have they fixed the where and when ?
And shall Trelawny die ?
Here's twenty thousand Cornish men
Will know the reason why !

Out spake their captain brave and bold,
A merry wight was he :
" If London Tower were Michael's hold,
We'll set Trelawny free !

We'll cross the Tamar, land to land,
The Severn is no stay,
With ' one and all ', and hand in hand,
And who shall bid us nay ?

And when we come to London Wall,
  A pleasant sight to view,
Come forth ! come forth, ye cowards all,
  Here's men as good as you !

Trelawny he's in keep and hold,
  Trelawny he may die ;
But twenty thousand Cornish bold
  Will know the reason why."

R. S. Hawker

THE COUNTRY MEMBER

How blest is he who leads a country life,
Unvexed with anxious cares and void of strife !
Who studying peace and shunning civil rage
Enjoyed his youth and now enjoys his age.
All who deserve his love he makes his own ;
And, to be loved himself, needs only to be known.
  Just, good and wise, contending neighbours come
From your award to wait their final doom ;
And, foes before, return in friendship home.
Without their cost you terminate the cause,
And save the expense of long litigious laws,
Where suits are traversed and so little won
That he who conquers is but last undone.
Such are not your decrees, but so designed,
The sanction leaves a lasting peace behind,—
Like your own soul serene, a pattern of your mind.

. . . . .

  No porter guards the passage of your door
To admit the wealthy and exclude the poor ;
For God who gave the riches gave the heart,
To sanctify the whole by giving part. . . .

. . . . .

  With crowds attended of your ancient race
You seek the champain sports or sylvan chase.

. . . . .

This fiery game your active youth maintained,
Not yet by years extinguished, though restrained.

You season still with sports your serious hours,
For age but tastes of pleasures youth devours.

. . . . .

Better to hunt in fields for health unbought
Than fee the doctor for a nauseous draught.
The wise for cure on exercise depend ;
God never made his work for man to mend.

. . . . .

You hoard not health for your own private use,
But on the public spend the rich produce.
When often urged, unwilling to be great,
Your country calls you from your loved retreat,
And sends to senates charged with common care,
Which none more shuns, and none can better bear.
Where could they find another formed so fit
To poise with solid sense a sprightly wit ?
Were these both wanting, as they both abound,
Where could so firm integrity be found ?
Well born and wealthy, wanting no support,
You steer betwixt the country and the court ;
Nor gratify whate'er the great desire,
Nor grudging give what public needs require.

. . . . .

Patriots in peace assert the people's right,
With noble stubbornness resisting might ;
No lawless mandates from the court receive,
Nor lend by force, but in a body give.
Such was your generous grandsire ; free to grant
In parliaments that weighed their prince's want ;
But so tenacious of the common cause
As not to lend the king against his laws ;
And, in a loathsome dungeon doomed to lie,
In bonds retained his birthright liberty,
And shamed oppression till it set him free.

John Dryden

HAPPY BRITANNIA

Heavens ! What a goodly prospect spreads around
Of hills and dales and woods and lawns and spires

And glittering towns and gilded streams, till all
The stretching landskip into smoke decays !
Happy Britannia ! Where the queen of arts,
Inspiring vigour, Liberty abroad
Walks unconfin'd ev'n to thy farthest cots,
And scatters plenty with unsparing hand.
  Rich is thy soil and merciful thy clime ;
Thy streams unfailing in the summer's drought ;
Unmatch'd thy guardian oaks ; thy vallies float
With golden waves ; and on thy mountains flocks
Bleat numberless, while roving round their sides
Bellow the blackening herds in lusty droves.
Beneath, thy meadows glow and rise unquell'd
Against the mower's scythe. On every hand
Thy villas shine. Thy country teems with wealth,
And property assures it to the swain,
Pleas'd and unwearied in his guarded toil.
  Full are thy cities with the sons of art ;
And trade and joy in every busy street
Mingling are heard : even drudgery himself,
As at the car he sweats or dusty hews
The palace-stone, looks gay. Thy crowded ports,
Where rising masts an endless prospect yield,
With labour burn and echo to the shouts
Of hurried sailor, as he hearty waves
His last adieu, and loosening every sheet
Resigns the spreading vessel to the wind.
  Bold, firm and graceful are thy generous youth,
By hardship sinew'd and by danger fir'd,
Scattering the nations where they go ; and first
Or in the listed plain or wintry seas.
Mild are thy glories too, as o'er the plans
Of thriving peace thy thoughtful sires preside :
In genius and substantial learning high ;
For every virtue, every worth renown'd ;
Sincere, plain-hearted, hospitable, kind ;
Yet, like the mustering thunder, when provok'd
The dread of tyrants, and the sole resource
Of those that under grim oppression groan.

James Thomson

THE INDEPENDENT BRITON

Fir'd at the sound, my genius spreads her wing,
And flies where Britain courts the western spring ;
Where lawns extend that scorn Arcadian pride,
And brighter streams than fam'd Hydaspes glide.
There all around the gentlest breezes stray,
There gentle music melts on every spray ;
Creation's mildest charms are there combin'd,
Extremes are only in the master's mind !
Stern o'er each bosom reason holds her state,
With daring aims irregularly great,
Pride in their port, defiance in their eye,
I see the lords of human kind pass by,
Intent on high designs, a thoughtful band,
By forms unfashion'd, fresh from Nature's hand ;
Fierce in their native hardiness of soul,
True to imagin'd right, above control,
While even the peasant boasts these rights to scan,
And learns to venerate himself as man.

Oliver Goldsmith

THE LITTLE VAGABOND

Dear mother, dear mother, the church is cold,
But the ale-house is healthy and pleasant and warm ;
Besides I can tell where I am used well,
Such usage in Heaven will never do well.

But if at the church they would give us some ale,
And a pleasant fire our souls to regale,
We'd sing and we'd pray all the livelong day,
Nor ever once wish from the church to stray.

Then the Parson might preach, and drink, and sing,
And we'd be as happy as birds in the spring ;
And modest Dame Lurch, who is always at church,
Would not have bandy children, nor fasting, nor birch.

And God, like a father, rejoicing to see
His children as pleasant and happy as He,
Would have no more quarrel with the devil or the barrel,
But kiss him, and give him both drink and apparel.

William Blake

THE WIDOW GOE

Next died the Widow Goe, an active dame,
Famed ten miles round and worthy all her fame ;
She lost her husband when their loves were young,
But kept her farm, her credit and her tongue.
Full thirty years she ruled with matchless skill,
With guiding judgment and resistless will.
Advice she scorned, rebellions she suppressed,
And sons and servants bowed at her behest.
Like that great man's, who to his Saviour came,
Were the strong words of this commanding dame ;—
" Come " if she said, they came ; if " Go ", were gone ;
And if " Do this ", that instant it was done.
Her maidens told she was all eye and ear,
In darkness saw and could at distance hear.
No parish-business in the place could stir
Without direction or assent from her.
In turn she took each office as it fell,
Knew all their duties and discharged them well.
She looked on want with judgment clear and cool,
And felt with reason and bestowed by rule.
She matched both sons and daughters to her mind,
And lent them eyes ; for Love, she heard, was blind.
Yet ceaseless still she throve, alert, alive,
The working bee in full or empty hive ;
Busy and careful, like that working bee,
No time for love nor tender cares had she ;
But when our farmers made their amorous vows,
She talk'd of market-steeds and patent-ploughs.
Not unemployed her evenings passed away,
Amusement closed as business waked the day ;
When to her toilet's brief concern she ran,
And conversation with her friends began,

Who all were welcome what they saw to share ;
And joyous neighbours praised her Christmas fare,
That none around might in their scorn complain
Of Gossip Goe as greedy in her gain.

George Crabbe

MEN OF ENGLAND

Men of England ! who inherit
  Rights that cost your sires their blood !
Men whose undegenerate spirit
  Has been proved on land and flood

By the foes ye've fought, uncounted,
  By the glorious deeds ye've done,
Trophies captured—breaches mounted,
  Navies conquer'd—kingdoms won !

Yet, remember, England gathers
  Hence but fruitless wreaths of fame,
If the freedom of your fathers
  Glow not in your hearts the same.

What are monuments of bravery,
  Where no public virtues bloom ?
What avail, in lands of slavery,
  Trophied temples, arch, and tomb ?

Pageants !—Let the world revere us
  For our people's rights and laws,
And the breasts of civic heroes
  Bared in Freedom's holy cause.

Yours are Hampden's, Russell's glory,
  Sydney's matchless shade is yours,—
Martyrs in heroic story,
  Worth a hundred Agincourts !

We're the sons of sires that baffled
  Crowned and mitred tyranny :—
They defied the field and scaffold
  For their birthrights—so will we !

Thomas Campbell

THE HAPPY WARRIOR

Who is the happy Warrior? Who is he
That every Man in arms should wish to be?
—It is the generous Spirit, who, when brought
Among the tasks of real life, hath wrought
Upon the plan that pleased his boyish thought:
Whose high endeavours are an inward light
That makes the path before him always bright;
Who with a natural instinct to discern
What knowledge can perform, is diligent to learn;
Abides by this resolve, and stops not there,
But makes his moral being his prime care;
Who, doomed to go in company with Pain,
And Fear and Bloodshed, miserable train!
Turns his necessity to glorious gain;
In face of these doth exercise a power
Which is our human nature's highest dower:
Controls them and subdues, transmutes, bereaves
Of their bad influence, and their good receives:
By objects, which might force the soul to abate
Her feeling, rendered more compassionate;
Is placable—because occasions rise
So often that demand such sacrifice;
More skilful in self-knowledge, even more pure,
As tempted more; more able to endure,
As more exposed to suffering and distress;
Thence, also, more alive to tenderness.
—'Tis he whose law is reason; who depends
Upon that law as on the best of friends;
Whence, in a state where men are tempted still
To evil for a guard against worse ill,
And what in quality or act is best
Doth seldom on a right foundation rest,
He labours good on good to fix, and owes
To virtue every triumph that he knows:
—Who, if he rise to station of command,
Rises by open means; and there will stand
On honourable terms, or else retire,
And in himself possess his own desire;

Who comprehends his trust, and to the same
Keeps faithful with a singleness of aim ;
And therefore does not stoop, nor lie in wait
For wealth, or honours, or for worldly state ;
Whom they must follow, on whose head must fall,
Like showers of manna, if they come at all :
Whose powers shed round him in the common strife,
Or mild concerns of ordinary life,
A constant influence, a peculiar grace ;
But who, if he be called upon to face
Some awful moment to which Heaven has joined
Great issues, good or bad, for human kind,
Is happy as a Lover ; and attired
With sudden brightness, like a Man inspired ;
And, through the heat of conflict, keeps the law
In calmness made, and sees what he foresaw ;
Or, if an unexpected call succeed,
Come when it will, is equal to the need :
—He who, though thus endued as with a sense
And faculty for storm and turbulence,
Is yet a Soul whose master-bias leans
To home-felt pleasures and to gentle scenes ;
Sweet images ! which, wheresoe'er he be,
Are at his heart ; and such fidelity
It is his darling passion to approve ;
More brave for this, that he hath much to love :
—'Tis, finally, the Man who, lifted high,
Conspicuous object in a Nation's eye,
Or left unthought-of in obscurity,—
Who, with a toward or untoward lot,
Prosperous or adverse, to his wish or not,
Plays, in the many games of life, that one
Where what he most doth value must be won ;
Whom neither shape of danger can dismay,
Nor thought of tender happiness betray ;
Who, not content that former worth stand fast,
Looks forward, persevering to the last,
From well to better, daily self-surpast :
Who whether praise of him must walk the earth
For ever, and to noble deeds give birth,
Or he must fall, to sleep without his fame,

And leave a dead unprofitable name,
Finds comfort in himself and in his cause ;
And, while the mortal mist is gathering, draws
His breath in confidence of Heaven's applause :
This is the happy Warrior ; this is He
That every Man in arms should wish to be.

William Wordsworth

NELSON AND PITT

To mute and to material things
New life revolving summer brings ;
The genial call dead Nature hears,
And in her glory reappears.
But O my Country's wintry state
What second spring shall renovate ?
What powerful call shall bid arise
The buried warlike and the wise ;
The mind that thought for Britain's weal,
The hand that grasped the victor's steel ?
The vernal sun new life bestows
Even on the meanest flower that blows ;
But vainly, vainly may he shine,
Where glory weeps o'er NELSON's shrine ;
And vainly pierce the solemn gloom,
That shrouds, O PITT, thy hallowed tomb !

Deep graved in every British heart,
O never let those names depart !
Say to your sons,—Lo, here his grave,
Who victor died on Gadite wave ;
To him, as to the burning levin,
Short, bright, resistless course was given.
Where'er his country's foes were found
Was heard the fated thunder's sound,
Till burst the bolt on yonder shore,
Rolled, blazed, destroyed,—and was no more.

Nor mourn ye less his perished worth,
Who bade the conqueror go forth,

And launched that thunderbolt of war
On Egypt, Hafnia, Trafalgar ;
Who, born to guide such high emprise,
For Britain's weal was early wise ;
Alas ! to whom the Almighty gave,
For Britain's sins, an early grave !
His worth, who in his mightiest hour
A bauble held the pride of power,
Spurned at the sordid lust of pelf,
And served his Albion for herself ;
Who, when the frantic crowd amain
Strained at subjection's bursting rein,
O'er their wild mood full conquest gained,
The pride he would not crush restrained,
Showed their fierce zeal a worthier cause,
And brought the freeman's arm to aid the
  freeman's laws.

Sir Walter Scott

THE VICAR

Some years ago, ere time and taste
  Had turned our parish topsy-turvy,
When Darnel Park was Darnel Waste,
  And roads as little known as scurvy,
The man who lost his way, between
  St. Mary's Hill and Sandy Thicket,
Was always shown across the green,
  And guided to the Parson's wicket.

Back flew the bolt of lissom lath ;
  Fair Margaret, in her tidy kirtle,
Led the lorn traveller up the path,
  Through clean-clipt rows of box and myrtle ;
And Don and Sancho, Tramp and Tray,
  Upon the parlour steps collected,
Wagged all their tails, and seemed to say—
  " Our master knows you—you're expected."

Uprose the Reverend Dr. Brown,
  Uprose the Doctor's winsome marrow ;
The lady laid her knitting down,
  Her husband clasped his ponderous Barrow ;
Whate'er the stranger's caste or creed,
  Pundit or Papist, saint or sinner,
He found a stable for his steed,
  And welcome for himself, and dinner.

If, when he reached his journey's end,
  And warmed himself in Court or College,
He had not gained an honest friend
  And twenty curious scraps of knowledge,—
If he departed as he came,
  With no new light on love or liquor,—
Good sooth, the traveller was to blame,
  And not the Vicarage, nor the Vicar.

His talk was like a stream, which runs
  With rapid change from rocks to roses :
It slipped from politics to puns,
  It passed from Mahomet to Moses ;
Beginning with the laws which keep
  The planets in their radiant courses,
And ending with some precept deep
  For dressing eels, or shoeing horses.

He was a shrewd and sound Divine,
  Of loud Dissent the mortal terror ;
And when, by dint of page and line,
  He 'stablished Truth, or startled Error,
The Baptist found him far too deep ;
  The Deist sighed with saving sorrow ;
And the lean Levite went to sleep,
  And dreamed of tasting pork tomorrow.

His sermons never said or showed
  That Earth is foul, that Heaven is gracious,
Without refreshment on the road
  From Jerome or from Athanasius ;

And sure a righteous zeal inspired
The hand and head that penned and planned
them,
For all who understood admired,
And some who did not understand them.

He wrote, too, in a quiet way,
Small treatises, and smaller verses,
And sage remarks on chalk and clay,
And hints to noble Lords—and nurses ;
True histories of last year's ghost,
Lines to a ringlet, or a turban,
And trifles for the *Morning Post*,
And nothings for Sylvanus Urban.

He did not think all mischief fair,
Although he had a knack of joking ;
He did not make himself a bear,
Although he had a taste for smoking ;
And when religious sects ran mad,
He held, in spite of all his learning,
That if a man's belief is bad,
It will not be improved by burning.

And he was kind, and loved to sit
In the low hut or garnished cottage,
And praise the farmer's homely wit,
And share the widow's homelier pottage :
At his approach complaint grew mild ;
And when his hand unbarred the shutter,
The clammy lips of fever smiled
The welcome which they could not utter.

He always had a tale for me
Of Julius Caesar, or of Venus ;
From him I learnt the rule of three,
Cat's cradle, leap-frog, and *Quae genus* :
I used to singe his powdered wig,
To steal the staff he put such trust in,
And make the puppy dance a jig,
When he began to quote Augustine.

Alack the change! in vain I look
For haunts in which my boyhood trifled,—
The level lawn, the trickling brook,
The trees I climbed, the beds I rifled:
The church is larger than before;
You reach it by a carriage entry;
It holds three hundred people more,
And pews are fitted up for gentry.

Sit in the Vicar's seat; you'll hear
The doctrine of a gentle Johnian,
Whose hand is white, whose tone is clear,
Whose phrase is very Ciceronian.
Where is the old man laid? look down,
And construe on the slab before you,
Hic jacet Gulielmus Brown,
Vir nulla non donandus lauru.

Winthrop Mackworth Praed

FIGHT ON

At the midnight in the silence of the sleep-time,
When you set your fancies free,
Will they pass to where—by death, fools think, imprisoned—
Low he lies who once so loved you, whom you loved so,
—Pity me?
Oh to love so, be so loved, yet so mistaken!
What had I on earth to do
With the slothful, with the mawkish, the unmanly?
Like the aimless, helpless, hopeless, did I drivel
—Being—who?

One who never turned his back but marched breast forward,
Never doubted clouds would break,
Never dreamed, though right were worsted, wrong would triumph,
Held we fall to rise, are baffled to fight better,
Sleep to wake.

No, at noonday in the bustle of man's work-time
  Greet the unseen with a cheer!
Bid him forward, breast and back as either should be,
"Strive and thrive!" cry: "Speed,—fight on, fare ever
    There as here."

Robert Browning

WANDERERS

As o'er the hill we roam'd at will,
  My dog and I together,
We mark'd a chaise, by two bright bays
  Slow-moved along the heather:

Two bays arch-neck'd, with tails erect
  And gold upon their blinkers;
And by their side an ass I spied;
  It was a travelling tinker's.

The chaise went by, nor aught cared I;
  Such things are not in my way;
I turn'd me to the tinker, who
  Was loafing down a byway:

I ask'd him where he lived—a stare
  Was all I got in answer,
As on he trudged: I rightly judged
The stare said, "Where I can, sir."

I ask'd him if he'd take a whiff
  Of 'bacco; he acceded;
He grew communicative too,
  (A pipe was all he needed,)
Till of the tinker's life, I think,
  I knew as much as he did.

"I loiter down by thorp and town,
  For any job I'm willing;
Take here and there a dusty brown,
  And here and there a shilling.

I deal in every ware in turn,
I've rings for buddin' Sally
That sparkle like those eyes of hern ;
I've liquor for the valet.

I steal from th' parson's strawberry-plots,
I hide by th' squire's covers ;
I teach the sweet young housemaids what's
The art of trapping lovers.

The things I've done 'neath moon and stars
Have got me into messes :
I've seen the sky through prison bars,
I've torn up prison dresses :

I've sat, I've sighed, I've gloom'd, I've glanced
With envy at the swallows
That through the window slid, and danced
(Quite happy) round the gallows ;

But out again I come and show
My face nor care a stiver,
For trades are brisk and trades are slow,
But mine goes on for ever."

Thus on he prattled like a babbling brook.
Then I, " The sun hath slipt behind the hill,
And my aunt Vivian dines at half-past six."
So in all love we parted ; I to the Hall,
They to the village. It was noised next noon
That chickens had been miss'd at Syllabub Farm.

C. S. Calverley

JUGGLING JERRY

PITCH here the tent, while the old horse grazes :
By the old hedgeside we'll halt a stage.
It's nigh my last above the daisies ;
My next leaf'll be man's blank page.

Yes, my old girl ! and it's no use crying :
  Juggler, constable, king, must bow.
One that outjuggles all 's been spying
  Long to have me, and he has me now.

We've travelled times to this old common :
  Often we've hung our pots in the gorse.
We've had a stirring life, old woman,
  You, and I, and the old grey horse.
Races, and fairs, and royal occasions,
  Found us coming to their call :
Now they'll miss us at our stations :
  There's a Juggler outjuggles all !

Up goes the lark, as if all were jolly !
  Over the duck-pond the willow shakes.
Easy to think that grieving's folly,
  When the hand's firm as driven stakes !
Ay, when we're strong, and braced, and manful,
  Life's a sweet fiddle : but we're a batch
Born to become the Great Juggler's han'ful ;
  Balls he shies up, and is safe to catch.

Here's where the lads of the village cricket :
  I was a lad not wide from here :
Couldn't I whip off the bail from the wicket ?
  Like an old world those days appear !
Donkey, sheep, geese, and thatched ale-house—I know them !
  They are old friends of my halts, and seem,
Somehow, as if kind thanks I owe them :
  Juggling don't hinder the heart's esteem.

Juggling's no sin, for we must have victual .
  Nature allows us to bait for the fool.
Holding one's own makes us juggle no little ;
  But, to increase it, hard juggling's the rule.
You that are sneering at my profession,
  Haven't you juggled a vast amount ?
There's the Prime Minister, in one Session,
  Juggles more games than my sins'll count.

I've murdered insects with mock thunder :
  Conscience, for that, in men don't quail.
I've made bread from the bump of wonder :
  That's my business, and there's my tale.
Fashion and rank all praised the professor :
  Ay ! and I've had my smile from the Queen :
Bravo, Jerry ! she meant : God bless her !
  Ain't this a sermon on that scene ?

I've studied men from my topsy-turvy
  Close, and, I reckon, rather true.
Some are fine fellows : some, right scurvy :
  Most, a dash between the two.
But it's a woman, old girl, that makes me
  Think more kindly of the race :
And it's a woman, old girl, that shakes me
  When the Great Juggler I must face.

We two were married, due and legal :
  Honest we've lived since we've been one.
Lord ! I could then jump like an eagle :
  You danced bright as a bit o' the sun.
Birds in a May bush, we were ! right merry !
  All night we kiss'd, we juggled all day.
Joy was the heart of Juggling Jerry !
  Now from his old girl he's juggled away.

It's past parsons to console us :
  No, nor no doctor fetch for me :
I can die without my bolus :
  Two of a trade, lass, never agree !
Parson and Doctor !—don't they love rarely
  Fighting the devil in other men's fields !
Stand up yourself and match him fairly :
  Then see how the rascal yields !

I, lass, have lived no gipsy, flaunting
  Finery while his poor helpmate grubs :
Coin I've stored, and you won't be wanting :
  You shan't beg from the troughs and tubs.

Nobly you've stuck to me, though in his kitchen
  Many a Marquis would hail you Cook !
Palaces you could have ruled and grown rich in,
  But your old Jerry you never forsook.

Hand up the chirper ! ripe ale winks in it ;
  Let's have comfort and be at peace.
Once a stout draught made me light as a linnet.
  Cheer up ! the Lord must have his lease.
May be—for none see in that black hollow—
  It's just a place where we're held in pawn,
And, when the Great Juggler makes as to swallow,
  It's just the sword-trick—I ain't quite gone !

Yonder came smells of the gorse, so nutty,
  Gold-like and warm : it's the prime of May.
Better than mortar, brick and putty
  Is God's house on a blowing day.
Lean me more up the mound ; now I feel it :
  All the old heath-smells ! Ain't it strange ?
There's the world laughing, as if to conceal it,
  But He's by us, juggling the change.

I mind it well, by the sea-beach lying,
  Once—it's long gone—when two gulls we beheld,
Which, as the moon got up, were flying
  Down a big wave that sparked and swelled.
Crack, went a gun : one fell : the second
  Wheeled round him twice, and was off for new luck :
There in the dark her white wing beckon'd :—
  Drop me a kiss—I'm the bird dead-struck !

George Meredith

THE ENGLISHMAN

I MET a sailor in the woods,
  A silver ring wore he,
His hair hung black, his eyes shone blue,
  And thus he said to me :—

'What country, say, of this round earth,
What shore of what salt sea,
Be this, my son, I wander in,
And looks so strange to me?'

Says I, 'O foreign sailorman,
In England now you be,
This is her wood, and there her sky,
And that her roaring sea.'

He lifts his voice yet louder,
'What smell be this,' says he,
'My nose on the sharp morning air
Snuffs up so greedily?'

Says I, 'It is wild roses
Do smell so winsomely,
And winy briar too,' says I,
'That in these thickets be.'

'And oh!' says he, 'what leetle bird
Is singing in yon high tree,
So every shrill and long-drawn note
Like bubbles breaks in me?'

Says I, 'It is the mavis
That perches in the tree,
And sings so shrill, and sings so sweet,
When dawn comes up the sea.'

At which he fell a-musing,
And fixed his eye on me,
As one alone 'twixt light and dark
A spirit thinks to see.

'England!' he whispers soft and harsh,
'England!' repeated he,
'And briar, and rose, and mavis,
A-singing in yon high tree.

'Ye speak me true, my leetle son,
So—so, it came to me,

A-drifting landwards on a spar,
  And grey dawn on the sea.

'Ay, ay, I could not be mistook;
  I knew them leafy trees,
I knew that land so witchery sweet,
  And that old noise of seas.

'Though here I've sailed a score of years,
  And heard 'em, dream or wake,
Lap small and hollow 'gainst my cheek,
  On sand and coral break;

'"Yet now," my leetle son, says I,
  A-drifting on the wave,
"That land I see so safe and green
  Is England, I believe.

'"And that there wood is English wood,
  And this here cruel sea,
The selfsame old blue ocean
  Years gone remembers me.

'"A-sitting with my bread and butter
  Down ahind yon chitterin' mill;
And this same Marinere"—(that's me),
  'Is that same leetle Will!—

'"That very same wee leetle Will
  Eating his bread and butter there,
And looking on the broad blue sea
  Betwixt his yaller hair!"

'"And here be I, my son, throwed up
  Like corpses from the sea,
Ships, stars, winds, tempests, pirates past,
  Yet leetle Will I be!'

He said no more, that sailorman,
  But in a reverie
Stared like the figure of a ship
  With painted eyes to sea.

Walter de la Mare

IF——

IF you can keep your head when all about you
  Are losing theirs and blaming it on you ;
If you can trust yourself when all men doubt you,
  But make allowance for their doubting too ;
If you can wait and not be tired by waiting,
  Or being lied about, don't deal in lies,
Or being hated don't give way to hating,
  And yet don't look too good, nor talk too wise :

If you can dream—and not make dreams your master ;
  If you can think—and not make thoughts your aim ;
If you can meet with Triumph and Disaster
  And treat those two impostors just the same ;
If you can bear to hear the truth you've spoken
  Twisted by knaves to make a trap for fools,
Or watch the things you gave your life to, broken,
  And stoop and build 'em up with worn-out tools :

If you can make one heap of all your winnings
  And risk it on one turn of pitch and toss,
And lose, and start again at your beginnings
  And never breathe a word about your loss ;
If you can force your heart and nerve and sinew
  To serve your turn long after they are gone,
And so hold on when there is nothing in you
  Except the Will which says to them : " Hold on ! "

If you can talk with crowds and keep your virtue,
  Or walk with Kings—nor lose the common touch,
If neither foes nor loving friends can hurt you,
  If all men count with you, but none too much ;
If you can fill the unforgiving minute
  With sixty seconds' worth of distance run,
Yours is the Earth and everything that's in it,
  And—which is more—you'll be a Man, my son !

Rudyard Kipling

THROUGH AMERICAN EYES

The English love their country with a love
  Steady, and simple, wordless, dignified ;
I think it sets their patriotism above
  All others. We Americans have pride—
We glory in our country's short romance.
  We boast of it and love it. Frenchmen when
The ultimate menace comes, will die for France
  Logically as they lived. But Englishmen
Will serve day after day, obey the law,
  And do dull tasks that keep a nation strong.
Once I remember in London how I saw
  Pale shabby people standing in a long
Line in the twilight and the misty rain
To pay their tax. I then saw England plain.

Alice Duer Miller

ENGLAND THAT SHALL BE

For all of England that is fair
Is what our dear Lord planted there ;
And all of England that is ill
Is where we've forced our pagan will ;
And all of England that shall be
Grows fine or false in men like me.

Frederick B. Watt

EPILOGUE

THE ENGLISH GRAVES

WERE I that wandering citizen whose city is the world,
I would not weep for all that fell before the flags were furled ;
I would not let one murmur mar the trumpets volleying forth
How God grew weary of the kings, and the cold hell in the north.
But we whose hearts are homing birds have heavier thoughts of home,
Though the great eagles burn with gold on Paris or on Rome,
Who stand beside our dead and stare, like seers at an eclipse,
At the riddle of the island tale and the twilight of the ships.

For these were simple men that loved, with hands and feet and eyes,
Whose souls were humbled to the hills and narrowed to the skies,
The hundred little lands within one little land that lie,
Where Severn seeks the sunset isles or Sussex scales the sky.

And what is theirs, though banners blow on Warsaw risen again,
Or ancient laughter walks in gold through the vineyards of Lorraine,
Their dead are marked on English stones, their loves on English trees,
How little is the prize they win, how mean a coin for these—
How small a shrivelled laurel-leaf lies crumpled here and curled :
They died to save their country and they only saved the world.

G. K. Chesterton

NOTES

THE MILKMAID'S LIFE (p. 9)

Martin Parker (*c.* 1600–*c.* 1656), probably a London tavern-keeper, wrote a large number of ballads. The best known is "When the King enjoys his own again" (1643), which became a favourite Jacobite song in the eighteenth century.

OUR VILLAGE (p. 28)

not Miss Mitford's Village: Mary Russell Mitford published in 1819 her prose sketches of rural life and character entitled "Our Village".

REMEMBRANCES (p. 33)

Enclosure: The poet alludes to the changes in the countryside brought about by the enclosure of common land to provide for increased production of corn. This policy was being actively pursued during the boyhood of John Clare (1793–1864).

TOUGH GUY (p. 38)

This is a ime: "Tough Guy" appeared in "The Observer", December 8, 1941.

DUNS SCOTUS'S OXFORD (p. 41)

Duns Scotus (*c.* 1265–1308), the great scholastic philosopher, was born in the village of Duns, in Scotland. He became a Franciscan and studied in Oxford; he afterwards lectured in Oxford and Paris. His followers, the Scotists, were in the sixteenth century attacked and ridiculed by the humanists and Protestant reformers, and the name "duns" or "dunce" came to mean "blockhead".

INDUSTRY TRIUMPHANT (p. 42)

The scene described belongs to the mid-eighteenth century. John Dyer's poem "The Fleece" was published in 1757.

DESCRIPTION OF A CITY SHOWER (p. 49)

templar: barrister or other occupier of chambers in the Temple.

ARSCOTT OF TETCOTT (p. 66)

John Arscott, the hero of this poem (published in 1852), was Sheriff of Devon; he died in 1675. The legend is that he still hunts in the county, his horn can be heard, and his hounds be seen passing by.

THE FISHER'S LIFE (p. 78)

This and another song by John Chalkhill (*fl.* 1600) are included in Izaak Walton's "Compleat Angler".

DANGERS OF FOOTBALL (p. 84)

The dext'rous glazier . . . pent-house sound: the glazier directs the football so as to break windows and get the job of repairing them.

Cricket (p. 85)

This song, written by "the Rev. Mr Cotton of Winchester", is inserted by John Nyren in his "Young Cricketer's Tutor", 1833. Another version is known in which the references to the Hambledon Club do not appear.

Pentathlum of Greece: The Pentathlon (Gk.) or Pentathlum (Lat.) was an athletic contest in which five exercises (leaping, running, throwing the discus, throwing the spear, and wrestling) were carried out by the same athletes on the same day.

Ballade of Cricket (p. 86)

The Envoy refers to Homer's "Odyssey", Book X, where the shade of Achilles tells Odysseus that he would rather be a poor man's thrall on earth than king among the dead.

The Armada (p. 95)

the royal blazon: the Royal Standard.

that famed Picard field: The Battle of Crécy (1346), when the army of Edward III defeated the forces of the French King Philip which included Genoese crossbowmen, a contingent of horse under John, King of Bohemia, and levies of other feudatories of the Holy Roman Empire ("Caesar's eagle shield").

The "Revenge" (p. 98)

The incident commemorated in this ballad took place in 1591 when Lord Thomas Howard was sent to intercept the Spanish treasure fleet homeward-bound from the Indies. Grenville had been second in command to Drake on board the "Revenge" in the fight against the Armada in 1588.

The Death of Admiral Blake (p. 103)

Admiral Blake (1599–1657) was a native of Somersetshire. He died of a fever while on the way home from England after destroying the Spanish West Indian fleet at Santa Cruz (1657).

Battle of the Baltic (p. 107)

In 1801 Sweden, Denmark, and Russia joined together in a policy of Armed Neutrality, and announced their refusal to be bound by the British claim to search neutral vessels which might be carrying French goods. The English fleet sent to attack the Danish fleet at Copenhagen was under Admiral Parker, with Nelson as second in command. The story of how Nelson used his blind eye on this occasion has become proverbial.

The Field of Waterloo (p. 109)

Harmodius: Harmodius joined with Aristogeiton and others to slay the brothers Hippias and Hipparchus who were tyrants of Athens, 527–514 B.C. He was honoured as a liberator of the State.

Admirals All (p. 112)

The exploits of Essex and Duncan here referred to are less familiar than those of Drake and Nelson. In 1596 Queen Elizabeth appointed the Earl of Essex, with Lord Howard of Effingham, Raleigh, and Lord Thomas Howard, to the command of the expedition against Cadiz. Essex defeated the Spaniards in a naval battle and took the town. Admiral Duncan became commander-in-chief of the North Sea fleet in 1795, and received instructions to harass the Dutch navy. In May 1797, owing to a mutiny in the British fleet, he had only two ships under his command. Nevertheless he proceeded to take up his station off Texel, where a Dutch fleet of 15 sail lay at anchor under Admiral De Winter. He adopted the stratagem of making signals as if to the main body of his fleet in the offing ; thus he was able to maintain his position until reinforcements arrived. In October he defeated De Winter at the battle of Camperdown.

WELLINGTON (p. 115)

Against the myriads of Assaye : In 1803 Wellington, then Sir Arthur Wellesley, was serving in India, where his elder brother, Marquis Wellesley, was governor-general. He gained two brilliant victories over the Mahrattas at Assaye and Argaum.

The treble works : During the Peninsular War, when he was given insufficient support by the home government, Wellington could not keep the field against the overwhelming French forces. He therefore constructed the chain of defensive entrenchments, known as the Lines of Torres Vedras, between the sea and the Tagus. Thus he was able to hold Lisbon.

Again their ravening eagle rose : Napoleon returned from his exile in Elba.

On that loud sabbath : The battle of Waterloo was fought on Sunday, June 18, 1815.

Be glad, because his bones are laid by thine : Wellington and Nelson were both buried in St. Paul's Cathedral.

BRAVE TOMB (p. 138)

Dryden's " Annus Mirabilis " dealt with events in 1666—the naval battles against the Dutch, and the Fire of London. *Our careful General* was George Monk, Duke of Albemarle.

THE ASPIRING SCHOLAR (p. 139)

These lines gain interest from their autobiographical character.

Bodley's dome : the Bodleian library at Oxford.

Bacon's mansion : Friar Bacon's tower, which formerly stood on the bridge over the Isis at Oxford. There was a legend that it would fall whenever a greater scholar than Bacon passed under it.

the jail : the debtors' prison.

Hear Lydiat's life and Galileo's end : Thomas Lydiat (1572–1646), though one of the greatest scholars of his time, lived in poverty. The old age of Galileo (1564–1642) was full of troubles : in 1639 he became blind, and a lingering disease caused his death.

ENGLAND (p. 145)

Oceana, Utopia such, and Plato's isle : The reference is to the ideal commonwealths described by James Harrington in " Oceana "

(1656), by Sir Thomas More in " Utopia " (1516), and by Plato in the account which he gives in the " Critias " of the legendary island of Atlantis supposed to have existed in the Atlantic Ocean and to have been overwhelmed by the sea.

The Friar (p. 157)

the ordres foure : the four orders of mendicant friars (Dominicans, Franciscans, Carmelites, Augustinians).

he was licenciat : He had a licence from the Pope to give absolution for all sins. The " curat " (parish priest) had to refer certain cases to the Bishop.

His tipet : his hood or cowl : this seems to have been used as a pocket.

For un-to such . . . Acorded nat : It was not becoming for such an important person as he was . . .

And over-al, ther as profit sholde arise : And everywhere, where profit was to be gained . . .

" *In principio* " : The begging friar said the opening words of St. John's Gospel (*In principio erat verbum*) in each house he visited.

His purchas . . . rente : The proceeds of his begging amounted to a greater sum than his income.

love-dayes : Certain days were appointed for settling disputes by arbitration without recourse to law. The friars took a hand on these occasions.

for his wantownesse : by way of affectation.

The Court of Fame (p. 160)

" The Garlande of Laurell ", from which this passage is taken, is an allegorical poem in which the author, writing in praise of himself, describes his coronation among the world's great poets. John Skelton was tutor to Henry VIII. His satirical poems directed against Wolsey made it necessary for him to seek sanctuary at Westminster, where he died.

A Bore (p. 163)

Holinsheds, or Halls, or Stows : the sixteenth-century chroniclers.

On the University Carrier (p. 164)

Hobson, the Cambridge carrier of Milton's poem, provided the origin of the phrase " Hobson's choice ". According to " The Spectator " he always obliged anyone who hired a horse from him to take the one standing nearest the stable door " so that every customer should have an equal chance of being well served, and every horse be used in its turn ".

The Tragedy of Wit (p. 166)

The Prologue to " Aureng-Zebe " (1676). This was Dryden's last play in rhyming verse ; it dealt with Aureng-Zebe's capture of the empire of India from his father and brothers.

THE ENGLISH BREED (p. 167)

In his satirical poem " The True-born Englishman " (1701) Defoe attacked the popular prejudice against King William III because he was of foreign birth.

SIR BALAAM (p. 169)

London's column : The Monument, on Fish Street Hill, built in memory of the Fire of London. The inscription attributed the fire to the work of the Papists.

JOHN BULL (p. 171)

In the poem " The Search after Happiness " the Sultan of Serendib, overcome by melancholy, seeks a cure. Physicians and councillors having prescribed in vain, he determines on his mother's advice to seek the shirt of a happy man. He travels far and wide, but can find no one who is really happy—not even John Bull. Eventually Paddy, a happy Irishman, is discovered ; but he has no shirt.

MR. LEAR (p. 174)

Edward Lear wrote his famous " Book of Nonsense " (1846) for the grandchildren of his patron the Earl of Derby. " The most remarkable of all nonsense-artists is Edward Lear ; if the rest are masters of nonsense, he is surely the Prince of Nonsense. He has raised nonsense, nonsense pure and simple, nonsense free of all sense, morals, and prettiness, to the heights of great art. His work is the very apotheosis of nonsense ; he is ' the prophet of the utterly absurd, of the patently impossible and vain ' " (Holbrook Jackson).

TO MRS. GAMP IN ELYSIUM (p. 188)

With Gram and Durandal: Gram, in the " Nibelungenlied ", is Sigurd's sword, given to his father by Odin. Durandal, in the " Chanson de Roland ", is the sword of the paladin Roland.

EDMUND SPENSER (p. 191)

our Colin : Edmund Spenser. The poet adopted the name of Colin Clout in " The Shepheards Calendar " and " Colin Clout's come home againe ".

Glorian : Gloriana was Spenser's name for Queen Elizabeth in " The Faerie Queene ".

AN ODE FOR BEN JONSON (p. 193)

As a young man Herrick belonged to the circle of wits who looked up to Ben Jonson as their master. He was adopted by Jonson as his poetical " son ".

TO WILLIAM WORDSWORTH (p. 197)

The " Poem on the Growth of an Individual Mind " is " The Prelude ", in which Wordsworth recorded his early spiritual development.

DEATH OF TENNYSON (p. 201)

Weimar : the home of Goethe.

Maro . . . the Mantuan : Virgil (Publius Virgilius Maro), born in a village near Mantua in Cisalpine Gaul.

In Memory of Wilfred Owen (p. 203)

Wilfred Owen, whose poems were published in 1920, served in the war of 1914–1918, was awarded the Military Cross, and was killed just before the Armistice.

Lascelles Abercrombie (p. 203)

Lascelles Abercrombie (1881–1939), poet and literary critic, was Professor of English Literature at Bedford College, University of London, 1929–1935, and later Goldsmith Reader in English Literature at Oxford University.

On Sir John Vanbrugh (p. 205)

Sir John Vanbrugh (1664–1726) was famous both as a writer of comedy and as an architect. As a designer of country mansions he favoured size. Blenheim Palace, which he planned, is probably the largest domestic building in England.

Sir Joshua Reynolds's Painted Window at New College, Oxford (p. 205)

Thomas Warton (1728–1790), professor of poetry, and later professor of history at Oxford, poet laureate, and historian of English poetry, was by reason of his admiration of mediaeval (" Gothic ") art a precursor of the Romantic school of criticism. But notwithstanding his predilection for the art of " Albion's earlier day ", he could not resist the classic genius of Reynolds.

Peele Castle in a Storm (p. 209)

Then, Beaumont . . . of Him whom I deplore : Wordsworth here alludes to the loss of his brother John, commander of an East India Company's ship, which was wrecked in February 1805. Sir George Beaumont (1752–1827) was a landscape painter and a noted patron of art.

To the Artists called P.R.B. (p. 211)

The Pre-Raphaelite Brotherhood, which included W. H. Hunt, J. E. Millais, D. G. Rossetti, W. M. Rossetti, and F. G. Stephens, professed to return to the ideals of art that existed before the time of Raphael.

Turner (p. 211)

And from the grave he challenged Claude Lorraine : Turner tried to break down the contemporary worship of the seventeenth-century French landscape painter Claude. In 1807 he painted " Sun rising through Vapour " in deliberate rivalry with the earlier master. This picture was included by him among those he left to the nation, on the express condition that it was hung beside the Claudes in the National Gallery.

In St. Paul's a while ago (p. 212)

Artemisia : Queen of Caria in the fourth century B.C. Overcome with grief at the death of her husband, Mausolus, she built the Mausoleum as a memorial to him.

the encircling mart: "St. Paul's Churchyard", in which (before the destruction of 1940–1941) shops and warehouses formed an important business centre.

VIROCONIUM (p. 216)

Viroconium was the ancient Roman city of which the remains can still be seen near Wroxeter. It was founded before A.D. 70, and may have been burned by the Saxons in 584.

TO A FRIEND IN PRAISE OF MUSIC AND POETRY (p. 218)

Dowland: John Dowland, lutanist and composer, published three books of "Songs or Airs" for the lute, 1597, 1600, and 1603.

MUSIC FOR THE MORRIS DANCE (p. 219)

the hobby-horse: The figure of a horse made of wickerwork was fastened about the waist of one of the performers in the morris dance.

TO MR. H. LAWES, ON HIS AIRS (p. 221)

With Midas ears: Midas, King of Phrygia, once declared that Pan was a finer flute-player than Apollo. To mark Midas's stupidity, Pan changed his ears to those of an ass.

POLITE MUSIC (p. 223)

Heydegger: John James Heidegger (1659 ?–1749) was manager of the opera at the Haymarket Theatre. For a time he was in partnership with Handel.

THE ORGANIST IN HEAVEN (p. 225)

Samuel Sebastian Wesley (1810–1876) was the leading organist and composer of church music of his day.

THE ROMAN CENTURION'S SONG (p. 231)

Rhodanus: The river Rhone.

Nemausus and Arelate: two Roman cities in Southern Gaul; now Nîmes and Arles.

Euroclydon: a stormy north-east wind of the Mediterranean.

THE PARSON (p. 242)

He sette nat his benefice . . . for soules: He did not leave his parish to be looked after by a curate while he went to St. Paul's in London to obtain a chantry for souls (*i.e.* an endowment providing for a priest to sing masses for the founder).

DRAKE'S CHAIR (p. 247)

Phaeton: son of Phoebus, the sun-god. According to the well-known legend, Phaeton begged his father to allow him to drive the chariot of the sun, but he could not control the horses, and he came so near the earth that he almost caused a great conflagration.

THE SONG OF THE WESTERN MEN (p. 249)

This song relates to Sir Jonathan Trelawny, Bart. (1650–1721), bishop successively of Bristol, Exeter, and Winchester. He was loyal to King James II until the Declaration of Indulgence, 1687. The following year he signed the petition against the second Declaration of Indulgence, and he was one of the seven bishops imprisoned in the Tower of London. He was a Cornish landowner.

Men of England (p. 255)

Russell's glory, Sydney's matchless shade : Lord William Russell (1639–1683) was an enthusiast for political liberty and took a leading part in the opposition to the pro-French and pro-Catholic policy of Charles II. Algernon Sidney (Sydney) (1622–1683) was a republican leader in the civil war against Charles I, and was later associated with Russell in opposition to Charles II. Both Russell and Sidney were executed on false charges of complicity in the Rye House Plot (1683).

The Vicar (p. 259)

marrow : spouse.

his ponderous Barrow : the collected sermons of Isaac Barrow (1630–1677), the great preacher, and mathematical and classical scholar.

Sylvanus Urban : was the pen-name of the editors of the "Gentleman's Magazine".

Hic jacet . . . lauru : Here lies William Brown, a man deserving to be crowned with every honour.

INDEX OF AUTHORS

THE END

Printed in Great Britain by R. & R. CLARK, LIMITED, *Edinburgh.*